# THE EXCAVATIONS AT DURA-EUROPOS

# PREVIOUSLY PUBLISHED

PRELIMINARY REPORT OF THE FIRST SEASON OF WORK, SPRING 1928. *Edited by* P. V. C. BAUR *and* M. I. ROSTOVTZEFF.

PRELIMINARY REPORT OF THE SECOND SEASON OF WORK, OCTOBER 1928—APRIL 1929. *Edited by* P. V. C. BAUR *and* M. I. ROSTOVTZEFF.

PRELIMINARY REPORT OF THE THIRD SEASON OF WORK, NOVEMBER 1929—MARCH 1930. *Edited by* P. V. C. BAUR, M. I. ROSTOVTZEFF *and* ALFRED R. BELLINGER.

PRELIMINARY REPORT OF THE FOURTH SEASON OF WORK, OCTOBER 1930—MARCH 1931. *Edited by* P. V. C. BAUR, M. I. ROSTOVTZEFF *and* ALFRED R. BELLINGER.

PRELIMINARY REPORT OF THE FIFTH SEASON OF WORK, OCTOBER 1931—MARCH 1932. *Edited by* M. I. ROSTOVTZEFF.

PRELIMINARY REPORT OF THE SIXTH SEASON OF WORK, OCTOBER 1932—MARCH 1933. *Edited by* M. I. ROSTOVTZEFF, A. R. BELLINGER, C. HOPKINS *and* C. B. WELLES.

PRELIMINARY REPORT OF THE SEVENTH AND EIGHTH SEASONS OF WORK, 1933–1934 *and* 1934–1935. *Edited by* M. I. ROSTOVTZEFF, F. E. BROWN *and* C. B. WELLES.

---

FINAL REPORT IV, PART I, FASCICLE 1. THE GREEN GLAZED POTTERY *by* NICHOLAS TOLL *with* TECHNOLOGICAL NOTES *by* F. R. MATSON. 1943.

THE

# Excavations at Dura-Europos

CONDUCTED BY

YALE UNIVERSITY AND THE FRENCH ACADEMY
OF INSCRIPTIONS AND LETTERS

---

PRELIMINARY REPORT
OF THE NINTH SEASON OF WORK
1935-1936

EDITED BY

M. I. Rostovtzeff

A. R. Bellinger, F. E. Brown, and C. B. Welles

---

PART I

The Agora and Bazaar

NEW HAVEN · YALE UNIVERSITY PRESS
London · Humphrey Milford · Oxford University Press
1944

# CONTENTS

# LIST OF PLATES

# LIST OF FIGURES IN THE TEXT

# PREFACE

THE departure of Professor Hopkins from Yale to the University of Michigan deprived us of his services as excavator, and the ninth campaign had to be undertaken without his experienced guidance. Professor Brown was Director of the year's work, with the Comte du Mesnil de Buisson as Assistant Director. Mr. Henry Pearson and Mr. Henry Detweiler were the architects, Dr. Toll and Mr. Francis Comstock assistants. We are indebted, as in all previous campaigns, to the generous coöperation of M. Seyrig and the *Service des Antiquités,* and of the military authorities.

The ninth campaign, of 1935–1936, explored the Agora, the headquarters of the Dux, the Necropolis outside the walls, the Dolicheneum, the temple of Zeus Megistos, the temple of the Gaddé, the house of Lysias, some private houses, and the ramp outside the walls. Circumstances have made it necessary to present this material in separate parts, of which this first deals with the Agora, while the second will include the Palace of the Dux and the Necropolis. The rest must await the return of Professor Brown, now in the government service in Syria.

Before his departure Professor Brown left his account of the Agora ready for the printer, and his colleagues have had to take care of only those incidental editorial problems which foresight never entirely avoids. The impracticability of communicating with him has occasionally forced them to resort to solutions which he might not have preferred, but these, of course, are mere trivialities which do not affect the meaning of his work.

Of the two Appendices, the excursus on the bronze plaque we owe to Professor Karl Lehmann-Hartleben, of New York University. The discussion of the difficult and important inscriptions from $G_5$, $C_2$ was written by Dr. Heinrich Immerwahr, then a graduate student at Yale. His induction into the Army before he could put his material in shape for publication has made it necessary for the editors to do more revision than they would have attempted under normal conditions, but the revision has been a matter of abbreviation and rearrangement, not of addition; it has been submitted for his approval and accepted by him. In this work we have been assisted by the expert advice of our colleague,

Professor Harald Ingholt, who has been very generous in his help to the editors.

E. L. Hildreth and Company and the Meriden Gravure Company have been most coöperative in dealing with problems which were intricate and sometimes acute, and the tireless patience of Dr. N. P. Toll has seen us through some difficulties with which only he could cope.

THE EDITORS

# I. SECTION G, THE AGORA AND BAZAAR

## I

## THE AREA AND ITS EXCAVATION
### (Fig. 78)

SECTION G in the excavators' plan of Dura comprises the area of eight city blocks, G1–G8. It is bounded by Main Street on the south, by Street 4 on the north, by Street D on the west, and by Street H on the east. These are the eight central blocks of the city. They lie north of Main Street in the angle of the "T" formed by Main and its crossbar H extending on either side to the heads of the natural ravine thoroughfares to the river plain below. It was both the geographical and vital center of the city. In the Parthian and Roman periods it was the quarter of the bazaars, the center of business life. In the Hellenistic period it was the agora. In the original city plan and throughout the city's history Main Street with the branches of Street H to the heads of the ravine roads, and probably Streets D, 4, and 5, were wider than any other streets of the city in accord with their function as arteries.

The bazaars, which in the later periods occupied almost all of Section G, consisted of a mass of small private houses and shops. They gave on streets many of which failed to fall into alignment with the regular block plan of the rest of the city, though for the most part they preserved its general orientation. The resultant blocks have been numbered as far as possible in accord with the general numbering scheme for the rest of the city, though for convenience they have not been made to follow it arbitrarily.

Of the total area of Section G, roughly 150 × 160 m. = 24,000 sq. m., somewhat more than three-fifths has been excavated completely or in part. The greater part of this has been fully explored down to bed rock. The excavations extending over a period of fourteen years proceeded as follows:

1923) The dwelling and shop known as Cumont's House at the southwest corner of Block G6.[1]

1924) Shops S64, S65, and S66 on Main Street at the southwest corner of Block G2; Alley G8 with rooms 1, 2, and 3 of House A, and

[1] Cumont, *Fouilles*, pp. 242–250.

rooms 1, 2, 3, 4, 5, 6, and 7 of House B in Block G8, superficially explored by soldiers garrisoned on the site.[2]

1931–32) The latest levels of the western portions of Blocks G1 and G3, the north portion of Block G6, and the excavated portions of Blocks G2 and G4, Alley G7, and Shop S1 of Block G7.[3]

1933–34) The greater part of Block G5 with House H of Block G7 adjoining. The excavation of Block G3 was pushed farther west, and the whole excavated portion was explored down to bed rock.

1936–37) The excavation of Blocks G1 and G3 was completed and everywhere carried to bed rock. The outlines of all the blocks in the section and of the adjoining blocks were trenched to at least the final level. Rooms C1, 2, and 3 of Block G8 in Street D were cleared, and the whole area was subjected to final cleaning.

The general ground level of the section as a whole before excavation lay some 1.60 m. to 3.00 m. above bed rock, and indicates the various heights to which the walls of the final period were found standing. The bed rock itself was approximately level over the entire area, but was pitted and uneven, crossed by ridges and depressions with a maximum variation of roughly 0.80 m. (219.58 m.—218.76 m. a.s.l.).

[2] Cumont, *Fouilles*, pp. 476 f.
[3] *Rep. V*, pp. 49–95. Alley G7 and Shop S1 of Block G7 not reported.

# II

## THE HELLENISTIC AGORA

(Figs. 78, 79, 80, 81, 82, 83)

BENEATH the structures of later periods in Blocks G1, G3, and G5 were found extensive remains of the earliest buildings in the area, the buildings of the Hellenistic agora. These remains consisted of the surviving portions of the stone foundations and socles of a complex of shop buildings which originally embraced the whole northern half of the section. They are best preserved in Block G3, especially in its western half, where in large part they continued to serve as the walls of later periods.[1] Elsewhere the destruction was in general more thoroughgoing. Both socle and foundations were for the most part replaced by later walls, though seldom without leaving their traces in the form of isolated bits of socle or foundation or of trenches for footing courses. It is only in the unexcavated western portion of the section, Blocks G7 and G8, that we are without direct evidence for the plan.

### A. Construction

(Fig. 8; Pls. I, II, IV, 1, VI, 1, VII, 2, VIII, 1, IX, XIII, 2)

The foundations and socles in question were built of carefully cut gypsum blocks to form single orthostate systems. In the north buildings in Blocks G3 and G5 this consisted when complete of a footing course or courses, a base course of headers, orthostate course, and capping course of headers. In the east building in Blocks G3 and G1 the base course of headers appears to have been omitted, and the same was presumably the case in the corresponding unexcavated west building. In the two north buildings the exterior socles were heavier than the interior and stood some 0.60 m. higher above the original ground level, 2.05 m. and 1.45 m. respectively. In the east and west buildings the interior socles stood some 1.05 m. above the original ground level. The exterior socles may be assumed to have been higher, but of this there is no direct evidence.

---

[1] The socles in this area which remained in use in the later houses A, F, and G were observed in 1931/32 by Hopkins, and discussed by him in *Rep. V*, pp. 75 f., 81–85. Their significance, of course, could not be appreciated at that stage in the excavations.

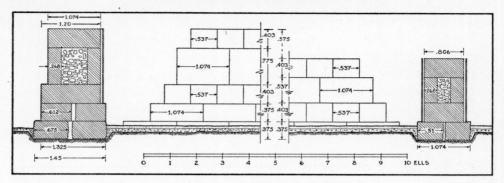

Fig. 1. Orthostate Socle. North Buildings

The individual blocks of the foundations and socles throughout the area were cut and laid to a cubit and foot measure slightly larger than the cubit and foot of approximately 0.525 m. and 0.35 m. used in the Hellenistic city wall socles[2] and in the city plan.[3] The cubit of the agora measured 0.537 m. to a foot of 0.358 m. The difference of ca. 0.008 m. per foot is not sufficient to indicate a different unit of measurement, and it may be assumed that both cubits represent the same ideal unit, the difference being due to the individual measuring sticks or cords used. It will be seen that the same cubit and foot of 0.537 m. and 0.358 m. were also employed in laying out the agora buildings themselves. Its determination was made easy by the relative exactitude of the cutting and fitting of the blocks and by the simplicity of the multiples and fractions employed.

In the north buildings in Blocks G3 and G5 the exterior socles were 1.074 m. or 2 cubits thick on footings 1.476 m. or 2¾ cubits wide. The capping headers were thus 1.074 m. or 2 cubits long × 0.537 m. or 1 cubit wide × 0.403 m. or ¾ cubit thick, the orthostates 1.074 m. or 2 cubits long × 0.268 m. or ½ cubit thick. Their height of 0.775 m. does not fall into the system and appears to have been fixed arbitrarily. Similarly the base headers were 0.537 m. or 1 cubit wide × 0.403 m. or ¾ cubit thick, while their various lengths of 1.20 m.–1.325 m. cannot be brought into the system. Below the base headers the footing stretchers, while uniformly 1.074 m. or 2 cubits in length, had an odd thickness of 0.375 m. and varied in width from 0.612 m. to 0.725 m. The interior

[2] *Rep. VII–VIII*, pp. 4 f.
[3] Below, pp. 24 f.

socles were 0.806 m. or 1½ cubits thick on footings of 1.074 m. or 2 cubits. Accordingly the capping headers were 0.806 m. or 1½ cubits long × 0.537 m. or 1 cubit wide × 0.403 m. or ¾ cubit thick. The base headers had the same dimensions. The orthostates measured 1.074 m. or 2 cubits long × 0.537 m. or 1 cubit wide × 0.268 m. or ½ cubit thick. The footing stretchers were uniformly 1.074 m. or 2 cubits long but had the odd thickness of 0.375 m. and averaged roughly 0.51 m. in width.

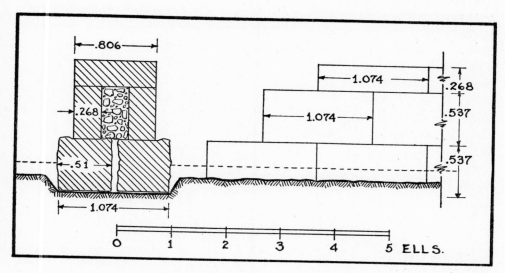

Fig. 2. Orthostate Socle. East Building

The exterior socles of the east building in Blocks G3 and G1 had footings of both 1.253 m. or 3½ feet and 1.343 m. or 2½ cubits. They were laid of stretchers 1.074 m. or 2 cubits long × 0.537 m. or 1 cubit wide and thick. Of the courses above nothing remains in situ. The interior socles were 0.806 m. or 1½ cubits thick on footings 1.074 m. or 2 cubits wide. The capping course was of blocks 1.074 m. or 2 cubits long × 0.806 m. or 1½ cubits wide × 0.268 m. or ½ cubit thick. The orthostates, 1.074 m. or 2 cubits long × 0.537 m. or 1 cubit high × 0.268 m. or ½ cubit thick, rested directly on the footings. The latter consisted either of a double row of stretchers 1.074 m. or 2 cubits long × 0.51 m. wide × 0.537 m. or 1 cubit thick or of headers 1.074 m. or 2 cubits long × 0.806 m. or 1½ cubits wide × 0.537 m. or 1 cubit thick.

The footing courses were uniformly set on a bedding grout of gypsum plaster in shallow trenches cut in the soft bed rock. When, as was normally the case, they were laid as double courses of stretchers, the two rows were set 0.07–0.15 m. apart leaving space between to take up expansion and contraction, seepage, or settling. The blocks of the footing courses were left rough-pointed save for the top joint bed which was worked smooth. Throughout the complex this course also served as the euthynteria. The smooth upper surface, ideally 219.355 m. a.s.l., was kept level with great accuracy by increasing or diminishing the depth of the trench or the thickness of the blocks. The maximum resultant deviation from the norm was only 0.06 m. The exceptions were dictated by necessity. A long depression in the bed rock caused the north exterior socle of the north building in G3 to be lowered 0.32 m. for a length of 72.00 m. and in two places required an additional course beneath for a short distance. Similarly a pronounced hummock in the bed rock surface caused the south exterior foundation in G1 to be raised the height of one course or 0.375 m. Where, as in the greater part of the exterior socles of the north buildings in G3 and G5, there was a second stretcher course below the base headers, this also was laid with a free space between the two rows save where its blocks served as thresholds.

The base and capping headers were laid with a fine gypsum plaster grout, 0.0015 m. or less thick, in the joints. Their vertical joints were generously pointed with plaster which spread 0.01–0.02 m. on either side of the joint. The exposed faces were not worked perfectly smooth but were left somewhat rough for the reception of plaster. The orthostates, on the other hand, had smoothly finished faces and were closely jointed without grout. Their dry joints regularly show a slight anathyrosis. The interior space of ½ to 1 cubit between opposite orthostates was packed with rubblework of red conglomerate chunks about the size of a lemon set in gypsum mortar. The same sort of rubblework was also used in the header courses at the intersections of the interior socles to fill spaces arising from the difference between the size of the normal header blocks and the dimensions of the space enclosed. This usage was part of a general tendency of which other examples will be encountered to avoid as far as possible cutting down the blocks of standard size in all courses.

The stone socles were of course designed to carry a superstructure of mud brick, though it is doubtful whether any of the original brick remained by the final period. It is possible, however, that the brick remaining on the party socles of area A in Block G3 is of the first construction

(Pls. I, II, IV, 1). At any rate it is of an early type compared with the rest of the mud brick extant in the section as a whole. The bricks, which are of fine grey mud mixed with chopped straw, measure 0.35–0.36 m. or 1 foot square and are 0.09–0.10 m. thick. It seems clear from the traces which remain that all the interior faces of the stone socles were originally hidden by the same rendering which covered the mud brick superstructure. It has been noted that the header courses were left rough to receive it, and, where chance has preserved it fragmentarily,[4] it is seen to have consisted of a heavy coat of mud and chopped straw rendered with a fine coat of plaster. On the other hand, the comparatively severe weathering of the stonework on the façades would seem to indicate that on the exterior the socle remained visible.

## B. Plan and Elevation

### (Figs. 9, 10, 11)

The excavated portions of the socle and its foundations are sufficient to give a fairly satisfactory plan of the whole agora complex. Of its four separate and symmetrical shop buildings only one remains completely unexplored. The areas of the north building in Block G3 and of the east building in Blocks G3 and G1 have been totally uncovered together with about three-fifths of the area of the north building in Block G5. Only the west building in Block G7 is still unexcavated. Fortunately the surviving portions of the north building in G3 are so abundant that the plan and elevation can be restored in every essential. Where the socle itself is not standing complete or in part, its foundations or the trenches to receive them are everywhere present. The scantier remains of the neighboring building in G5 suffice to show that it was at all points identical. This correspondence implies a similar correspondence of the east and west buildings, and the unexcavated west building may accordingly be restored with full confidence on the pattern of the building opposite.

The two north buildings formed a pair separated by Street F, an interval of 6.33 m. Each was 76.73 m. long and 21.48 m. wide on the exterior as measured along the orthostates. This length in each case comprised the width of two city blocks together with the intervening street. The width was equal to 40 cubits of 0.537 m. Both buildings were

[4] Below, p. 15, Pl. I, 1.

mechanically laid out as double series of two-room shops. As may be seen in the north building in G3, the long rectangle of the plan was systematically subdivided into forty-eight square and rectangular cells, twenty-four on either side of a longitudinal partition which ran the full length of the building without openings.[5] These cells formed the series of twelve identical double shops on either side of the longitudinal partition. Those to the south gave on the open area before the buildings, those to the north on Street 4 behind. Each pair consisted of a square shop room with a rectangular work- or storeroom in the rear.

The shop rooms opened on the exterior by wide doorways which were seldom precisely on the axes of the rooms. It is evident that their exact positions depended on the normal termination of the series of socle blocks between doorways, and were determined by the general desire to avoid cutting down the blocks of standard size. The interior doorways communicating with the rear rooms were narrower. They were located on the same principle and at the same time as far as possible to one side or other of the outer door axis, in order to prevent a direct view from the outside into the rear room. Since the thresholds were in both cases simply the blocks of the course beneath, the difference in the coursing of the exterior and interior socles brought the interior doorsills some 0.03 m. higher than the exterior. None of the doorways retained traces of trim of any kind. In the orthostate course the reveals of the exterior doorways were simply faced off with standard orthostates extending through the full thickness of the socle (Pls. I, 2, VII, 2). In the interior doorways the practice apparently varied. Two, A2–A4 and A2–A5, are intact (Pl. I, 1). Each has an orthostate facer as its west reveal and the east reveal formed by bringing the end orthostates together in a joint, each with the thickness of 0.403 m. Doorway G4–G3 lacks only the facing orthostates which it had in each reveal. Doorways B6–B7, B10–B11, and K2–S4 each have one reveal preserved, in the first case the west, in the others the east, always with the orthostate facing. Nowhere were there traces of the fittings for the doors.

In most if not all cases the double shop units on either side of the unbroken longitudinal partition were likewise without direct communication. The narrow openings, 0.715 m. or 2 feet wide and originally faced with orthostates, between rear rooms A5 and A3 (Pl. II, 2), A3

[5] The breaches which appear in Fig. 8, cf. Fig. 79, between rooms A4 and F2, G3 and G6, K4 and K5 were effected in later periods to provide doorways.

and G3, B11 and H5, are quite exceptional. It is possible that they were not intended as doorways at all but designed to receive wooden shelves or cupboards.

If we may judge from the two shops which originally made up room A2, all the shops were floored with carefully tamped and smoothed clay mixed with chopped straw and laid on a bed of fine gypsum detritus from the construction. This inevitable product of stonecutting was employed in all the Hellenistic constructions of Dura as a leveller for the bed rock surface.

The mechanical uniformity of the general plan was reflected in the dimensions given to its units. As we have seen the building measured 40 cubits wide on the exterior, giving with subtraction of the exterior socles an interior width of 36 cubits. Each pair of double shops on either side of the longitudinal partition had an interior width of 5.37 m. or 10 cubits save the last pair to the east which measured 6.45 m. or 12 cubits wide. This departure from strict uniformity was apparently forced on the architect by the necessity for laying out his units in round numbers and at the same time conforming to an area whose length was already fixed by the dimensions of the city block plan. As a result the front shop rooms of this east pair alone were not perfectly square, 10 × 10 cubits. The rectangular rear rooms appear to have been planned as ideally 6 cubits, 3.225 m., deep. Actually they measure only 3.08 m.–3.12 m. This difference would seem to have been caused by the discrepancy between the sum of the ideal dimensions of the walls and rooms which total 40½ cubits and the given width of the building of 40 cubits.

In the twin north building in Block G5 the destruction of the stone socle and foundations was much more thoroughgoing. Only the west exterior socle with the immediately adjacent portions of the north and south exterior socles (Pl. XIII, 2) and of the central longitudinal partition were found standing to their full height. At four other points remains of the exterior base header course give the position of exterior doorways. Moreover the first meter or so of the third interior cross wall from the east has been preserved between rooms F3 and D3. Its position 18.76 m. from the inner face of the west exterior socle establishes the fact that the oversized pair of double shops with a width of 12 cubits was here, exactly as in the other north building, introduced at the east end.[6] Other remains of interior foundations and footing trenches in rooms C1, C2,

---

[6] I.e., 18.76 = 5.37 (10 cubits) + 0.806 (1½ cubits) + 5.37 (10 cubits) + 0.806 (1½ cubits) + 6.45 (12 cubits) = 35 cubits.

F4, E2, E1, F2, H7, H9, and H1 fall into their places in the plan with perfect regularity, and furnish evidence as far as the sixth interior cross wall from the east. Remains of the north exterior socle carry some 5.00 m. farther to the west, and the restoration of the missing portions of the plan along the same lines is obvious.

Both buildings unquestionably had simple gabled roofs. The evidence beyond the plans themselves consists of numerous fragments of terra-cotta roof tiles and a single antefix attached to a fragmentary end cover tile. The fragments of roof tiles were found at scattered points all over the area of the two buildings. The greater part of them were found imbedded in the floors of the lowest levels beneath the pavings of later periods. In three or four cases they had been used as caementa in later rubblework socles. They were of two types: (1) almost semicircular cover tiles, and (2) flatter concave tiles. None was complete, but the number found was sufficient to make a reconstruction possible (Fig. 3).

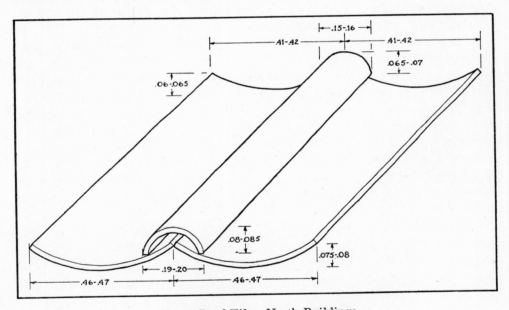

Fig. 3. Roof Tiles. North Buildings

The cover tiles were approximately 0.80 m. (1½ cubits?) long with walls some 0.016 m. thick. They tapered from 0.19 m.–0.20 m. in outside width at the large end to 0.15 m.–0.16 m. at the small on an arc of about 16° less than a semicircle. The flat tiles were 0.46 m.–0.47 m. wide at the large end and 0.41 m.–0.42 m. at the small with a curve of about 75° of a circle. The latter of course were laid edge to edge concave side up on a bed of clay or clay and straw with the end joints overlapping. The adjacent edges were covered by the overlapping cover tiles leaving effective water channels of about 0.27 m. between. Many tile fragments bore indications that the overlapping joints were secured with plaster.

The antefix[7] was found built into an early rubblework foundation beneath the later court levels of G7, H1. Its female mask measured 0.168 m. wide and 0.152 m. high. The remaining stump of cover tile behind had the vertical radius of 0.098 m. normal for the large end of the tile, but its horizontal radius was only 0.082 m. and the curve had a stilted form. This would seem to indicate that the end tiles bearing antefixes, since they were not required to overlap another tile, were almost without taper in width and maintained a uniform height from one end to the other. Such shaping provided for the maximum of free channel space between the antefixes at the eaves and had the effect of lifting the antefix tiles slightly along the roof edge.

It is plain that the plan of the buildings was calculated to make possible the construction of a gable in the most economical manner, an important consideration in a land devoid of large timbers. The whole gable could easily be carried on the walls with the central longitudinal partition built up to the ridgepole, the other longitudinal walls to the height required by the pitch of the roof, and the cross walls finished off on the angle of pitch. Tie beams and principal rafters could be eliminated, and the tiling carried solely on short purlins and common rafters. There is no evidence for the overhang of the eaves, but it must have been sufficient to carry water well beyond the line of the walls and foundations. It has been restored in Fig. 11 as roughly 0.50 m. (cf. Fig. 5).

A space of 5.37 m. or 10 cubits separated the north wing of the east shop building in Blocks G3 and G1 from the south façade of the north shop building in Block G3, forming a passage from Street H to the open agora area enclosed by the buildings. Its opening on the street was narrowed to 3.22 m. or 6 cubits by heavy piers projecting 1.074 m. from the corner of either building. Of the northern pier the footing and base courses are preserved, of the southern merely the footing course (Pl. VIII, 2). It is conjectural whether these piers carried or were intended to carry a lintel of some sort, or whether they served as imposts for an

[7] Below, p. 165, Fig. 88.

arch similar to the contemporary arches of the city gates and citadel. Either solution presents difficulties, and further evidence is wanting. No blocks that might be identified as voussoirs were found in the excavations.

The east shop building was a narrow structure in the shape of an inverted "L," 50.09 m. long overall as measured on the foundations, or 49.88 m. as measured on the orthostates. This length like that of the north buildings was fixed in advance by the dimensions of the blocks and streets of the city plan. The full extent of the agora buildings on the east, comprising the length of the east building + the width of the north building + the passage space between, occupied the length of one city block with the street bounding it on the south and totalled 76.73 m.

The foundations of the north wing are preserved almost in their entirety in addition to a segment of socle containing a door (Pls. VII, 2, VIII, 1). Only the foundation of the west exterior socle is missing, and its position is well marked by the termination of the south socle as at a corner and by later wall L4–L1 which preserved its line. Thus in plan the north wing originally consisted of three shops each 5.37 m. or 10 cubits deep and respectively 5.37 m., 4.30 m., or 8 cubits, and 4.30 m. wide from east to west. The preserved doorway was that of the westernmost shop. It was 1.43 m. or 4 feet wide and opened south on the open market place. The doorway of the middle shop may be restored as identical. The position of the doorway in the south wall of the eastern shop is indicated by the slight projection of the foundation blocks which formed its sill. It opened from the shop to the south.

The foundations of the remainder of the east building were found in a much more fragmentary state, but the general layout emerges clearly. The long east wing consisted of a series of ten identical small shops each 5.37 m. or 10 cubits deep. The foundation of the east exterior socle is preserved for 26.90 m. southward from the north wing. Separate segments of the foundation of the west socle were found to extend 38.85 m. southward from the north wing. The stumps of the foundations of the first seven interior partitions from the north remain in most cases at the points where they bonded into the east exterior foundation. An important segment of the south exterior foundation is still in situ, built over by the later wall F122–S124. The void south of the last partition of which traces remain is exactly equal to the area of three normal shops with their partitions.

The ten shops had an average width of 3.15 m. between foundations (= some 3.42 m. between socles). This irregular dimension of about 0.20 m. over 6 cubits probably merely represents the equal division among ten shops of the predetermined available space of 42.58 m. It is noteworthy as offering a different solution of the same problem faced in the laying out of the north buildings.

Although the foundation course which alone is preserved must also have served as doorsill in the openings of the east shops, no certain traces of doorways remain. General considerations, however, and the analogy of the preserved doorway of the north wing suggest the restoration of doorways 1.43 m. or 4 feet wide giving on the open market place to the west. The absence of direct evidence for the roofing of the shops makes its restoration likewise conjectural. In this case the relatively slight width to be covered points to a roof with a single pitch. These features are assumed for the corresponding unexcavated west shop building opposite, which has been restored as identical in every respect.

The south exterior wall of the east shop building was projected westward to serve as a southern enclosing wall for the open market area. A considerable stretch of its foundation was found in area 71$^1$–102–91 of Block G1 (Pl. IX, 2), and the bedding trench for its continuation was uncovered as far as the east wall of Shop S100, while traces of it were picked up in Block G6 to the west. The position of the opening or openings in this enclosure wall remains somewhat problematical. They would presumably have been in alignment with the regular city streets as laid out in the city plan. Indeed there is evidence of a sort for such an opening on the line of Street G, for, when at a later date buildings were erected against the wall on either side, an opening appears to have been walled up at this point.[8]

The four shop buildings together with the open space which they enclosed occupied the area of four of the original city blocks including that of the three north-south streets, E, F, and G, and that of Street 2 on the south, a total area of 159.79 m. × 76.73 m., or approximately 12,260 sq. m. Of this, 8,015 sq. m., roughly ⅔, was open market place. On it faced the twenty-four two-room shops of the north buildings and the twenty-four single shops of the east and west buildings. Onto Street 4 behind opened twenty-four more two-room shops of the north buildings. This complex, however, took up only a little more than half of the

[8] Cf. below, p. 37.

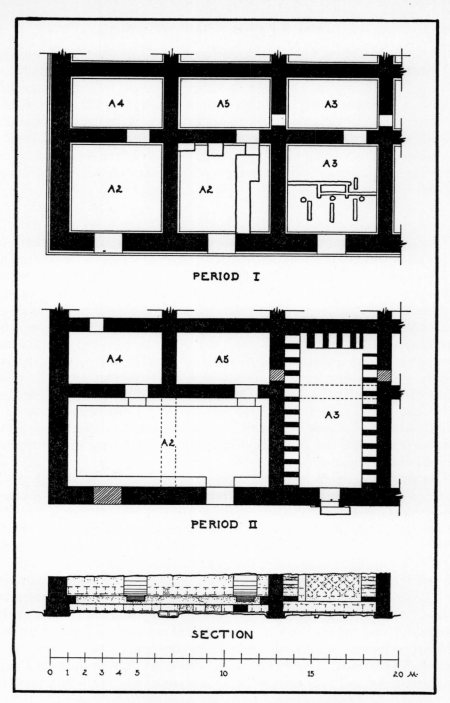

PERIOD I

PERIOD II

SECTION

Fig. 4. G3, A2–5. Periods I and II. Restored Plans

entire section. Between the south enclosing wall of the shop buildings and Main Street stretched an expanse 159.79 m. $\times$ 70.40 m. which was also a part of the agora, although never encompassed by permanent shop buildings. Excavations within this area in Blocks G1, G2, G4, G6, and G8 were carried in many places down to bed rock but failed to reveal any traces of structures contemporary with the shop buildings. It is to be assumed that all through the Hellenistic period this portion of the agora lay open and unoccupied save by temporary booths and stalls on market days.

## C. The Shops

Within the area originally occupied by the shop buildings little remains of the floor levels associated with the stone socles. The continuous processes of building and rebuilding, which brought in their train the removal of the original socles and foundations and the sinking of new rubblework foundations to bed rock, have for the most part effectively destroyed the floors and furnishings of the shops. These factors operated most destructively in Blocks G1 and G5. Even in Block G3 those sharp rises in floor level accompanied by a fill to meet the rise in the adjacent streets, which might have preserved important vestiges of the original floors, came mostly at a much later time. Here and there, as in the later rooms G3 and G4, J3 and J4, and K5 of Block G3, isolated patches of the original level can be identified, but there are actually only two areas, both in G3, where the original disposition of the shops of the earliest period may be studied.

The first is area A in the southwest corner of the block. Here the essential plan of the three original double shops, A2–A4, A2–A5, and A3–A3 was preserved relatively without alteration all through the city's history, and such changes as were made have not destroyed the evidences of the primitive arrangements (Figs. 4 and 5; Pls. I, 1, II). All three shops retained their original flooring of tamped clay and straw laid on a levelling bed of fine gypsum detritus. The mean level of 219.265 m. a.s.l. lay some 0.46 m.–0.50 m. below the doorsills and must have necessitated the installation of some sort of temporary step, no trace of which remains. Along the east wall of room A2 below the floor level of the succeeding period ran a strip of the original covering of wall and socle. It consisted of a coat, 0.03 m.–0.05 m. thick, of fine mud mixed with chopped straw and rendered with a fine coat of plaster, 0.003 m. thick on the average. Double Shop A2–A5 was clearly arranged with its fore-

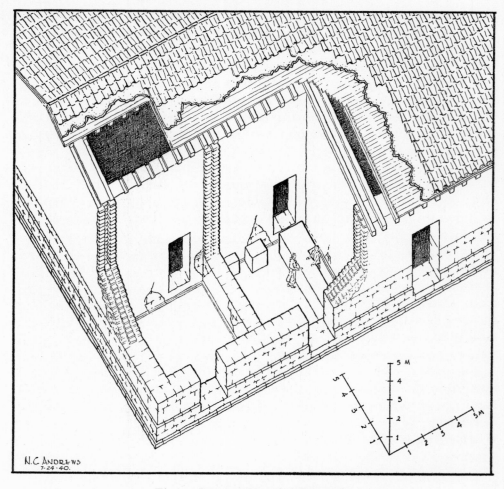

Fig. 5. G3, A2. Restored Isometric

room A2 as the place of sale and its rear room A5 as a storeroom. Across
the east end of A2 ran a counter of mud-rendered mud brick flush with
the east reveal of the entrance and terminating 0.80 m. short of doorway
A2–A5 in a broad table-like projection. Between the end of the counter
and the doorway was a mud brick step, 0.35 m. high. In the northwest
corner of the shop and nearby against the north wall were benches or
tables of pisé with a thin plaster rendering. How high these furnishings
stood can only be conjectured, since in the following period they were

razed to the new floor level. Double Shop A3–A3 appears to have followed a similar general arrangement. The only surviving vestige of its appointments was a system of shallow trenches across the south end of the front shop, cut through the original floor and 0.12 m.–0.20 m. deep into the bed rock. The trenches, which are 0.15 m.–0.20 m. wide, were evidently designed to receive the framework of some sort of superstructure, probably of wood, possibly of thin stone slabs. Neither their position nor their pattern lends itself to the cuttings necessary for a loom, the most obvious possibility. Probably one must imagine a low partition across the room with a counter or table in the center and bins or benches before it. Nothing remains of the original appointments of double Shop A2–A4. Only its outer doorway is remarkable as showing cuttings apparently intended for door fittings. Though cut after the original construction of

the doorway, they clearly belong to the earliest period, since this doorway went out of use and was blocked up in the succeeding period. There were five cuttings in the west reveal and one in the sill which seems somewhat too far forward to have been a bolt socket.

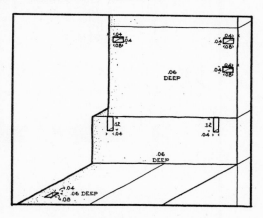

Fig. 5a. Cuttings in Doorway of A2

The second such area lies at the opposite end of the block at its southeast corner. It comprises the later rooms M1–M4, L1, and the neighboring portion of Alley G3 (Fig. 6, Pl. VIII, 1). Here room M2, originally the corner room of the north wing of the east shop building and hence the rear room of the first shop in the series to the south, retained much of its original character beneath the later levels. It was clearly a work room. Its flooring was of burnt bricks, 0.35 m.–0.36 m. or 1 foot square and 0.075 m.–0.085 m. thick, laid directly on the gypsum detritus leveller. These bricks were much less thoroughly burnt than the later bricks of the Parthian and Roman periods and had a distinctive yellowish color which approximated that of Neo-Babylonian bricks. They are of exceptional interest as the earliest burnt bricks found at Dura, certainly of local manufacture and carrying on the Neo-Babylonian tradition of the region. Near the center of the north side of the room the place of nine bricks was taken

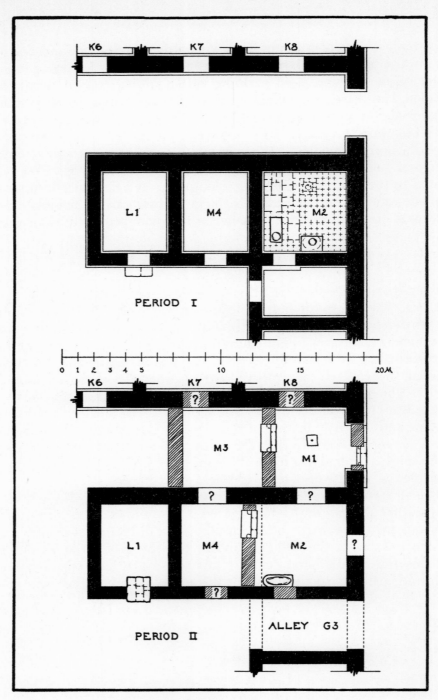

Fig. 6. G3, M1–4. Periods I and II. Restored Plans

by a small hearth of gypsum flags with a deeply charred and calcined area in the center. Against the south wall opposite was a low platform of fine plaster mortar, 0.085 m. high, with a slightly raised circular depression, and there was a similar platform, 0.12 m. high, with a circular sinking at the south end, to the left beside the west wall. Presumably these circular depressions were intended for the support of large jars or bowls, and the whole arrangement implies the manufacture or preparation of some commodity for sale in the adjacent shop. Room M2 existed in this original state long enough for its brick floor to wear out in places and to be patched with large gypsum flags, notably in the northwest corner and near the center of the room before the doorway.

### D. Date

The area and the shop buildings just described constituted the agora of Dura. They were the first buildings on their site, their floors only a few centimeters above the virgin surface of the bed rock. Dura itself was a Seleucid royal colony, planted around the turn of the fourth and third centuries B.C. as the heavily fortified halfway house on the direct road between the capitals of Antioch-on-the-Orontes and Seleucia-on-the-Tigris. The grid of its streets was laid down and its fortifications were planned by the royal architects. An agora was the focal point of Greek city life and the basic feature of the planned Greek city. There is therefore a strong probability that the agora of Dura was an essential part of the original colonial project. This inherent probability is abundantly confirmed by a mass of other evidence.

The agora buildings form one of a small group of buildings at Dura which differ sharply in plan and purpose from the later buildings of the city, and are all known on other grounds to be of Hellenistic date. These are the Palaces of the Citadel[9] and of the Redoubt,[10] the Temples of Artemis-and-Apollo[11] and Zeus Olympius,[12] and at least one unexplored and unidentified structure.[13] With these may be taken the socle of the

---

[9] *Rep. II*, pp. 15, 53 f.; cf. Rostovtzeff, *Dura-Europos and Its Art* (1938), pp. 12, 35–39; and forthcoming *Rep. X*.

[10] Preliminary account of final period, *Rep. IV*, pp. 21–25; cf. Rostovtzeff, *op. cit.*, pp. 35–37, 141; and forthcoming *Rep. X*.

[11] *Rep. VI*, pp. 404–411.

[12] To be described in a later part of *Rep. IX*.

[13] To be described in a later part of *Rep. IX*.

west front of the city wall.[14] As a group they constitute the official Seleucid buildings of the Hellenistic colony. Their plans are of western derivation, almost uninfluenced by the architectural tradition of the region. Their construction is equally foreign to a vicinity long accustomed to build with brick and plaster after the Babylonian manner. They share alike in the characteristics unique at Dura of socles of dimension stone built in an orthostate system of familiar Greek bond or full Hellenistic Doric orders or both. The agora buildings share with them their Western conception and plan which are purely Greek or Hellenistic having no parallels in the later architecture of the city, in Parthian architecture, or in the earlier architecture of the Near East. They too have the characteristic orthostate socles of dimension stone, and this constructional similarity extends to the smallest details of the cutting, laying, and coursing of the stonework. Attention has already been drawn, e.g., to the careful use of the by-product of stonecutting to level off the inequalities in the bed rock surface in preparation for laying floors.[15] A typical feature is the type of doorway employed. All later buildings in the city have monumental stone door trim of one sort or other. The Seleucid buildings along with the agora were characterized by the use of simple openings without projecting jambs, raised sill, or for the most part door sockets, which were evidently intended to receive additional fittings of wood or fine stone. Furthermore we can posit for the agora buildings a significant architectural feature of which none of the other buildings of its group has left evidence. This is the gabled roof. Here for the first and last time at Dura, a city of flat roofs in a world of flat roofs, we meet the Greek tiled gable with antefixes.

This evidence from design and construction is borne out by the ceramic finds. The original clay floors of the north building in Block G3 were apparently laid down at the time of construction. None of them contained potsherds. The ceramic evidence thus comes exclusively from the immediately succeeding layers of occupation, though in the southeast corner of Shop A3 the neck of a stamped Thasian amphora[16] found sunk in the bed rock may probably be associated with the earliest period. In rooms G3 and G4, J3 and J4, and K5 of Block G3, where the accumulation of debris and the rise in floor level were gradual and to a large

---

[14] *Rep. VII–VIII*, pp. 5–23; cf. Rostovtzeff, *op. cit.*, pp. 11 f.; and forthcoming *Rep. X*.

[15] Above, p. 9.                    [16] Below, pp. 169–176, no. 938.

extent undisturbed, the lowest distinguishable level above the original floor contained no datable pottery other than sherds of fine local "common ware" of the earliest type and late fourth or early third century "Attic" black glaze sherds. In area A1 of Block G3, some 3.50 m. before the façade of Shops A2–A4 and A2–A5 a pit had been sunk 2.06 m. into bed rock and carefully sealed over with a large gypsum slab. It had apparently been used as a receptacle for rubbish and broken vessels from the two shops, and fell into disuse and was covered over at or shortly before the end of the first period of this part of the building when rooms A2–A5 ceased to function as shops. It contained a stratified deposit, the lowest layers of which furnished datable sherds of only the types associated with the floors described above.

Finally a *terminus ante quem* for the earliest period of the agora is provided by the approximate date of the beginning of the period immediately following. This is shown by architectural, epigraphic, and ceramic evidence to have fallen in the last quarter of the second century B.C. or, at the latest, in the early years of the first century.

Architecturally the agora buildings identify themselves with a group of structures known to be of Hellenistic origin (ca. 300–120 B.C. at Dura), the evidence of pottery suggests a date in the third century, and the period to which the buildings belong can scarcely have lasted beyond the second century. The probability arising from the general circumstances surrounding the creation of the colony may therefore be regarded as confirmed, and it may be assumed that the initial period of intense building activity which produced the first necessary official buildings also included the agora. A somewhat closer consideration of the general plan and elevation of the buildings will suggest further conclusions.

Their stripped and barren look devoid of all architectural ornament save the row of antefixes at the eaves is probably due to the fact that they were purely utilitarian, colonial structures put up with the maximum economy of means and effort. Instances of the sacrifice of precise design to the thrifty use of stone in standard sizes have already been noted.[17] This does not, however, explain the curious truncated appearance of the whole complex, nor the absence of that most constant feature of ancient market places, the continuous portico. A comparison with other Hellenistic agoras makes it almost certain that the agora of Dura was the

[17] Above, pp. 6, 8.

result of a compromise solution of the problem arising from a plan which it proved impossible to complete. The original project must have called for the continuation of the east and west shops southward as far as Main Street to enclose the agora area on either side and produce the characteristic "horseshoe" form and for continuous colonnades down either side and across the rear, interrupted if at all only by the projecting north wings of the east and west buildings. This project was not carried out. The porticoes were never started. It was decided to terminate the east and west shops on the line of the south side of Street 2, and the south enclosure wall was erected setting off the completed portion from the open area in front. The east shop building in the form in which it was completed bore unmistakable traces of the change. It has been noted that the ten shops south of its north wing had the incommensurable average width of 3.42 m., some 0.20 m. over 6 cubits, and that this dimension appeared to be the result of the parcelling out of the available length of 42.58 m. It is highly unlikely in view of the consistent use of simple multiples of the cubit in the dimensions of the north buildings that this could have been intended in the original project. On the contrary a simple calculation shows that in an original plan for shops extending as far as Main Street twenty-eight units of exactly 6 cubits each would just fill the space of 113.030 m. Such a scheme would provide thirty instead of twelve shops on either side, giving a total of eighty-four shops opening on the market place and twenty-four on Street 4 behind, one hundred eight in all.

As to the reason for the failure to carry out the original plan we can only conjecture. Presumably either the royal treasury failed to supply the requisite appropriation for the whole project, which it was planned to complete in the future, or the builders could foresee that the portion eventually completed would be sufficient for the needs of the colony and were content to go without porticoes. In any case the agora buildings merely shared the fate of other over-ambitious projects for the Seleucid colony. In a similar way both the Seleucid west wall of the city and the Citadel were left unfinished whether for lack of time or funds.

If this interpretation of the evidence be correct, we may conclude by assuming that the project for the shop buildings of the agora, begun soon after the foundation of the colony, was altered to conform with circumstances in the course of the work, and completed in its present partial form not later than the middle of the third century B.C.

## E. Relation to the City Plan

### (Fig. 12)

The agora as originally planned occupied the canonical position in the city plan. It covered the area of a fixed number of the regular city blocks lying in the approximate center of the city, and had one side open to the main thoroughfare. The individual character of the site added an exceptional feature of adaptation. The northward prolongation of the main thoroughfare in Street H skirted its eastern flank, and Streets D and 4, where they skirted its western and northern flanks, were intended to form an alternative route for descent to the river plain. Accordingly this portion of Street 4 was treated as a market street, and the two north buildings were doubled to present a row of shops to the street as well as to the agora area proper. The same sort of adaptation was made in the east building of the south agora at Miletus.

The area of eight city blocks which was assigned to the agora in the original plan measured 159.79 m. × 147.13 m. or 23,510 sq. m. This was only slightly less than the area of the agora of Magnesia-on-the-Meander or that of the south agora of Miletus. It was more than four times the area of the agora of Priene, and gives an excellent index of the founder's ambitious conception of the future of the colony. Yet, as compared with the whole townsite, this area was not excessive by the standards of Hellenistic commercial centers. The agora area of Dura accounted for approximately 5% of the total city area exclusive of the Citadel, while the entire agora complex of Miletus amounted to about 5.4% of that city's area.

Since the agora buildings were an essential part of the original plan of the city and were set out with remarkable precision, they furnish valuable information about the dimensions of the original blocks and streets of Seleucid Dura. This information is of the highest importance, because it is difficult if not impossible on the evidence of the dimensions of the blocks and streets of the city in their final aspect to arrive at a mean which in any sense represents the dimensions employed in the original Hellenistic layout. Though throughout its history the city retained the outlines of the basic rectangular grid of the original plan, considerable irregularities crept in in the course of time and with the spread of the inhabited area from its original nuclei. These may be accounted for principally by the tendency of the buildings to encroach continually on the streets, and for the streets to make up as far as possible on one side for what they had lost on the other. In this way the dimensions and even the course of streets might change appreciably. These factors operated more freely in areas which had not been previously built on nor permanently staked out in the original survey. For these reasons the blocks and streets of the final period of the city are found upon close analysis to exhibit a disconcerting diversity and irregularity, which in general increases toward the periphery.

The Hellenistic agora buildings, on the other hand, offer a group of blocks and streets which preserve their exact original dimensions. As such they furnish the key to the city plan as a whole. The length of each of the north shop buildings was 76.73 m. and comprised the width of two city blocks together with the street between. The width of this included street is given by that of Street F between the two north buildings. It was 6.33 m. The width of the original blocks was therefore half of 76.73—6.33, or 35.20 m. Again, the east and west sides of the agora buildings measured 76.73 m., and comprised the length of one city block together with the street adjacent to the south. Given the street width of 6.33 m., the length of the original blocks was 76.73—6.33 = 70.40 m. or twice the width. The dimensions 35.20 m. and 70.40 m. correspond to 100 and 200 feet of 0.352 m. or $66\frac{2}{3}$ and $133\frac{1}{3}$ cubits of 0.528 m., while 6.33 m. = 18 of these feet or 12 cubits. We may conclude that the original city plan of Dura was based on a unit foot of 0.352 m. and a fundamental subdivision into blocks of 100 × 200 feet separated by streets of 18 feet.

This foot and cubit closely approximates the cubit of about 0.525 m. found by Gerkan to have been employed in the city walls and is probably identical with it. The cubit of 0.537 m. used in the agora buildings was presumably a larger variation of the same unit.

Most of the ordinary streets of the final period of the city were considerably less than 6.33 m. wide. Where earlier foundations have been found to underlie the walls on either side, they show the progressive encroachment of the buildings on the streets which resulted in the narrowing of their planned width. However Streets D and 4, where they bound the agora area, and the north and south prolongation of Main Street as Street H were even in their final form markedly wider than 6.33 m. and about of a size. The original width of Street H, which may also be assumed for the others, is preserved between the north shop building in Block G3 and an apparently contemporary ashlar socle across the street.[18] It measured 8.45 m., 24 feet of 0.352 m. or 16 cubits of 0.528 m. The original width of Main Street is not so easily determined, since no Hellenistic foundations have been located on its borders. In its final state it had an average width of about 8.00 m. save in the vicinity of the Main Gate where it measured more than 10.00 m. At this period, moreover, the gate was not centered on the street, which gives the appearance of being displaced toward the south. In fact, however, it seems clear on the basis of the original block measurements that the buildings along the north side of the street have encroached 3.00 m. to 4.00 m. over the original north side of the street as planned, while the buildings along the south side are approximately in their intended original position. It will be seen that this general encroachment of the buildings on the north side of Main Street probably reflects the irregularities attending the building up of the open south portion of the agora area. In any case the evidence points to an original width for Main Street of 12.00 m. to 13.00 m., most probably 12.67 m., 36 feet or 24 cubits, twice the width of the ordinary streets. The basic subdivisions of the plan were thus handled flexibly to meet the requirements of circulation, and the rectangular grid, though perfectly regular, was skillfully adapted to the particular features of the site.

Dura's streets of 18, 24, and 36 feet were much broader than the norm in the planned cities of Asia Minor. Its blocks with their 2,480 odd sq. m. of area and their length to width ratio of 2 : 1 were likewise bigger than those of Miletus and Priene and longer in proportion. Olynthus' blocks of ca. 3,144 sq. m. with the length to width ratio of 5 : 2 (ca. 88.65 m. × 35.46 m.), on the contrary, were somewhat bigger than those of Dura and longer in proportion. Its streets of 17 and 24 feet (5.02 m. and 7.08 m.) were considerably narrower. These earlier planned cities thus fail to show any close or direct relationship to the Dura plan. On the other hand the planned Seleucid cities of Syria and Iraq do display a striking affinity. Antioch, Apamea, Laodicea, Damascus, and Aleppo all appear, as far as may be judged, to have been laid out in blocks of a common size and with the length to width ratio of 2 : 1. The average common dimensions are roughly 110 m. × 52 m. which perhaps represent 300 and 150 feet of 0.352 m. and yield blocks some 2¼ times as large as those of Dura. The blocks of Seleucia-on-the-Tigris have the same 2 : 1 proportion and can probably be reduced to the same unit of measure.

[18] Below, pp. 26 f.

They would appear to have been planned as 400 × 200 feet, just four times the size of the Dura blocks. The Dura plan on this evidence falls into place as an exemplar of a uniform and standardized Seleucid planning system which employed the same unit and the same proportions in varying simple multiples as the circumstances required. The development of such a system was the natural outcome of what was in the early Hellenistic period very literally a mass production of cities.

## APPENDIX. THE STONE SOCLE IN BLOCK B7

A trench carried to bed rock along the west side of Block B7 revealed beneath the rubblework socles of later structures the remains of the west exterior stone socle of a building on the opposite side of Street H from the north and east agora buildings. With the exception of a gap of 9.67 m. the footing course of the whole west side of the building was found in place together with a segment 4.03 m. long of the orthostate socle above. The socle when complete consisted of the footing course of two rows of stretchers, a base header course, an orthostate course, and a crowning header course. No blocks of the latter remained in situ.

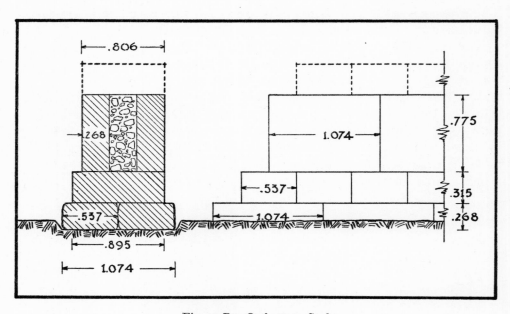

Fig. 7. B7, Orthostate Socle

The blocks were cut and laid to the same cubit and foot unit as the agora buildings. The levels were different. The footing course of the building in Block B7 had the mean level of 219.13 m. a.s.l., 0.225 m. lower than the corresponding course of the agora buildings.

The footing course was 1.074 m. or two cubits wide. It consisted of two rows of stretchers, 1.074 m. or two cubits long × 0.537 m. or 1 cubit wide and ideally 0.268 m. or ½ cubit thick, left rough pointed save for the upper joint surface. They were laid in a shallow trench cut in the bed rock without free space between the rows but also without fitted joints. The top level was kept uniform by increasing or diminishing the depth of the trench or the thickness of the blocks. The base headers were 0.895 m. or 2½ feet long × 0.537 m. or 1 cubit wide and had the incommensurable thickness of 0.315 m. They were thus set back 0.089 m. (1 palm?) from either face of the footing course. They were finished as smooth as possible and closely jointed with the use of the finest plaster grout without exterior pointing. The socle above was 0.806 m. or 1½ cubits thick. The orthostates like those of the north agora buildings were 1.074 m. long, 0.775 m. high, and 0.268 m. thick. They were finished smooth with close dry joints which showed definite anathyrosis. The space of 0.268 m. was packed with fine rubblework in gypsum mortar. The whole gives the impression of being somewhat more finely and carefully constructed than the socles of the agora buildings.

The two west corners of the building are preserved at either end of the footing course. As measured on the footings its western dimension was 36.16 m. or 101 feet of 0.358 m. which would give 35.80 m. or 100 feet as the length along the orthostates. If as is probable the building occupied the full width of the block, it was almost a perfect square in plan, 35.80 m. × 35.20 m. The block remains unexcavated, and nothing is known of the nature, destination, or plan of the early building it contains. We may assume that it was of Hellenistic origin and probably of a public character.

# III

## THE BAZAAR QUARTER
### A. *Origins*

THE history of Section G during the next period or periods is the history
of the gradual conversion of the carefully planned agora with its shop
buildings to a crowded bazaar quarter. The change proceeded slowly
over a long period of time and in a sense was never completely accomplished. For many reasons it is not possible to present a detailed picture
of each step in the process. The excavation of the section is far from complete. Even in the excavated Blocks G2 and G4 many areas have not
been explored beyond their final levels. Since the bazaar quarter was not
the result of a sweeping transformation or transformations, its history
does not fall into a series of sharply defined building periods. It was a
continuous and unceasing process of growth and change without definite
plan or purpose, the general aspect of which at any given time was the
almost wholly fortuitous result of a sum of separate and unrelated inci-
dents. The largely planless mass of buildings and open spaces which
was the end result of more than three hundred fifty years of development was in itself the record of almost every step along the way but had
at the same time progressively obliterated more and more the traces of
its earliest stages. Under the circumstances dating must be for the most
part essentially relative and the general view of the state of the whole
area at any given time highly approximate.

The critical initial stages in the transformation can fortunately be
observed at certain isolated points where special circumstances have
operated to preserve their traces. Three such points in particular present themselves: Rooms A2–A5 and M1–M4 of Block G3, which have
already been discussed for the evidence they give of the arrangement of
the Hellenistic shops,[1] and area 70–71[1], 83–102, 126 of Block G1.

G3, A2–A5 (Figs. 4, 79, 81, 82; Pls. I, II, III, 1). This group of
three double shops at the southwest corner of the north agora building in
G3 was converted to a public office of four rooms. The removal of the
partition between the front rooms of Shops A2–A4 and A2–A5 created

---

[1] Above, pp. 15–19.

the single room A2, 11.55 m. $\times$ 5.37 m. with its length perpendicular to the axis of the entrance. The partition was completely demolished leaving only the trench for its footing course, and the blocks obtained were used to wall up the old exterior doorway to A2–A4. The old entrance to A2–A5 served as the entrance to the new room, and at the level of its sill a new floor level was established with a floor of rammed earth 0.45 m. above the old. In the process the counter and benches of the old shop were razed to this level. About the room ran a narrow bench of packed mud lightly rendered with plaster, 0.47 m. high $\times$ 0.50 m. broad on the west, north, and east sides of the room and 0.58 m. broad on the south. It was interrupted at the entrance, and before the doorways to rooms A4 and A5 sank to a low step, 0.16 m. high. Inner rooms A4 and A5 received new floors at the level of that of A2. A narrow doorway, 0.81 m. wide, was cut through the rear wall of A4 to the inner room beyond, but unfortunately the state of the evidence does not permit the reconstruction of the arrangement of this room (F2) during this period. In any case the doorway was subsequently walled up again. The blocks obtained in cutting it were used in room A5 to wall up the narrow opening A5–A3.

Double Shop A3–A3 like its neighbor was made into a single long room, 9.28 m. $\times$ 5.37 m., but with its length on the axis of the doorway. The east-west partition was razed to the footing course, and the narrow opening through to room G3 was closed with mud brick. A new floor level was established 0.66 m. above the old, some 0.20 m. above the sill of the original doorway. Accordingly the floor of the doorway was raised 0.30 m. by a paving of gypsum slabs, and the old opening was fitted with a complete stone trim consisting of a raised sill and projecting sectional jambs cut on the ends of the slabs which formed the new reveals. In the process the doorway was narrowed to a width of 1.18 m. between the jambs, since the western reveal slabs were simply added against the old reveal and the east slabs only slightly mortised into it. Against the east, north, and west walls of the room on a plinth of mud brick mortared and rendered with plaster and 0.31 m. high were built the tiers of deep square bins or compartments described in *Rep. V,* p. 82. The tiers were built up on a lozenge system of partitions at an angle of 45°. Each compartment was 0.80 m.–0.85 m. deep, 0.50 m. across, and 0.35 m.–0.36 m. on a side save in the bottom tier and at the ends, where gabled shapes and half compartments occurred. These dimensions were determined by the fact that the framework of the compartments was as far as possible constructed of undivided mud bricks 0.35 m.–0.36 m. or 1 foot square set on edge and heavily mortared with plaster, the angle joints being packed with clay. The compartments along the west wall extended its full length and numbered eleven and a half in each tier. Those along the east wall were ended for accessibility 1.16 m. short of the north wall numbering ten in each tier. For the same reason the compartments along the north wall were separated by a space of 0.43 m. from the west compartments and by a space of 0.82 m. from the west wall. They numbered three and one-half in each tier. There were thus twenty-five compartments in each tier about the room and at least four complete tiers, as indicated by the compartments found standing to this height in the north end of the room.

The function of the room and of the compartments is made clear by the numbers and letters inscribed to the left of each compartment.[2] The latter were pigeonholes for filing annual rolls of documents and their accompanying registers several to each pigeonhole. The room itself was the city archive. The entire complex A2–A5 containing the archive is thus identified as the chreophylakion or register-office of the city. Room A2 with its inner offices A4 and A5 doubtless served for the drawing up, attesting, and registration of documents, the payment of the requisite fees, etc. The central location on the market place was appropriate to this function, and in fact the presiding official was presumably the agoranomos.[3] The permanent character of this group of rooms as a public bureau is sufficiently indicated by the fact that they alone of all the structures in the area of the original agora buildings remained essentially unchanged throughout the subsequent history of the city.

The remodelling of Shops A2–A5 and the creation of the register office can be dated by ceramic, architectural, and epigraphic evidence to the end of the second century B.C.

The stratified deposit in the pit before Shop A2–A5,[4] which presumably was covered over at the time of the conversion of the shops, closed with layers containing a scattering of earlier datable sherds amid a preponderance of early "Pergamene" sherds and the local imitations both of it and of "Attic" black glaze in similar copied shapes. Such a distribution is characteristic of the late second century. The sealed fill beneath the new floors of rooms A2 and A3 and the packing within the benches of

[2] Below, pp. 169–175.
[3] For this official at Dura, *Rep. V*, p. 21, no. 388.
[4] Above, p. 21.

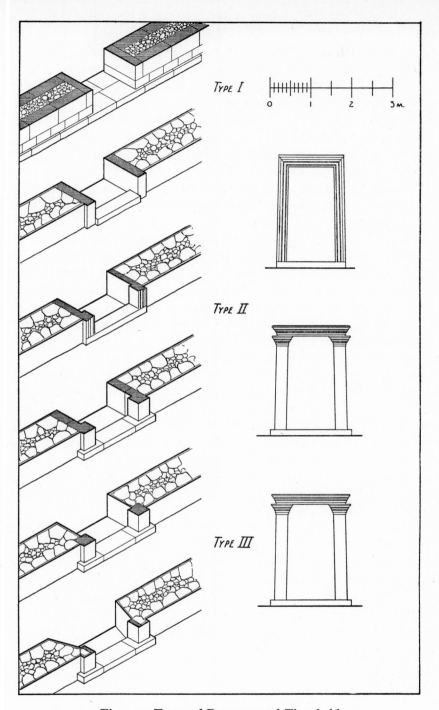

TYPE I

TYPE II

TYPE III

Fig. 12a. Types of Doorway and Threshold

A2 and the plinth of A3 contained large numbers of sherds which corroborate this dating. The sherds, which must have been accumulated at the time of the remodelling, were more heterogeneous and had a larger proportion of the earlier black glazes and fine local "commonware," but they exhibited the same preponderance of early "Pergamene" types and imitations. Both fill and packing also contained sherds of Rhodian or other island jars and altogether eight sherds of the typical early imported green glaze bowls.

The only datable architectural feature was the new door trim of room A3. This was of the second general type with its slightly projecting sectional jambs worked on the ends of reveal slabs which are set without splay. It is the earliest form in which the normal doorway with projecting monumental jambs and raised sill occurs at Dura, and is characteristic of just this period, late second and early first centuries B.C.

The evidence from the epigraphy of the inscribed year numbers and letters on the pigeonholes in room A3 fully confirms this dating and is discussed in detail below, pp. 169–176.

G3, L1, M1–M4 (Figs. 6, 79, 82; Pl. VIII). This group of shops at the north end of the east shop building underwent radical changes typical of the transformation which was taking place in other parts of the agora area. As seen above[5] inner room M2 retained its original form and appointments long enough for its brick floor to require extensive patching with stone flags. Some time later, along with its neighbor M4, it became part of a complex of at least four rooms created out of this portion of the agora buildings. The essential feature of this development was the obstruction of the passage between the east and north shop buildings and its conversion to two rooms, M1 and M3. At the outer end of the passage the space between the projecting piers was closed by a wall largely made up of reused Hellenistic socle blocks and pierced by a doorway 1.26 m. wide. Between the sill blocks and the north pier two reused header blocks, 1.074 m. long, served as foundation. In the wall itself old orthostates were used, two of which were found in situ, one on either side of the doorway. The reveal slabs were missing, but the traces of weathering on the sill indicated that they were not cut with projecting jambs. The two blocks of the threshold, however, were cut back to form a slightly raised sill, behind which on either side were shallow square

[5] Pp. 17, 19.

sinkings for the door sockets. Some 4.80 m. to the west a second wall was thrown across the passage. Its socle was found standing an average of 1.00 m. high above bed rock beneath later wall M1–M3 which was in part footed on it. It was 0.78 m. thick and constructed of large roughly shaped stones mortared with mud with an occasional reused socle block. Its doorway, 1.80 m. wide, had likewise lost its reveal slabs, but the threshold of gypsum slabs, which projected about 0.07 m. beyond the socle face on either side, showed clearly that they had been without projecting jambs. The slabs of the threshold were laid so as to form a raised sill on the east side of the doorway, behind which were the shallow rectangular cuttings for the door sockets. Some 5.00 m. farther west the passage was closed by a wall on the line of the Hellenistic shop partition L1–M4 which rested on a socle of similar construction but without openings. Its lowest 0.40 m.–0.60 m. remains beneath the later wall M3–L2. The systematic demolition of the south exterior socle of the north shop building eastward of this point within the area of complex M indicates that this wall formed from the beginning the western limit of the complex.

Of the two rooms created by these operations M1, which opened directly from the street, was adapted to serve as a house court and was provided with a shallow cesspool. M3 formed an inner living room. Whether the Hellenistic Shops K7 and K8 to the north were brought into the new complex there is no certain means of knowing. Their area was so thoroughly altered in later remodellings that practically no trace of the intermediate stages remains. Perhaps it is more probable that they remained outside, that their original south doorways were blocked up, and that they were given an opening on Street H and formed the nucleus of the later House K. In any case, however, the presence of Hellenistic blocks in the new socles of M1 and M3 may possibly be taken as evidence that the demolition of the south exterior socle of K7 and K8 and the encroachment of complex M on their original area had already begun when the new socles were erected.

To the south, original Shop M4 and rear room M2 were clearly joined to the new rooms. The entrance to M2 from the shop south of it was walled up, as is demonstrated by the placing of a large oval rubblework basin directly before it on the level of a new rammed earth floor 0.12 m.– 0.16 m. above the old brick and flag paving. The shop itself was thrown open by the razing of its east and west walls, and was converted to a passage to the open market place to replace the old passage taken up by

rooms M1 and M3. It is probably to be assumed that the original doorway of Shop M4 was walled up at the same time, though direct evidence
is wanting and it is possible that it continued to function as a shop. At
any rate the original partition between Shops M4 and M2 was demolished almost completely and replaced by a new one slightly west of the
old line, whose socle still stands some 0.70 m. high above bed rock beneath the floor of the later room M2. Like the socles of M1 and M3 it
was built of large rough-shaped stones mortared with clay with a reused
block here and there, and had the same width of 0.78 m. Near the north
end was the doorway, 1.80 m. wide and of the same type and construction as doorway M1–M3. The stump of the plain stone facing of its
north reveal remained in place. It had a threshold of gypsum slabs
which had a raised sill and sinkings for door sockets and projected
slightly beyond either face of the socle.

Either M2 or M4 presumably served as a shop. If it be assumed that
the south doorway of M4 was walled up, an exterior doorway on Street
H must probably be restored for M2. If, on the other hand, M4 continued to function as a shop, M2 must be restored as an inner room
accessible from M1. The problem of these doorways is rendered practically insoluble by the almost total later destruction of the Hellenistic
socle in this area. Fortunately this fact does not seriously impair the
general impression to be gained from the evolution of the complex M
out of the Hellenistic shop buildings as typical of the process that was
going forward in all parts of the agora. The development of such small
house complexes of which one unit served as a shop, the obliteration or
displacement of the original avenues of access to the open market place
were the characteristic first steps in the transformation of the agora to
the bazaar quarter. In this instance the southern limit of the future development of Block G3 was permanently fixed by the new approach to
the dwindling open area created by the haphazard formation of Alley
G3.

The date at which these changes took place is approximately indicated by the constructional technique of the new socles and doorways
and by the beginning of the deposit of broken pottery in the cesspool of
court M1. The socles with their large stones and clay mortar taken by
themselves might rightly be assigned to a time before the perfection of
the plaster rubblework technique for socles with its plaster mortar and
uniformly graded small caementa. These considerations, however, are
not decisive since this general type of wall continued to some extent in

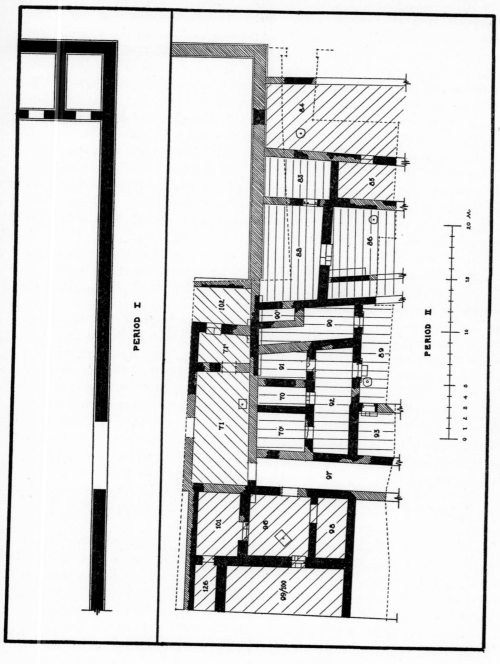

PERIOD I

PERIOD II

Fig. 13. G1, Area 70–71,[1] 83–102, 126. Restored Plan

use below ground and in cheap construction throughout the city's history. In this case the evidence of the doorways provides the needed confirmation. They were of an early transitional type between the first and second general types, having a raised sill but not projecting jambs. They were thus somewhat earlier in type than the new doorway of archive room A3 and probably date from the last quarter of the second century B.C. This rough date is confirmed by the scanty sherds from the lowest layers in the cesspool and by the relatively slight rise in the surface level of Street H as indicated by the new exterior doorway of M1. Its sill lay 0.18 m. below the old high exterior sill level of the north agora building and 0.19 m. above the old low sill level of the east agora building.

G1, 70–71[1], 83–102, 126 (Figs. 13, 80, 81, 82; Pl. IX, 2). This area, the southeast portion of Block G1, was in its original state merely a part of the open market place lying on either side of the wall which set off the half of the agora enclosed by shop buildings. It is possible to form an idea of its immediate post-Hellenistic development largely because at a much later period the buildings which had come to occupy it were razed to ground level, and the area became once more an open place. Owing to this circumstance the foundations, socles, and floors of its earliest buildings were not progressively disturbed or obliterated by later rebuildings but were preserved beneath the later ground level. The area of the later open place, however, was naturally circumscribed by the buildings about it, and these limits were without relation to the plan of any earlier building or buildings. All the early house plans save one, therefore, that can be reconstructed from the remaining foundations are more or less truncated and partial. They are cut off to the west, north, and east by the houses of later periods and to the south by a row of small shops.

In all five houses can be distinguished. They were built in what was then open ground on either side of the south enclosure wall of the agora buildings. The wall itself at the time they were built was in part completely done away with, in part replaced by a wall of rubblework on the same line, which at one point retained a segment of the older footing course as foundation. It was within the area of House 96–126 which lay athwart its course that the wall was fully demolished and its line ignored in the plan, though the trench in the bed rock for its footings is still traceable. The other four houses lay wholly to one side or the other of the wall, and, since it served them as a party wall, its line at least was respected. Between Houses 70–93 and 71–102 to the east the stone socle was replaced by a narrower socle of clay-mortared rubblework. Bits of the latter adhere to the nine blocks of the old footing course which remain here. Where such traces are totally lacking, as between rooms 70$^1$–70 and 71, the abutment of the remaining house walls at right angles indicates the continuation. Here the party wall was clearly without openings save at its western extremity where it was broken for the entrance to court 71 of House 71–102. This entrance fell at the end of the long alley or corridor, 97, which probably also afforded means of access to House 96–126. Its width of 2.55 m.–2.65 m. occupied the western half of a strip lying on the projection of Street G of the original city plan, and the opening at its northern end, of which one side is preserved, thus fell within the limits of an opening in the Hellenistic socle on the produced axis of Street G. This coincidence is probably not fortuitous, and we may see in entrance 97–71 a bit of evidence for the presence of the earlier opening at this point. Farther east beyond room 102 the course of the Hellenistic socle lies outside the later open place within the area of the later rooms S100, F121, F122, and S124, and there are no means of judging its condition at the time in question. At a later date it had been completely removed save for a short segment of the footing course preserved where it was crossed by wall F122–S124.

House 96–126 was the only one which lay completely within the open place of later times. Its floors lay at an average of about 219.65 m. a.s.l. or 0.25 m.–0.30 m. above bed rock, while its socles of rubblework mortared with clay stand 0.45 m.–1.25 m. high above it. Their faces were built up of large rough-shaped stones and the interior space packed with smaller stones and clay. Originally these faces were probably pointed and rendered with clay of which all trace has long since disappeared. House 96–126 was a compact structure of five rooms. Its court, 96, probably entered directly from corridor 97, was approximately 5.50 m. square and was provided with a shallow cesspool, 3.68 m. deep, covered by a well-worn rectangular slab of gypsum pierced in the center with a circular hole, 0.12 m. in diameter. In the northeast corner stood a small rectangular bench or table. The wall which separated it from small rectangular room 98 to the south had been razed to below the level of the threshold, but the doorway was probably, as restored, at the east end where the socle was lowest. Larger room 101 to the north was entered from the court through a doorway 1.70 m. wide, a plain opening without projecting jambs. Its flat threshold was composed of two slabs marked by square cuttings for the door sockets joined by a deep groove.

Its west wall was broken by the simple opening, 1.02 m. wide, of the doorway to narrow chamber 126. The threshold was a single flat slab with sinkings for the door sockets at either side. A doorway only 1.19 m. wide in the west wall of the court gave access to room 99–100, the chief room of the house. It was long and narrow, 10.75 m. × 4.12–4.27 m. The reveals of the doorway were faced off with plain gypsum slabs, and its threshold was made up of seven small slabs, three of which, projecting 0.12 m. beyond the east face of the socle, formed a slightly raised sill. Behind it against the south reveal was a circular cutting for the door socket, and in the north reveal opposite was the slot for the bolt, 0.76 m. from the sill.

Rooms 99–100 alone were reused and to some extent remodelled to serve as shops giving on the open place of the later period. As part of their renovation at this time their original socles were pointed and rendered with plaster. Although the west socle of these rooms now appears to be continuous and throughout contemporary with the other socles of the house, it is possible that in room 126 it was partially rebuilt obliterating all trace of a doorway which may have stood at the west end of this chamber. One cannot, therefore, be perfectly certain that 126 was not at one time as its plan might suggest the entrance passage to the house from the open market place to the west. In any event this entrance, if it ever existed, was soon closed by the building of House D adjacent.[6]

Of House 71–102 only three rooms can be identified and of one of these only the southern portion is known. The rest extended northward in the area later occupied by House A and were demolished to the last vestige when that house was built. The remaining socles are of the same construction as those of House 96–126 and in addition contain numerous fragments of Hellenistic socle blocks. It is evident that the east wall of room 102 and walls 71[1]–102 and 71–71[1] originally abutted on the party wall which replaced the Hellenistic enclosure wall. That 71 was the house court is indicated by the cesspool closed with a small pierced gypsum slab close beside the south party wall. Entry was, as we have seen, from corridor 97, and the plain west reveal of the doorway faced with a gypsum slab has been preserved, though the threshold is missing. The walls of the court must be largely restored in continuation of what remains together with a doorway in the north wall giving access to the rooms on that side. How far these extended it is impossible to say with

[6] Below, pp. 47, 135 f.

certainty. Probably not more than the width of one range of rooms to judge from the fact that the north wall of House D on the west long represented the northern limit of building into the open area there. In all likelihood there was a shop or shops opening north on the market place and two or three other rooms. Room 102 extended northward beyond the north side of the court and room 71¹ and formed a part of this north portion of the house. Whether the house extended eastward beyond room 102 with another room or rooms, the existing condition of the east socle of 102 makes it useless to conjecture. Of room 71¹ little can be made out beyond its bare outline. Even its doorway from the court is conjectural. Fortunately the threshold of doorway 71¹–102 is preserved. The opening was 1.32 m. wide and without jambs of any sort. Two slabs formed a rough sill which projected 0.11 m. beyond the west face of the socle. There was no trace of the door sockets.

The plan of what was unquestionably the major portion of House 70–93 can be recovered. The missing portion to the south which included the balance of court 89 and room 93 and contained the entrance to the house cannot have been very extensive. It probably extended no farther than the approximate line of the façades of the later row of shops along Market Street, some 5.00 m.–7.00 m. southward. Here we have only to restore the remainder of court 89 and room 93, an entrance, presumably a shop or shops, and the outer end of corridor 97. The same considerations apply with equal cogency to the neighboring House 83–88. The position of the south façades of these early houses with their entrances on the open market place was determined solely by convenience and the natural extension of dwellings of this size southward of the old enclosure wall in front of which they were built. Once established, however, it formed the necessary limit of building in this direction, and in the course of time, when the area to the south was built up, defined the north side of a street, the later Market Street. This course of development was exactly parallel to that of Alley G3, which, after its casual opening as a substitute passage to the open market place, came in time to form the natural southern limit of Block G3.

All the remaining socles and foundations of House 70–93 were originally of the same construction as those of Houses 96–126 and 71–102. At a later date the north socle of court 89 and all the socles south of it were rebuilt above the contemporary ground level in solid plaster rubblework of early type on the old foundations. The original floor level of ca. 219.44 m. a.s.l., only 0.20 m.–0.30 m. above bed rock, remained throughout almost unchanged. The single extant doorway in the north part of the house, doorway 92–70, was of the same type as the doorways of Houses 96–126 and 71–102. It had no projecting jambs. Its reveals were faced with plain gypsum slabs, and its threshold consisted of a single large slab, which projected 0.09 m. beyond the south face of the socle to form a raised sill block, and three smaller slabs behind. They showed no trace of the door sockets. The doorways of the southern part of the house are of two sorts. Doorway 89–93 was of the second general type like the door-way of archive room A3 in Block G3.[7] It had a raised sill and projecting sectional jambs cut on the ends of the reveal slabs. It is clear that it was inserted in the old socle at some intermediate period of renovation before the general remodelling of this part of the house. Doorways 89–92 and 89–90, on the other hand, were of the third general type. Each had a nar-row raised sill of three blocks on which rested projecting monolithic jambs. The reveals of doorway 89–92 were not revetted. Those of door-way 89–90 were faced with thin gypsum slabs distinct from the jambs. Unmistakable proof that these doorways of a later type were installed at the time when the socles of this part of the house were rebuilt is furnished by the fact that they were provided for in the construction of the socle. The projection of the stone jambs was continued for about 0.20 m. on either side of each doorway in the rubblework.

Court 89 was some 9.25 m. long. Its cesspool situated close beside doorway 89–92 was 4.17 m. deep and covered with a pierced circular lid of stone. The principal living room of the house was room 92. Like room 99–100 of House 96–126 it was long and narrow, 9.50 m.–10.00 m. × 3.20 m.–3.40 m. From it opened the three smaller domestic chambers 70[1], 70, and 91. The south walls of rooms 70[1] and 91 no longer stand to the height of the doorsills, so that the doors can only be approximately restored. Rooms 90 and 93 were secondary units which retained nothing that would characterize them further. The northeast corner of room 90 appears to have been occupied by a large closet, 90[1].

Of House 83–88, which adjoined House 70–93 on the east, the court and two or three rooms are distinguishable. The southern portion of court 86 together with the entrance to the house from the market place and an additional room or rooms are missing. The remaining portions of the socle show the same type of rubblework in clay mortar found else-where in the area. The original floors lay approximately 219.43 m. a.s.l.,

[7] Above, p. 32.

only 0.10 m.–0.20 m. above bed rock. The two preserved doorways were of the familiar early type. Doorway 86–88 was a simple opening without jambs or stone revetment 1.93 m. wide. Its threshold consisted of five gypsum slabs, three of which, projecting 0.13 m. beyond the south face of the socle, formed a raised sill. There were no remains of the door sockets. Doorway 88–83, 1.22 m. wide, had stone-faced flat reveals and a single threshold slab, on which were worked the raised sill with rectangular sinkings for the door sockets and a slot for a vertical door bolt. Court 86 had a greatest east-west dimension of 6.62 m. Its cesspool near the east wall was found partially fallen in and filled with miscellaneous debris from the razing of the house. Along the west wall from the northwest corner ran a high rubblework bench or table, 3.30 m. long and 0.68 m. wide, which stood some 0.70 m. above the floor. The west wall was a relatively slight partition only 0.48 m. thick which shut off what appears to be a long narrow chamber or closet of which only the north end remains. Room 88, the chief living room of the house, measured 9.10 m. × 5.20 m. in greatest dimensions and had as its dependency living room 83 to the east.

Room 85 appears to fall within the general limits of House 83–86, but its socles show no trace of any possible opening from court 86 or room 83. On the other hand, in the extant doorway in its west socle the position of the doorsill on the west side of the threshold indicates that the doorway opened from this direction, and consequently that room 85 was part of the house of which 84 was the court. The latter is identified by its cesspool, found open and filled with debris. Presumably the entrance for this house, 84–85, was on Street H to the east. Although the scanty vestiges reveal very little of the original plan, it is clear that the house belonged integrally with the group under consideration. This is shown not only by the site overlapping that of House 83–88, but also by doorway 84–85 which is of the same early type as the other original doorways in the area. The paucity of remains is to a large extent due to the fact that the house was suppressed at an intermediate period before the formation of open space and replaced by a row of shops. The remains of the socle of the rear wall of these shops in continuation of the west wall of Shop S124 cut through area 84 from north to south, and the west walls of later Shops S44 and S45 are partially footed in it.

The approximate date of the five original houses can be deduced from their plans, the construction of their socles, their doorways, and the scanty ceramic evidence furnished by the contents of their cesspools.

Their near contemporaneity is demonstrated by the practical identity of these features throughout. The plans are rather exceptional for Dura and appear to show the influence of a Hellenistic house plan related to that familiar from Olynthus. The type of construction universally employed in the original socles, faces of large roughly shaped stones mortared with clay with a filler of smaller stones in clay, was closely similar to that of the new socles in area M1–M4 of Block G3. In both cases it gives a presumption of a date before the perfection of rubblework of uniform small caementa and gypsum plaster, and abundant evidence from elsewhere in the city shows that this technique was firmly established by the mid first century B.C. In both cases the presumption is borne out by the type of doorway associated with the original socles. In area 70–71[1], 83–102, and 126 all the original doorways were of the same early transitional sort between the first and second general types, while a doorway of the second type occurred at an intermediate stage in House 70–93. Though the covered cesspools of courts 96, 71, and 89 yielded relatively few datable sherds, they were in full accord with the architectural evidence. In each case the lowest layers of the deposit contained only sherds of the third to early first centuries B.C., "Attic" black glaze, early "Pergamene," and the local imitations of both. The combined evidence points unmistakably to the last quarter of the second century.

The development of the area in the one hundred fifty odd years before the erection of the five houses may probably be envisaged somewhat as follows. The open market place stretching away on either side of the south enclosure wall of the Hellenistic agora buildings lent itself, particularly on market days, to the setting up of many structures of a temporary sort to meet the needs of a lively trade—booths, stalls, or stands in the open air or covered with planks or awnings. The unencumbered stretches of the enclosure wall were especially adapted to the erection of lean-to booths of this sort along either side. As time went on there was an ever increasing tendency for such constructions to become more or less permanent, to grow larger, and at length to provide living quarters for the tradesman and his family. The natural end result of such a process unhindered by legislation or effective control was the creation of permanent dwelling places normally in conjunction with a place of business. In our area they presumably preserved in general the location of the temporary structures that had preceded them, but brought about as varying circumstances demanded the destruction or alteration of the old wall against which they had originally leaned.

In each of the three specific areas which have been examined in detail the first decisive step in the transformation of the Seleucid agora to an Oriental bazaar seems to have taken place at about the same time, the decades immediately preceding the turn of the second and first centuries B.C. This is the transitional period of the end of Seleucid and the beginning of Parthian political domination at Dura. All our evidence indicates clearly that with the withdrawal of Seleucid rule and of direct and sustained Hellenistic influence on Dura was bound up the abandonment of the Greek conception of the agora as the characteristic expression of the economic life of the city. Neither as a formal concept nor as a reality could the agora subsist by itself under the new conditions. Its existence at Dura had been solely by virtue of the Seleucid program of Hellenization and the Seleucid ability to invest money and services in it. With the reversion of the city to local rule and local traditions of life went inevitably its gradual conversion to an Oriental bazaar quarter.

How this conversion came about in actual practice the areas under examination have shown. The development in each case was typical. The shops of the Hellenistic agora buildings had no doubt originally been leased by the city to individual tradesmen. With long tenure and the relaxation of administrative vigilance they tended to lapse into private ownership. Then they might be combined in groups and remodelled to form modest dwellings in connection with the owner's shop (G3, M1–M4). Temporary structures in the open agora area were under similar circumstances enlarged and made permanent (G1, 70–71[1], 83–102, 126). In either case the original plan of the area was modified and gradually obliterated. Old avenues of access and circulation disappeared; new lines of streets and alleys more or less fortuitously created became the limits of future development. At the same time the conversion of Shops G3, A2–A5 to a public clerk's office reflects vividly the necessity for keeping some portion of the old agora as an indispensable public building free from encroachment at the hands of private individuals.

## B. Development. Period I

### (Fig. 78)

The process of change once initiated proceeded without ceasing until the end of the city's history. The obstacles which confront any attempt

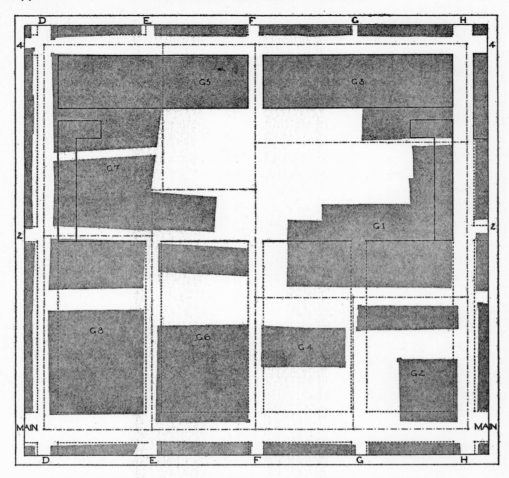

Fig. 14. Section G, Bazaar. First Century B.C.—Second Century A.D.

to present and analyze each step in this gradual and unsystematic development have been described at the beginning of this section. The procedure adopted here will be that of sketching the general lines of growth up to and after a certain arbitrarily selected intermediate point of time. The steps in the development of the individual buildings concerned will be examined in detail as far as the evidence permits in the following section on the houses and shops of the final period.

The date chosen as a convenient point of reference is the turn of the first and second centuries of our era, though it must be understood that reference made to it is never more than approximate. By this time the open area which had been enclosed by the Seleucid shops had shrunk to about one-half its original size, encroached on by buildings from all sides. The old avenues of access to it had for the most part been replaced by others. Only the short stretch of Street F between the shop buildings to the north remained unchanged. On the east access was by narrow Alley G3, created in the first instance, as has been seen,[8] by the suppression of the northernmost shop in the original east building. On the west there were two approaches: a similar but longer and somewhat oblique alley, G5, originally broken through the second shop from the north in the west building; and a street approximately in alignment with Street 2 of the city plan. Access from the south was by a broad opening roughly on the line of Street F but with its axis shifted toward the east. The open Hellenistic market place south of the original shop buildings had to a great extent filled with blocks of shops and dwellings separated by north-south streets in approximate continuation of Streets E, F, and G of the city plan. The northern part of this area was traversed by a broad open strip of varying width, the so-called Market Street.

The general course of this development was the following. In Block G3 (Fig. 79) the creation of House M[9] had apparently been accompanied or immediately succeeded by that of House K and Shops S1–S5 in their earliest form.[10] They evolved from the six easternmost double shops of the old Seleucid north building. The conversion of the rest of the shop building proceeded slowly from the periphery to the center, from east to west where the three double shops, A2–A5, had already been remodelled to form the public clerk's office.[11] Houses H and J in their original form[12] were followed by the early House B[13] and House G,[14] and the transformation was completed by the formation of House F[15] and the closing of doorway F2–A4. The extent to which the Hellenistic stone socles remained in evidence down to the end of the city gives a rough index of this sequence of building. Within the area of the older houses toward the east end of the block the course of a longer existence

[8] Above, p. 34.
[10] Below, pp. 69 f.
[12] Below, pp. 80 f.
[14] Below, p. 91.
[9] Above, pp. 32–36.
[11] Above, pp. 28–32.
[13] Below, pp. 90 f.
[15] Below, pp. 99 f.

involving continual remodelling and repairing brought about the almost total destruction of the original socles, whose materials were broken up and used in the construction of new socles of rubblework. Within the area of the more recent houses toward the west end of the block this process had not had time to go so far, and considerable portions of the original socles remained in use. The progression from east to west can be followed chronologically in a general way by means of the evidence of the construction of the earliest independent house socles, by the typology of doorways and moldings, by the relation of successive exterior doorway levels to the ever rising levels of the streets, and here and there by the ceramic contents of cesspools. This evidence, scanty, fragmentary, and inconclusive as it frequently is, will be treated in the discussion of the individual houses.

During the same time, though well after the construction of the original Houses J and H, Houses D and L[16] were erected in that order in front of the old shop building area with their façades in prolongation of the north side of Alley G3. When built both gave on the open market place to the south, and beyond House D the façade of the Hellenistic shop building long remained the southern boundary of the block. This is clearly indicated by the fact that the exterior thresholds of D and L, particularly after the erection of House A in Block G1 opposite, were several times raised to meet the rapid rise in the level of narrow Alley G3.[17] The outer doorways of the much later Houses C and B,[18] opening on what had continued to be an arm of the open square and therefore not subject to the rapid accumulation of rubbish, were built to a much lower level which never required correction.

In Block G1 (Fig. 80) the area of the Seleucid east shop building together with a strip of some 8.00 m.–10.00 m. west of it had come to be occupied by a series of ten or more shops, most of them of two rooms, and at least two dwellings. Already by the turn of the first and second centuries after Christ these units were the result of a long process of growth and change. The earlier stages, which apparently consisted largely of a haphazard replacement of the Seleucid shops with a double row of much smaller shops on rubblework socles and turned about so as to open from Street H, have left many disconnected vestiges in Shops S116, S118, S115, S117, G103, and room F123.[19] At the time under discussion the

[16] Below, pp. 70–72, 81.
[18] Below, p. 91.
[17] Below, pp. 70 f., 74.
[19] Below, pp. 124, 126.

western boundary of this area was constituted by the west walls of Shops S111[1] and S114, rooms F113, F106, F105, F107, and court F109. South of F109 it apparently made two right angles, its continuation being represented by the socle cutting across later room F123, the west wall of later Shop S124, and the fragmentary socle beneath and beside the west wall of later Shops S44 and S45. This portion south of F109 adjoined the early houses of area 70–71[1], 83–102, 126, the court of one of which, House 84–85, it bisected leaving only a narrow space with access to the cesspool.[20] These early houses, whose façades formed part of the south side of the enclosed open square and part of the north side of Market Street, were continued on the west by partially excavated Houses D[21] and E which were doubtless originally created under very similar circumstances on either side of the old enclosure wall. To House D belonged Shop S76 which gave on the broad entrance to the open square. To House E belonged Shops S65–S68 which gave on Market Street. Houses A, B, and C and Shops S74, S75, S80, S82, S79–79[1], and S69 were of much later construction.

The progressive transformation of the Seleucid north shop building in Blocks G5 and G7 (Fig. 83) was closely parallel to that of its twin on Block G3.[22] In Block G5, however, no single group of shops, like A2–A5 of G3, was reserved for public use and kept in something like its original form. The conversion to small dwellings was complete and thoroughgoing. In G5 and G7 the process of change appears, as in G3, to have proceeded from the periphery toward the center, in this case from west to east. Here again the preservation of the Hellenistic socle serves as an index. Although only the eastern three-fifths of the area of the whole original shop building has been explored, it is only at the extreme east end of that portion, presumably the last to be converted, that any appreciable segments of the Hellenistic socle were found to remain. All the excavated houses show the same general succession of alterations, repairs, and raisings of the levels of exterior thresholds to meet the rises in street level as the houses of Block G3. All present the same meager criteria of construction, typology of doorways, and pottery for dating, and these will be considered in the section dealing with the individual houses. It is clear, moreover, that at the west end of the shop building in Block G7 a series of changes took place which duplicated

[20] Above, p. 41.                    [21] Below, pp. 135 f.
[22] Below, p. 102.

those which occurred at the east end of the building in G3. The passage between the north and west shop buildings was partitioned off into rooms. To replace it a new passage to the open market place was broken through the second shop to the south of the north wing, and came, like Alley G3, to define the northward and southward limits of building in its vicinity. The position and extent of this passage and of the structures north and south of it at the beginning of the second century of our era can be restored from the lines of the later blind alleys G5 and G7. These narrow blind passages of the final period leading in from the street and open square to the entrances of houses and shops were simply vestigial survivals of the through alley and the free façade on the open square which were left perforce to preserve access when the thorough-fare was blocked off and the façades obstructed by later buildings. The south and west sides of Alley G5 represent what were once the limits of the open market place, the north and east façades of the shops and houses opening on it. The north and south sides of Alley G7 represent the façades of shops and houses developed southward from the original north shop building and eastward from the original west shop building on either side of the original alley. If the west side of Alley G5 be pro-duced it meets the south side of the old north shop building at the point where the westernmost vestige of the stone socle is preserved and east of which the south façade of the shop building continued to be the south façade of the houses which had come to occupy it. The old façade here long remained the boundary of this portion of Block G5, and House F,[23] originally built to open south directly on the market place, was subse-quently, when threatened with obstruction by later buildings, provided with a long entrance passage, F5, with an opening to the east. Similarly if the sides of Alley G7 be produced it is seen that the through alley of which it is a vestige passed some 15.00 m.–18.00 m. south of the façade of the old shop building. This is about the width of a row of small houses and betrays a development closely parallel to that of Alley G3 or the north side of Market Street in Block G1.

Farther south the area about the Seleucid west shop building and south enclosure wall in the south portion of Block G7 and the north portion of Blocks G6 (Fig. 85) and G8 developed somewhat differently from the corresponding area in Block G1. In this case the temporary

[23] Below, pp. 113 f.

lean-to structures against the Hellenistic enclosure wall were converted to permanent installations only along the south face of the wall. The north face was kept free, and the strip of ground before it was treated as a street in continuation of Street 2 of the city plan. It was originally broken through the southernmost shops of the west shop building to provide access to the enclosed market place. In time the Seleucid wall disappeared completely leaving only the fragmentary traces of its bedding trench. By the end of the first century of our era the street, approximately on the line of Street 2, was bounded on the north by a row of shops and dwellings of which the excavated remains are Shops S16, S4, S7, and rooms C5 and C4 of House C in Block G6.[24] Its south side was formed by the façades of two narrow blocks of shops separated by a street roughly on the axis of Street E of the city plan. The foundations of the eastern of these blocks were in part preserved beneath the level of the later market building in G6. They indicate an "island" only some 11.00 m. wide from north to south consisting of two rows of shops set back to back and presumably opening respectively north and south. The remains are those of five or six rather large shops out of an original fourteen or fifteen. Of the western block in G8 only the west, north, and east façades have been laid bare. It may be restored, however, as originally 17.00 m.–19.00 m. wide from north to south, since the approximate position of its south façade is well indicated by the sharp difference in alignment between the original east and west façades and the later walls which continued them southward.

The buildings enumerated above grew up around the original Seleucid shop buildings. They found their natural southern limit of proliferation along an irregular line which remained in Block G1 as the north side of Market Street. At the period under review Market Street was a broad open strip from 9.00 m. to 21.00 m. in width which traversed the entire section from east to west. It separated the northern portion of the bazaar quarter from four blocks of shops and dwellings erected in the free southern portion of the old agora along the approximate continuations of Streets E, F, and G of the city plan.

G2 (Fig. 84), the easternmost of these blocks, was gradually built up in two sections separated by Alley G2, an open strip 10.00 m. to 11.50 m. wide. Only the northern section has been completely explored. On the

[24] Below, pp. 153 f.; Fig. 78.

circumference of the southern section Shops S1, S2, S4–S6, S8–S14, S64–S66, and rooms A3 and A7 have been cleared, together with the remainder of the façades on the streets. At the turn of the first and second centuries after Christ the northern section consisted of a narrow island of shops similar to that in the north half of Block G6. There were twenty-four or twenty-five small shops set back to back in a double row and opening north and south save for the end shops to the east. The island even as it stood was the product of a long process of accretion, as the examination of the remaining original butt joints of its rubblework socles shows. Moreover, the southwestern corner was later radically altered by the construction of two dwellings, B and C, built partly of the original shop rooms and partly by addition to the south.[25] Fortunately these alterations may be readily distinguished both by the absence of bonding between the older and newer socles and by the fact that the southwest corner buttress of the original island of shops together with a reused bit of the adjoining south socle was preserved at the west side of court B38.

In view of the incomplete excavation of the southern section, the determination of its precise state at the time under discussion is more hazardous. As it is, three distinct stages in its growth are evident. The earliest distinguishable nucleus comprised the eastern half of the section, less Shops S8, S5, and S6 at the northeast corner. Its original west façade has been exposed at either extremity: at the north, the northwest corner with its buttress; at the south, the last 9.00 m. or so of wall. The western three-quarters of its original south façade lay about a meter in front of the later south façade of the section, and the greater part of its razed foundation remains. To this nucleus were added at various times the three shops at the northeast corner and, as a unit, the western half of the section. The former involved considerable remodelling of the adjacent portions of the earlier structures, the details of which could be cleared up only by further excavation. The latter apparently consisted of a single large dwelling and the three excavated shops, S64–S66, with their portico. In both cases the evidence of construction, doorways, and other architectural features points to dates in the Roman period, probably in the early third century. On the other hand, certain architectural details and in particular the construction of the razed south socle which

[25] Below, pp. 60, 148 f.

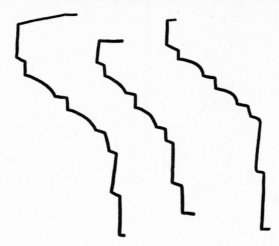

Fig. 15. G6, Roman Market. Lintel Profiles

is of an early type of plaster rubblework indicate that the eastern nucleus in its original form was, at any rate in part, built about the beginning of our era. It may therefore be assumed that this part alone falls within the limits of our period.

Of Block G4 (Fig. 84) only the four façades and the northeastern portion have been cleared. The latter comprises all or part of three small houses, A, B, and C, and eight shops, S45–S47, S49–S53.[26] Even these partial excavations suffice to show that Block G4 was built up in at least two distinct main building periods. The northern portion was first built. Its southeastern corner with its massive corner buttress on the exterior of room A60 was uncovered in the excavations, and a clean unbonded break in the west socle opposite gives the position of the southwest corner and the line of the south façade. The sharp difference in alignment between the east and west halves of the north façade indicates that this northern portion itself was built up bit by bit. Although it seems clear from the surviving evidence of construction, confirmed by the ceramic contents of the cesspool of court A57, that the northern portion of the block in its original form came into being in the course of the second half of the first century B.C., there is no conclusive indication as to when

[26] Below, pp. 151–153; Fig. 78.

the rest of the block was added to the south. The two doorways on Main Street appear to be of relatively late construction, but doorways were frequently remodelled. It is here simply assumed for convenience of exposition that the addition was made after 100 A.D.

However that may be, it is certain that by this time the southern section of Block G6 was completed, with its outline substantially as excavated. Its northern façade was on approximately the same line as that of G4, and comprised the seven shops, S5–S9, S11, S20, and the house entry B10, which served long after as the south side of the large Market Building. The rest of the section remains unexcavated save for Cumont's House, D, at the southwest corner.[27] Both this house and the northern row of shops bear many traces of relatively early construction, and the exterior doorway of the house was several times adjusted to meet the rising level of Street E. The faces of the exterior socles on all fronts maintain the same alignment and show no breaks or essential differences in construction.

The excavation of Block G8 is even less advanced, and material for dating is almost wholly lacking. The superficially explored house rooms are known only in outline, and conclusions must be drawn almost entirely from the state of the façades. The northern section of the block has already been discussed. The line of the north façade of the southern section at this time, i.e., the south side of Market Street, is approximately indicated by the south side of Alley G8 and the south wall of rooms A2 and A3. This alley, like Alleys G5 and G7, was evidently the vestige of an originally free façade preserved to give access to doorways which would otherwise have been blocked off by later buildings. One of the later buildings in this case was House A, which was built in this stretch of the original Market Street. The other façades appear to be uniform except on the south and southwest. On the south the original façade of the block is represented by the three central shop doorways behind a porch of three columns. At a later time, when the walls to either side were moved forward some 3.00 m., the central portion remained unchanged, and the porch was added to compensate. On the southwest the structures in Street D belong to the late Roman period.

The long process of development outlined above exhibited beneath its apparent planlessness certain intrinsic tendencies of growth which controlled the general process itself and gave the outcome its peculiar

[27] Below, pp. 156–158.

stamp. These tendencies were those inherent in the organization of economic life in a bazaar quarter. They were part of the traditional pattern
of life in the ancient Orient, and their operation at Dura was in this
sense almost unconscious. The bazaar as an expression of concentrated
urban economy is the antithesis of the agora or open market place. It is
essentially a close-knit, permanent nexus of streets lined with shops. Behind or in connection with the shops there may be dwelling places, places
of manufacture, or warehouses, but the essential is the avenues of circulation and the crowded places of sale. The open, public place is fundamentally foreign to it.

It was toward this goal that the business center of Dura was develop-
ing during the period just reviewed. It was to this sort of bazaar quarter
that the Seleucid agora was in process of being transformed as its broad
open spaces gradually filled with buildings and streets, and this under-
lying tendency is evident in every step of the process. The permanent
shop buildings about the periphery of a Greek agora opened inward on
the enclosed area. When at Dura such shops were being converted to the
shops of a bazaar quarter, they were wherever possible remodelled so as
to open outward on the bazaar streets. The tradesman in the Hellenistic
agora lived apart from his place of business in some other portion of the
town. The tradesman in the bazaar lived behind or beside his shop or in
the closest proximity. From the beginnings of the bazaar at Dura the
practice was for the shopkeeper to incorporate his shop in his dwelling,
and the quarter took on the general character of a mass of modest private houses, each presenting one or more shops on the street. This character it retained, but, as building grew more concentrated and certain
locations commercially more desirable, shops were erected in continuous
rows without dwellings. Their proprietors perforce dwelt elsewhere
close by, many no doubt in the numerous small shopless houses in the
quarter.

This development of the central section of the city, proceeding at a
time when the city itself was rapidly expanding and being built up all
about it, inevitably exerted an important influence on the adjacent areas
and on the city plan as a whole. The tendency of the growing buildings
of the bazaar to encroach on the streets of the original plan where these
were not already delimited by buildings was especially marked. The
south side of Main Street opposite the agora was apparently largely
built up during the Hellenistic or early in the Parthian period. The

north façades of these buildings were erected approximately true to the line of the street as laid down. The north side of the street, however, was not so defined and the bazaar buildings in Blocks G2 and G6 were allowed to trespass from 3.00 m. to 4.00 m. over it. The new line thus established was followed in later building, and eventually produced a permanent narrowing and apparent displacement toward the south of much of Main Street. The south side of Street 4 where it skirted the agora was fixed by the two north shop buildings, and the buildings along the north side opposite here maintained their approximate planned distance. Similarly the portion of Street H between Blocks G3 and G1 on the west and Block B7 on the east was strictly delimited by the Seleucid shop buildings and the Hellenistic structure in B7. South of this portion, however, these restrictions were inoperative, and the bazaar buildings of Block G2 encroached 1.50 m.–2.00 m. on the street, with the result that the west façade of Block B8 when built was set back an equivalent distance from the original street line. The planned line of the west side of Street D had apparently not been given permanence by building when the formation of the bazaar quarter was in its early stages. In this case the presence of the original shop buildings in Blocks G5 and G7 was not sufficient to prevent the bazaar buildings from encroaching 2.00 m.–4.00 m. on the east side of the street. The west side, when built up, was set back an average of about 2.00 m. to compensate, and this displacement was perpetuated in the subsequent course of Street D to the north.

The streets which developed within the bazaar quarter itself played a decisive rôle in the growth of the city blocks to the east. During the Hellenistic period Block B7 appears to have been unoccupied save for the Seleucid building in its northern half. In the subsequent building up of Blocks B8 and B7 the original block plan was in so far maintained that the continuation of Street 2 east of the agora was observed by a thoroughfare roughly on the planned lines. The influence of the bazaar development, however, proved decisive, for a street was also created in continuation of the east end of Market Street, which eventually superseded the continuation of Street 2. The west end of the latter was blocked and filled with buildings, and the eastern portion continued to exist only as a typical blind alley giving access to the shops and houses on the original street. The continuation of Market Street came to determine the block plan of this entire section of the city, and was eventually developed as a stepped descent to the lower town.

## C. Development. Period II

### (Fig. 78)

The next century and a half down to the end of the city about 256 A.D. witnessed in general the uninterrupted growth and progress of the bazaar quarter toward its goal. Certain tendencies, which, as we shall see, appear to work against the general trend, made themselves felt with the change in the city's political status to Roman rule, but by and large

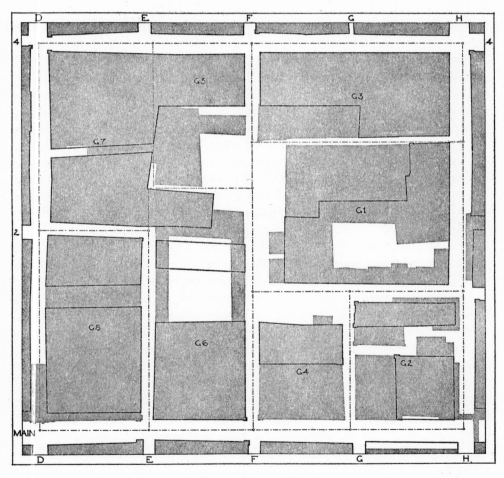

Fig. 16. Section G, Bazaar. Second Century A.D.—256 A.D.

development proceeded along the same lines as before. As a result the central open place continued to dwindle in size, until finally it had only about a quarter of the area it possessed at the end of Period I, about one-eighth the original enclosed area of the agora.[28] At the same time continued building altered its approaches and the bazaar streets in general. Alley G7 was swallowed up save for its western end. The continuation of Street 2 and Market Street where they traversed Block G6 were obliterated, and the section of Market Street across Block G8 disappeared with the exception of the vestige, Alley G8. Toward the end of the period Street D at the southwest corner of G8 was blocked by the construction of rooms C1, C2, and C3. The practicable approaches to the central place were thus reduced to Street F whether from north or south and Alley G3, and efficient through circulation within the bazaar itself was restricted to its eastern and more especially its southeastern portions.

The sum of the building operations which brought about these changes may be enumerated block by block as follows.

Block G3 (Fig. 79) was filled out to the line of Alley G3 by the erection of Houses C and B and courtyard A1.[29] House C, built against the original façades of Houses H and B6–B11, was closely followed by House B1–B5, which masked the south façades of Houses B6–B11 and G. Houses C and B1–B5 originally communicated by a doorway, B5–C6. This opening was walled up at a later time, when Houses B6–B11 and B1–B5 were thrown together to form a long rambling dwelling extending through the block.

This progressive masking of the original south façade of the block by an additional range of houses threatened to obstruct the approach to the public record office, A2–A5. The emergency was met by the construction of a monumental courtyard, A1, before its entrance (Fig. 34, p. 101, Pl. III, 2). The enclosing walls were strongly buttressed at the exterior corner and by four interior piers, and the gateway was provided with doors and a small covered gatehouse. Probably at the same time room A2 was extensively remodelled. The Seleucid shop-doorway which had served as its entrance was walled up with mud brick, and a new doorway, 1.81 m. wide, was cut approximately on the axis of the room. Its

---

[28] The three rubblework bases or altars in the central square present a problem of dating which is insoluble in the actual state of the evidence.

[29] Below, p. 91.

sill was slightly more than one course, 0.47 m., higher than the old and flush with the tops of the benches about the room. The latter were accordingly dispensed with. The floor level was raised 0.47 m. by a fill of earth and debris, and a new floor of plaster was laid at the level of the bench tops. The benches had been twice replastered during the preceding period, and the top coat of the north bench beside doorway A2–A5 bore a fresh graffito which may probably be dated about the turn of the first and second centuries of our era.[30] The bench was thus still in service at this time, though, as its relatively unworn surface and the fresh appearance of the graffito show, not for long thereafter. The remodelling of the room may well be put in the second quarter of the second century. The sherds found in the fill beneath the new plaster floor also suggest this approximate date.

Considerably later a stone-faced rubblework plinth, 1.57 m. × 0.82 m., with a plain projecting base course and a narrow rubblework step before it, was erected against the north wall on the axis of the new doorway. Found standing to a height of 1.03 m., its capping course was missing. The statue or statues which it was built to carry are no doubt represented by the fragmentary bronze foot and silver radiate crown found in rooms A4 and A2 respectively.[31] Presumably at about the same time a larger solid stone plinth, 1.86 m. × 1.68 m., with a similar unmolded projecting base course, was built against the façade of courtyard A1 just west of the entrance. It too lacked its capping course, and stood when found some 1.20 m. high. The sculpture which it bore has left no traces.

Block G1 (Fig. 80) was also filled out, to the line of Alley G3 on the north and to the line of the façades of Houses D and E on the west. The development in this case, however, was accompanied by profound changes in the earlier portions of the block. The first step was taken, apparently early in the second century, with the erection of House A,[32] which entailed the razing of the greater portion of the existing buildings in the southeastern portion of the block. The owner of this imposing dwelling, surpassed in size among the excavated houses of Dura only by the House of Lysias[33] and the House in Block E4,[34] was evidently one of the city's great merchants. His house was merely part of a complex

---

[30] Below, p. 168.
[32] Below, pp. 136 f.
[34] *Rep. VI*, pp. 4–48.

[31] *Rep. V*, pp. 81 f.
[33] To be described in a later part of *Rep. IX*.

planned to provide not only appropriate quarters for himself and his family but also the areas required by commercial activity on a large scale. The whole covered both the vacant area west of Shops S111[1] and S114 and rooms F113, F108, and F109 and a broad strip already encumbered with buildings[35] across the southeastern portion of the block from Houses D and E on the west to Street H on the east. All traces of the older structures were eradicated from the northern edge of this strip which fell within the area of House A proper. The greater part of the remainder was cleared to the desired level, graded, and left to serve as an open yard, presumably for the loading and unloading of goods, the parking of caravans, etc. On it at the rear of the house gave four large warehouse or storage rooms, S1, S1[1], A19, and S120, communicating directly with the house through rooms A19 and A12 (Pl. IX, 2). At the western end of the yard, rooms 126 and 99–100 of the early House 96–126 escaped destruction and were remodelled to form the four rooms S126, S100, S99, and S95 used for shops or storage. The method by which the open yard was originally enclosed on the south and east has left no traces. It was clearly a temporary expedient. The permanent solution was at once shrewd and practical. It is found in the row of twenty-three shops, S41–S42, S44–S64, along Market Street and Street H, which was the product of a relatively short but discontinuous building period. The owner, it appears, sold or leased an irregular strip along the south side of the newly cleared and graded yard to individual tradesmen who one after another built shops of the size they desired, singly or in blocks of two, three, or four. Building progressed in a general way from west to east as is clear from the unbonded abutments of the rubblework socles, and there was a sharp set-back of about 2.30 m. in the general façade line east of Shop S42. Shops S44 and S45 on Street H in their final form were part of the same development. North of S44 an arched opening of 2.71 m. and an entrance passage preserved access to the yard from Street H.

The shops were completed and the exterior walls of S42 had been twice replastered when a continuous portico of nineteen columns was erected before the seventeen easternmost shops along Market Street at an average distance of about 2.10 m. from their façades. The accuracy with which the columns were aligned without reference to the irregular shop façade and the absolute uniformity of dimensions and construction indicate that the portico was built as a unit. The westernmost column

[35] Above, pp. 36–42.

was engaged to the free corner of Shop S42. The easternmost was treated as a three-quarter column with an engaged pilaster on the east side, and was connected by a rubblework sill and short spur wall with the free corner of Shop S46. The columns were of rubblework, 0.61 m. in lower diameter, and rested on square rubblework plinths capped by square gypsum bases on which a quarter-round torus was worked. The gypsum Doric capitals were identical in form with the bases, difference in function being indicated merely by difference in size. The lower diameter of the echinus was 0.51 m., so that the columns had a taper of 0.10 m., roughly 0.03 m. per meter. Although the columns were spaced without regard to the shop doorways behind, their axial intervals, especially toward the eastern end of the portico, showed considerable irregularity. The maximum variation was as great as 0.70 m., between 1.82 m. and 2.52 m. The average was 2.22 m., the median 2.37 m.

The demolitions attending the construction of House A, its yard, and storehouses made it possible for the owner of the older House F to enlarge his dwelling southward, adding rooms F121–F123.[36]

The northwestern portion of Block G1 was filled soon after the construction of House A by House B[37] and House C[38] with its two shops, S22 and S72. During the building of the latter, room S6 was created and attached to the dependencies of House A. Finally, a series of six shops, S69, S74–S75, S79–S80, and S82, was erected against the west façades of Houses D and E.

It cannot have been long after the beginning of the second century that Alley G5 was created as a result of the eastward expansion of Block G5 into the market place. The new extension remains unexcavated, but most probably comprised two houses, each with its shop on the market place. The building of the northern of these two dwellings brought about the construction of corridor F5 to preserve access to House F. Later still a narrow wing of shops was thrust out into the market place from the new east façade.[39] It passed through three stages of growth and alteration before the end of the city, and in its final form consisted of four shops extending to the approximate line of the west side of Street F (Fig. 83).

In Block G7 the details of the development which led to the blocking of the original Alley G7 still await excavation.

The progressive development of Block G2 (Fig. 84) resulted in the

[36] Below, p. 129.
[38] Below, p. 147.
[37] Below, pp. 142 f.
[39] Below, pp. 122 f.

transformation of Alley G2 from a broad open strip to a narrow alley with two right-angle turns, and in the westward expansion of the southern section to the line of Street G. The construction of Houses B and C in the northern section of the block has been discussed above.[40] A final change in the aspect of this section was brought about by the addition of a portico of sixteen columns before the north, east, and south façades at the eastern end. The portico was built as a unit on a continuous rubblework stylobate, 0.64 m. wide, laid at a mean distance of 1.75 m. from the north, 1.00 m. from the east, and 1.70 m. from the south façade. The stylobate was founded on bed rock, and its surface was only some 0.04 m. above the late street level to which it was built. The rise in the level of Market and H Streets in this area had been relatively slight, but sufficient to cause the previous raising of most of the doorsills. The north flank of the portico was terminated on the west by an anta engaged to the end of a spur wall on the line of partition S33–S22. The face of the wall behind it showed four previous coats of plaster. To the final column of the south flank corresponded a half-column added against the south façade of S16. The rubblework columns were uniformly 0.58 m. in lower diameter. They rested on low rubblework plinths rising from the stylobate and capped, like those of the G1 portico, with square gypsum base blocks molded with a crude quarter-round. The capitals again were identical in all but size, and gave evidence of an upper column diameter of ca. 0.50 m. The irregularities in column spacing were in this case apparently dictated by an effort to avoid placing columns opposite doorways. The greatest variation in the axial interval was almost a meter, between 2.48 m. and 3.46 m., but the average and median were fairly consistent, 2.81 m. and 2.72 m. respectively. At a later time the column opposite the free corner of Shop S17 was engaged to the wall with a spur of rubblework, and an additional column was added to the south flank beyond the original stylobate.

A portico of eight columns was also added before the old east façade of the southern section. Unlike the porticoes of Block G1 and the northern section, it was not built as a unit but in three separate stages. The first was the northernmost, a porch of four columns before house entry A3 and Shop S2. The rubblework columns were 0.62 m. in lower diameter and rested on separate square plinths of rubblework capped with gypsum bases molded with a rough quarter-round. They were spaced at an average of 1.45 m. from the façade so as to fall on the axes of the

[40] P. 50; cf. below, pp. 148 f.

walls of the rooms behind with one column interpolated directly before the doorway of A3. From the first and third plinths from the north, rubblework sills were laid across to the façade of A3 where flat pilasters were run up the wall as responds. The area covered by the porch and extending south across the front of Shop S1 was paved with plaster mortar at the time of construction. The level of this pavement, which was never raised, corresponded to the second level of the doorsill of A3 and the third of Shops S1 and S2.

Somewhat later a similar porch of three columns was put up before Shops S10–S13 at a distance of 1.44 m. from the façade. Its square rubblework plinths were spaced at axial intervals of 2.46 m. The rubblework columns, 0.60 m. in lower diameter, rose from unmolded gypsum bases. No capitals were found. As in the neighboring porch, the end columns were connected with the façade by low rubblework sills, and the area was paved with plaster mortar. At a subsequent date the porch was closed off by the addition of waist-high rubblework parapets on the sills. The partitioning off of Shop S13 occurred after the construction of the porch. The new doorway to Shop S10 was cut well above the porch level with a step bedded on the porch paving before its sill.

About 231 or 245 A.D.[41] the monumental stone arch was thrown across Main Street at the east side of its intersection with Street H, and the pendant rubblework arch was erected across Street H. Shortly after, a single rubblework column 0.63 m. in lower diameter was inserted midway between the porch of S10–S13 and the northward projection of the west pier of the arch on the axis of partition S11–S12. The column rested directly on a square rubblework plinth without a stone base and was crowned with a plain gypsum abacus. The newly covered area before the doorways of Shops S11 and S12 received a pavement of plaster mortar. Along its edge for 1.75 m. north of the plinth a low curb was later run, presumably as a precaution against the invasion of the portico by the dirt and debris of the street.

In contrast to these colonnades added to preexisting buildings, the porticoes of Shops S8, S5, S6, and S64–S66 were laid down at the same time as the new rooms behind them.[42] The façade of Shops S8, S5, S6 was planned to include two pilasters as responds on the axes of the lateral walls of S8 and a spur projecting from the north wall of S6 to engage the terminal column on the east. The columns themselves, rest-

---

[41] *Rep. IV*, p. 73; *Harvard Theological Rev.*, XXXIV (1941), p. 102.
[42] Above, p. 50; Pl. XIV, 1.

ing on separate rubblework plinths, were 0.66 m. in lower diameter and built without bases or, apparently, capitals of stone. They were spaced at about 1.70 m. from the façade with considerable irregularity in relation to the openings behind them, the axial intervals from west to east being 2.36 m., 2.52 m., 2.36 m., and 3.08 m. A sill between the central column and pilaster distinguished the respective porches of Shops S8 and S5, and a rubblework curb some 0.46 m. high from column to column set the whole portico off from the street.

The addition of the large western house with its three shops to the southern section of G2 involved a rebuilding of the existing south fa-çade, the reason for which is obscure. The entire old façade west of Shop S14 was demolished to its foundations, and a new façade put up 0.90 m.–1.30 m. behind it, though still 0.80 m.–1.25 m. in advance of the new shop front to the west. The latter's portico of nine columns was carried across the junction point so as to mask the discrepancy. In the construc-tion of the new shops the west wall of Shop S64 was carried 1.86 m. be-yond the façade to close the portico with an anta, and spur walls were thrown across from three points on the façade to subdivide it into three porches. The columns, which rested on deep rubblework plinths capped with plain gypsum base-blocks, were 0.70 m. in lower diameter. They carried gypsum Doric capitals of the normal debased form, and tapered to a diameter of 0.61 m. at the top. The axial intervals were uniformly 2.15 m. with the exception of the fifth from the west which measured 2.51 m. Rubblework sills were later laid between the columns before Shop S64.

The southward extension of Block G4 (Fig. 84) to Main Street re-mains unexcavated save for the street façades. The most probable con-clusion from a study of the exterior doorways is that it consisted of three houses with five dependent shops. Shops S46 and S47 of the older north-ern portion were at a very late period provided with a deep porch of four columns. The ground level to which the rubblework plinths were built was the latest in this portion of Market Street and meets the doorsills of Shops S45, S46, and S47 well above the last level to which they had each been raised at various times. The rubblework columns were large, 0.81 m. in lower diameter, and rested directly on the plinths. They were evenly spaced at axial intervals of 2.40 m. No capitals could be iden-tified.

In Block G6 (Fig. 85; Pl. XIV, 2) alone the consistent development of the bazaar quarter was forcibly interrupted. The disjointed elements of the earlier G6 were united in a structure which stood in sharp contrast to the buildings of the rest of the quarter. It consisted essentially of an open market place surrounded on the west and south by shops, on the north by shops and a colonnade, and on the east by an enclosing wall and colonnade. Four openings fitted with doors gave access from the exterior: a principal entrance from Street F and Market Street in the east wall; a lesser entrance from Street E at the southwest corner; and entrances at the northwest and northeast corners, which when open made the north colonnade a thoroughfare in continuation of Street 2.

The builders found a straightforward and practical way of adapting the earlier buildings on the site to their purposes. The double row of shops between Street 2 and Market Street was razed. The row of Shops S20, S11, S6–S9, which with house entry B10 formed the north façade of the southern section of the block, and the row of Shops S4, S7, C4, which with room C5 formed the south façade of the northern section, were made to serve as the ends of the new building. It was necessary only to continue the north end eastward as far as the line of Street F with Shops S1–S3 and to join the ends by lateral walls on east and west. Within, a row of six new shops, S13–S15, S17–S18, and S21, was built against the new west wall and a portico of seventeen columns before the new east wall and the north side. The two wings of the latter were built on continuous rubblework stylobates which carried the square rubblework plinths from which the columns rose without the interposition of stone bases. The interaxial spacing was somewhat irregular, especially on the east flank where it varied between extremes of 3.05 m. and 4.20 m. with an average of 3.71 m. On the north the variation was less, between 3.18 m. and 3.56 m. with an average of 3.32 m.

The building grade chosen for the new structure was approximately that of the older shop doorways on the north, which had all been raised from 0.35 m. to 0.45 m. in various stages during their previous existence. The old doorways on the south had remained almost as built, and were simultaneously raised to the new level of ca. 219.50 m. a.s.l. at which the new entrances were built. Only the upper 0.22 m. of the plinths of the portico was intended to be visible above ground. The stylobate, which was founded on bed rock, served merely as a general foundation and leveller. Its surface was carefully brought to the uniform level of 219.14 m. a.s.l.

The intrusion of so distinctively foreign a type of building amid the homogeneous architecture of the bazaar quarter could only be due to outside influence, and its relatively late appearance makes it probable that the influence was Roman. The late date is confirmed by the construction. It shows the most advanced form of local rubblework technique with carefully laid up faces of hard red limestone, pointed and heavily rendered with plaster, and a loose interior filling of red limestone caementa with a minimum of plaster grout. The trim of the new doorways exhibits a late and vertically compressed form of the cavetto-fillet profile. Fig. 15 (p. 51) shows examples from the lintel of the north-west entrance, the jamb capitals of the entrance to Shop S3, and the lintel of Shop S17. The probability of Roman influence is borne out by the plan, which is essentially that of a small provincial forum or market place reduced to its simplest terms. Practical certainty is assured by the abundant evidence for the use of the Roman foot of 0.296 m. in the layout of the new portions of the building. The builders contrived even within the framework of the earlier structures to work in large, simple multiples of this alien unit.

The length of the east portico between the axes of the terminal columns was 29.67 m. or 100 feet. The length of the north portico from the axis of the east column to the face of the anta was the same. The depth of the east portico from column axis to wall face was 3.56 m. or 12 feet, that of the north portico 4.16 m. or 14 feet. The plinths of each portico were 0.592 m. or 2 feet high, the columns 0.89 m. or 3 feet in lower diameter. The overall exterior length of the new west shops was again 29.66 m. or 100 feet. The width was increased from 4.74 m. or 16 feet at the north end to 5.04 m. or 17 feet at the south in order that the central open area might have a uniform width of 25.26 m. or 85 feet. The original width of the new doorway openings has in most cases been obscured by the addition of stone trim, splayed reveals, repairs, etc. The doorways of Shops S21 and S18, however, remained unaltered, 1.63 m. or 5½ feet wide, and the original width of the principal east opening can be measured as 2.97 m. or 10 feet. Four widths of wall were employed, of which the largest, 1.04 m. or 3½ feet, the smallest 0.75 m. or 2½ feet, were simple multiples of the foot.

In short, like the baths at either end of Main Street, our building may be taken to represent one of the first steps in the systematic Romanization of the life of the city, part of the program of the Roman administration to introduce the characteristic forms of the civilization of the empire to its outpost on the Euphrates.

The evolution of Block G8 during the second and third centuries must be read chiefly from the excavated façades. House A, in whole or in part, was erected during this period in the area formerly occupied by the western portion of Market Street. As noted above,[43] the south façade of the block on either side of the three central shops was set forward some 3.00 m., and a porch of three columns was built before the remaining portion of the old façade. The columns, 0.80 m. in lower diameter and placed at axial intervals of 1.47 m., rested directly on separate rubblework plinths. The southwest corner of the new façade was originally free. Later, and presumably at about the same time as the erection of the arches at the other end of the quarter, it was rebuilt as part of the monumental arched façade of complex C1–C3 which was inserted in Street D. Rooms C1 and C2 formed part of an unexcavated structure within the block. C3, which also communicated with the interior of the block, was designed as a hall of some sort with a flat roof carried on five transverse rubblework arches sprung from shallow piers along the east wall. At their foot ran a broad low bench. The side arches of the entrance were hardly more than slits with full span of 0.72 m. reduced to 0.38 m. by the jambs. The full span of the central arch was 2.12 m., the width between the jambs 1.76 m. This central opening was framed by half-columns with a radius of 0.38 m. resting directly on rubblework plinths, 0.94 m. high. Nothing which could be identified as a capital or cornice molding was found among the scanty fragments of the arch itself and the half-columns.

The point reached by the bazaar about 256 A.D. (Figs. 17, 78) was in no sense the final goal of its development. It was merely a stage in a process fortuitously interrupted. The fact of its interruption, however, obliges us to attempt to assess the general results of its three and one-half centuries or more of operation. The business center of Dura had come to consist essentially of some fifty-six private dwellings and one hundred eighty-two shops. To these must be added the shops along the adjacent portions of the south side of Main Street, the east side of Street H, and the north side of Street 4, which number about fifty-three and bring the total of shops to some two hundred thirty-five. Of these, thirty-two houses and one hundred forty-one shops have been fully excavated. The great majority of shops were simple single rooms with an average floor area of 14.30 sq. m. In all only eighteen were two-room units.

[43] P. 52.

These places of business were not equally distributed over the entire area (Fig. 18). The slow growth of the bazaar quarter out of the original agora had brought with it a general shifting of the commercial center of gravity. The shops of the agora had been grouped about the north end of a great open square, removed from the main arteries of traffic which skirted it. The shops of the developed bazaar, exception made of the Roman market place in Block G6, were concentrated in the southeastern portion of the area along the main arteries of traffic, Main Street, Street H, and Market Street, and the alleys leading directly off

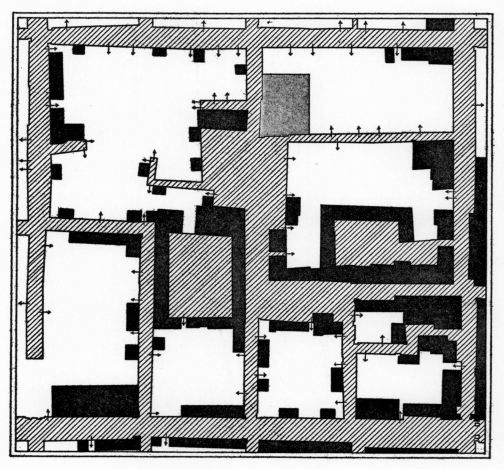

Fig. 18. Section G, Bazaar. Distribution of Shops

them. Here the shops were packed close together. Over the rest of the area the distribution was more sporadic and the space given over to dwellings much greater in proportion.

From its inception down to its final stages this development of the bazaar quarter of shops and houses was consistent and homogeneous. Toward the end the advent of Roman influence introduced new tendencies exemplified by the market place in Block G6 and the monumental arches over the streets. The same tendencies were probably at work in the porticoes which make their appearance in the most frequented streets during this last period. As we have seen, the streets of the bazaar originally lacked them. Although the column as a legacy from Hellenistic times had been continuously if sparingly employed at Dura, it had never been used to form street porticoes or stoas. It was just these years, however, of the late second and early third centuries that saw the cities of Syria under Roman influence bordering their streets with long rows of columns. Nothing more natural than that along with Roman rule the influence of these developments in the great centers to the west should make itself felt at Dura, and that the great colonnaded streets of Antioch and Palmyra should find a distant echo there. Characteristically the new influence found expression in purely local forms. There is no trace of the imperial Corinthian architecture of the West. The columns were without exception of the traditional local type, of rubblework with the debased Doric capitals handed down from Hellenistic times. They show the wide and freely erratic spacing which is the result of the substitution of wood-reinforced rubblework lintel members for entablatures of stone. The Dura porticoes were plainly not the result of civic planning or public effort. In each case they seem to have been put up by individual tradesmen or by a group of associated tradesmen before an individual shop or range of shops. They were not conceived of as sheltered thoroughfares, but were usually closed at one or both ends and often partitioned into porches before single shops.

If the bazaar quarter in its final aspect permits us to form a general notion of the volume and organization of the city's economic life, it tells us very little about it in detail. The shops yield disappointingly little evidence as to the nature of the business carried on in each of them, and it is quite impossible to trace any coherent system of a division of the bazaar into quarters based on commodities or occupations.[44] Shops were

[44] Cf., however, *Rep. V*, pp. 85–95.

stripped of all objects of value. The commodities themselves and all perishable furniture have of course disappeared. The scanty permanent appointments and objects of common use which remain are in most cases of so commonplace and ubiquitous a sort as to yield little specific information of value. Typical of the former are niches, benches and tables of brick or rubblework, tubs or basins often in the form of broken jars sunk in the floor, small hearths of brick or rubblework, bins, and large plaster "mortars" or "coolers."[45] Typical of the latter are the ordinary pottery vessels of all kinds, lamps, coins, bits of bronze or iron fittings, common objects of personal adornment such as fibulae, etc. The difficulty and danger of interpreting material of this sort as evidence of the owner's occupation are well illustrated by the House of Nebuchelus, B8, H.[46] The owner is known from the graffiti to have traded in textiles, garments, shoes, unguents, and probably wine. Yet there is nothing in the nine shops surrounding his residence, including the two which seem more particularly his own, B8, 8 and 9, which could be taken to point clearly to the sale of any of these specific commodities. Even in exceptional cases like Shops S3 and S4 of Block G3[47] or House C of Block G6 with its Shops C4 and C8[48] the relatively abundant remains may well indicate either the brewing or storage and sale of beer, or the mixing, preparation, or storage and sale of wine, or of oil, etc.

[45] Cf. *Rep. VII–VIII*, pp. 141, 305 f.
[47] Below, p. 79.
[46] *Rep. IV*, pp. 79–140, Pl. XVI, 1.
[48] Below, pp. 153–156.

# IV

## HOUSES AND SHOPS OF THE FINAL PERIOD

### A. *Block G3*

#### 1. Eastern Portion, Houses K, L, M, Shops S1–S5

##### (Figs. 78, 79; Pls. VI, VII, VIII)

###### a. History

THE formation of House M toward the end of the second century B.C. has been studied above.[1] At the same time or even a little earlier, House K and Shops S1–S5 in their original form developed from the first three double shops of the north and the first two of the south row of the Seleucid north shop building. The third double shop of the south row, later rooms K5 and K6, was not at first included in House K, but continued to exist separately as a shop for some time. Similarly the end shop of the north wing of the Seleucid east shop building, the later L1, also continued its independent existence as a shop adjoining House M, while the end of the original passage behind it was left free to preserve access to K5–K6.

House K in its original form consisted of a court, K2, five rooms, K8, K7, K3, K4, and S4, and a shop, S5. The south wall of the Seleucid shop building formed its southern limit. The court was originally larger than later, for its south wall, of which a fragment remains as foundation for the later hearth in room K8, was on the same line as partition K3–K7. The latter was built approximately on the line of the Seleucid partition and largely of its materials. The Seleucid partition which remained as the north wall of the court also at this time formed the north wall of rooms K3 and K4. The remains of its foundations in rooms K3 and K4 stand well above the original floor levels. The older shop walls were similarly retained as the west walls of rooms K4, K3, and K7. Only the central north-south wall, K3–K2, K7–K8, was a completely new wall on a new line. Here, as in wall K3–K7, the remains of the original socle, where they are preserved below ground or have survived later repairs and alterations, show the same construction as the early

[1] Pp. 32–36.

socles of House M. They are of rubblework consisting of large pieces of gypsum, mostly the broken blocks of the Seleucid socles, mortared with mud.

None of the openings of this early stage exists in its original form. All the existing openings were either first built or completely rebuilt at a later date, and even the exact location of many of the original door-ways can no longer be determined. There is nothing, for example, to show that the original entrance to the house occupied the place of the later one. On the other hand, doorway K2–K3 seems from the condition of the socle at either side always to have remained in the same position, while doorway K2–S4 was simply the old Seleucid shop doorway.

The area of the three Seleucid front shop rooms north of House K was completely made over. A new exterior socle of the same early rubble-work found in House K replaced the masonry of the Seleucid socle above the foundation courses and the base headers. The original interior partitions were razed, and new ones of rubblework were erected so as to redistribute the interior space in five parts: a two-room shop and a large single shop in area S1–S3, room S4 and Shop S5 of House K. Here again the position of the original openings is far from certain. It is most probable that the two-room shop and its neighbor used the old doorways with rebuilt upper portions. The entrance to Shop S5 was pretty clearly in its later position, but partition S4–S5 was later so thoroughly rebuilt above the floor level that no clear evidence as to doorway S4–S5 remains.

The proximity in date of House K and the adjacent shops to the early House M is confirmed both by the construction of the early rubblework socles and by the stratified deposit in the cesspool of court K2, the lowest layers of which furnished potsherds typical of the late second cen-tury B.C.

The next step in the development of the eastern portion of the block was brought about by the construction of House L. During the inter-vening period House D had been erected to the west, and the doorway of Shop L1 had been raised some 0.34 m. by the addition of a new threshold with a broad stone platform on the interior and a stone step in the street before it. The four rooms of House L simply incorporated Shop L1 and partitioned the free space, some 8.00 m. wide, between Houses M and D. In the process the remaining Hellenistic socles in the area were in vary-ing degrees suppressed. The original west socle of L1, which became the court of the new house, was completely razed and rebuilt in rubble-work on the same line. The footing course of socle L1–M4 and about half that of the north socle of L1 together with the three lower courses of the adjacent section of the old south exterior socle of the north shop building were left in place as foundations for new socles of rubblework. The south socle of L1 was retained almost intact. The shop doorway was walled up with orthostates from the razed socles, and a new rubblework socle was erected on top. Walls L3–L2 and L3–L4 were built new, and the east wall of House D was to some extent rebuilt and narrowed in L4. The new socles were all of an early type of plaster rubblework with large pieces of gypsum, mostly debris of the Seleucid socles, laid solid through the wall. They were pointed but not rendered with plaster below ground.

With the exception of doorway L1–L2, none of the original openings remained unchanged down to the end of the city. The street entrance to court L1, however, was merely raised from its original level on top of the Hellenistic socle without change in dimensions or trim. It was a doorway of the second general type, like doorway A1–A3,[2] 1.12 m. wide, with slightly projecting jambs cut on the ends of sectional reveal slabs set without splay. Its moldings may be restored from those of doorway L1–L2. The latter, 1.26 m. wide between the jambs, was of exactly the same type and in addition retained its original lintel and jamb capitals (Figs. 19, 20). Each bore an identical series of moldings: cavetto, Les-

Fig. 19. G3, L1–
L2. Lintel Profile

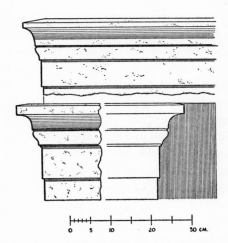

Fig. 20. G3, L1–L2. Jamb Capital
and Lintel Restored

[2] Above, p. 32.

bian cyma, fillet, two fasciae. Doorways and moldings provide an approximate terminus for the date of the house. Doorways of this type were no longer built at Dura after the middle of the first century B.C. (Type II; Fig. 12a). The well-turned Lesbian cyma is associated almost exclusively with continuous running moldings about the openings of doorways of this type. It did not survive the third quarter of the first century B.C. Doorway L1–L2 shows the cavetto and cyma lintel molding of this type applied to form a jamb capital in the manner which was to prevail from the late first century B.C. on. Doorway L1–L2 may confidently be dated in the last half of the century.

The cesspool of the court in this case afforded no confirmation. It was found almost without deposit, having apparently been cleaned out shortly before the end of its history. A singular find, however, in room L3 lends general support. There, in a shallow pit scooped out of the bed rock and sealed in by two undisturbed rammed earth floors, was found a pair of bronze figurines of musicians, which by their style are of Hellenistic date.[3]

The erection of House L had important consequences for the adjacent buildings. Shop K5–K6 was now effectively cut off from the exterior and was incorporated in House K. Its west wall had already been rebuilt in rubblework, apparently at the time of the formation of House H.[4] Its east wall was now torn out and replaced with rubblework partitions containing doorways K3–K5 and K7–K6. Partition K5–K6 was likewise replaced in rubblework but without openings. Presumably at the same time doorway K4–K5 was cut in the remaining Seleucid socle, and wall K4–K3 was rebuilt in rubblework.

The rubblework of K4–K3 is of a piece with that of the socle of a new rear wall of Shops S1, S2, and S3, built some 1.40 m. north of their original Seleucid rear wall, and of partitions S1–S2 and S2–S3. It was at this time, then, that the early rubblework socle of the western two-room shop was razed to its foundations, and that Shops S1, S2, and S3, together with rooms K4 and K3, emerged in their final form. Probably as part of the same program room S4 was detached from House K by the blocking of doorway K2–S4. It was converted to an independent shop with a street entrance and a communicating doorway from Shop S3. It is also to this approximate time that we must assign the first dis-

---

[3] Below, pp. 160 f.                    [4] Below, p. 81.

tinguishable doorsill level of the street entrance to House K in its final position.

From this general period doorways K3–K4, K3–K5, S3–S4, and S4–S5 came down unchanged. All were already of the normal later type. The preserved lintel of K3–K4 has the flattened ovolo molding characteristic of the century between 50 B.C. and 50 A.D. (Fig. 21). The jamb capitals and lintels of S3–S4 and S4–S5 show an early form of the standard cavetto-fillet molding. The stone trim of the five exterior doorways of Shops S1–S5 appears to be of the same date, but the doorways themselves were many times altered.

The final major development resulted from the acquisition by the owner of House M of room K6. To secure an entrance from room M3 it was necessary to create a short corridor, and this was done by tearing out the old party wall between Houses M and K and rebuilding it 1.90 m. to 2.30 m. farther north. The loss of space to room K8 was partially made good by the rebuilding of wall K2–K8 1.30 m. farther north. This in turn reduced the size of court K2. Doorway K7–K6 was walled up.

In House M these operations were the occasion for a general remodelling of the interior. Wall M3–M1 was razed to its foundations and rebuilt some 0.50 m. to the west. Wall M4–M2 was similarly moved 1.05 m.–1.30 m. to the profit of room M2. The exterior walls were repaired, pointed, and rendered with plaster. The old street entrance was walled up, and a new one was cut in its final position. The renovation was accompanied by a general raising of the floor level by means of a fill of earth. It ranged from 0.82 m. to 1.02 m. in the various rooms. In court M1 the orifice of the cesspool was correspondingly built up to the new level by a shell of rubblework. In both houses the changes were accompanied by the construction or complete reconstruction of the stair units in their final form. The new socles throughout were built in the developed technique of plaster rubblework with wide use of secondhand material of all sorts as caementa.

All the doorways of House M date from this final reconstruction. All are of the normal later type with monolithic stone jambs. The extant capital and lintel of doorway M2–M4 show a developed form of the regular cavetto-fillet moldings (Fig. 22). In House K only doorway K2–K8, which is of the same type, can definitely be assigned to this period (Fig. 23). A date in the second quarter or about the middle of the first century of our era is suggested by the distribution of the potsherds found in the sealed fill beneath the plaster floor of room M2.

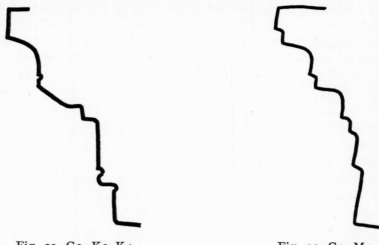

Fig. 21. G3, K3–K4.
Lintel Profile

Fig. 22. G3, M2–
M4. Lintel Profile

The later changes in the area were relatively insignificant. To match the rise in street level the entrance to House L was raised a total of 0.47 m., those of Shops S1–S4 0.37 m., 0.37 m., 0.39 m., and 0.37 m. respectively, that of Shop S5 0.26 m., that of House K 0.45 m. Only the entrance of House M remained at its original level, to which as time

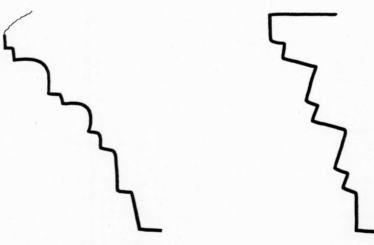

Fig. 23. G3, K2–K8.
Lintel Profile

Fig. 24. G3, K2–K3.
Jamb Capital Profile

went on a more and more marked depression in the adjacent street surface came to correspond. Within House M the original cesspool was abandoned and filled in. A new one was dug close beside it. Houses M and K were brought into direct communication by a rough opening, some 0.80 m. wide, broken through partition K5–K6. Another narrow doorway was cut at the southeast corner of room K3 to give direct access to room K7. Late in the history of House K doorway K2–K3 was completely remodelled. Its massive new jambs were typical of the latest phase in door construction at Dura. Stone trim was reduced to a minimum, a mere inset in the exposed corner of a jamb carried out in rubblework. The late and angular form of the jamb capitals is especially characteristic (Fig. 24). In House L doorway L2–L3 was at some indeterminable date reduced about 0.40 m. in width.

## b.  Description. House M. Five Rooms

### M1, Court (Pl. VIII, 2)

The street entrance at the northeast corner was a single door with a bar socket. It opened into a covered vestibule beside the stair unit, M5. The court was paved with rammed earth, and the opening of its cesspool was covered by a square pierced gypsum lid. The stair unit in the northwest corner had the stair entrance at the left and at the right a doorway to a closet beneath the stair. The stair ascended clockwise about a central rubblework newel. In the northwest corner of the space beneath the stair was a low plaster platform with an inset basalt grinding stone; in the southeast corner was a plaster "cooler."[5]

### M2, Diwan

The doorway from the south side of the court had a stone step before it and was hung with double doors. The threshold was of stone, and the splayed reveals projected on the interior. The diwan was floored with plaster. In one of the walls was set a bas-relief of Hercules.[6]

### M4, Chamber

The doorway from the diwan was hung with double doors. The room contained a large dolium. A bas-relief of Hercules was set in one of the walls.[7] The floor was of rammed earth.

### M3, Diwan

The doorway from the west side of the court was hung with double doors. Along the north wall of the room ran a broad plaster bench, 0.22 m. high. In the wall above it was a wide niche. The floor was of rammed earth.

[5] *Rep. VI*, p. 269; *Rep. VII–VIII*, p. 141, n. 18.
[6] Below, p. 159.            [7] Below, pp. 159 f.

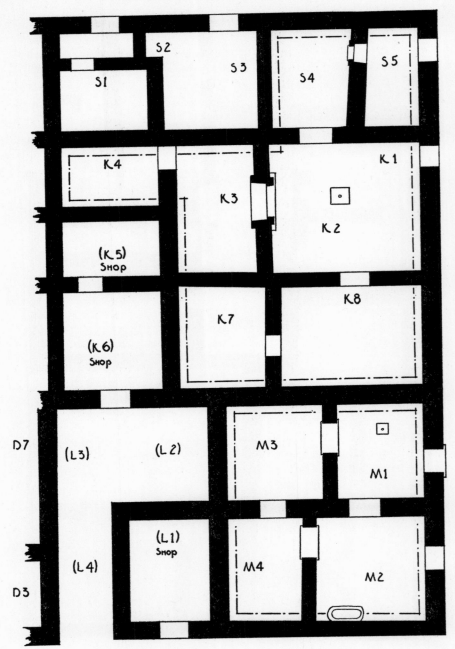

Fig. 25. G3, K–L–M. Early State. Restored Plan

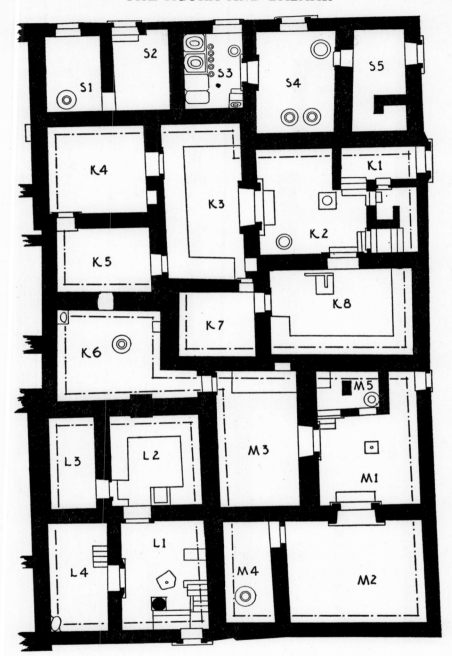

Fig. 26. G3, K–L–M. Final State. Restored Plan

### K6, Women's Chamber ( ? )

The doorway opening from room M3 into the connecting corridor had a single door with a bar socket and a stone threshold. Against the east wall of the room was a rubble-work seat or table, 0.44 m. high. In the northwest corner was an oval terra cotta tub set in a plaster frame. The room contained a large dolium. The floor was of rammed earth.

## House K. Seven Rooms

### K1, Vestibule

The street entrance had a single door with a bar socket. The low doorway in the south wall leading to a closet beneath the stair was similar. Three steps through an opening, probably arched, descended 0.71 m. to the level of the court.

### K2, Court (Pl. VI, 2)

The court was paved with rammed earth, and the opening of its cesspool was covered with a square pierced gypsum lid. Near the south wall stood a plaster "cooler." The stair unit on the east side of the court had the stair entrance on the right, two steps up from the court, and on the left a doorway to the space beneath the stair. The stair itself ascended counter-clockwise about a newel wall. The first flight of two steps is pre-served, and the newel bears the imprint of the second flight of five. The average tread was 0.31 m., the average riser 0.18 m. The stair probably made two full turns of eight flights and reached the roof by two or three additional steps at about 5.60 m. above the court level. Access was presumably provided from the seventh landing to the roof of the vestibule and of Shops S4 and S5.

### K8, Diwan

The doorway from the south side of the court had a stone step before it and a stone threshold. It was hung with double doors. About three sides of the room ran a broad rubblework bench, 0.21 m. high. Before the west reveal of the door was a fireplace com-posed of twelve deeply charred bricks, 0.31 m.–0.32 m. square, with a T-shaped rubble-work screen, 0.43 m. high. The floor was of rammed earth.

### K7, Chamber

The doorways from rooms K8 and K3 both had single doors with bar sockets. The floor was of rammed earth.

### K3, Diwan

The doorway from the west side of the court had a stone step before it and a stone threshold. It was hung with double doors, and its splayed reveals projected on the in-terior. The room was floored with rammed earth, and about three sides ran a broad plaster bench, 0.09 m. high.

### K4, Women's Chamber (?)

The doorway from room K3 had a stone threshold and double doors. That from room K4 also had a stone threshold but was hung with a single door. The doorway to room K6 was a rough opening without trim save for a sill of rubblework. The floor was of rammed earth.

## Shops S1–S5

### S1

The street entrance was equipped with double doors. The shop was floored with rammed earth and contained a large dolium.

### S2

The street entrance had double doors and a rubblework step leading down to the shop's rammed earth floor. Opening S1–S2 was probably arched.

### S3 (Pl. VII, 1)

The street entrance was fitted with double doors. Against the west wall was an installation consisting of two oval terra cotta tubs set in rubblework and shielded by a thin parapet of upright gypsum slabs, 0.17 m. high, and two smooth flat gypsum slabs forming a table. Five pointed amphorae were set in the rammed earth floor before the tubs. In the southeast corner of the shop was a three-step rubblework counter with an oval basin let into the top step. Near the northeast corner was a small "cooler."

### S4

Both the street entrance and the doorway from Shop S3 were fitted with double doors. The latter had a stone threshold and splayed reveals which projected beyond the wall face. The shop was floored with rammed earth and contained two large dolia and a "cooler."

### S5 (Pl. VI, 1)

The street entrance had double doors; the doorway from Shop S4 a single door with a bar socket. The southeast corner of the shop was screened off by a mud brick partition to form a closet. The floor was of rammed earth.

## House L. Four Rooms

### L1, Court (Pl. VII, 2)

The street entrance had a stone threshold and was fitted with a single door. Beneath an interior porch supported by a rubblework column on a square gypsum base, two broad stone steps led down some 0.49 m. to the rammed earth paving of the court. The mouth of its cesspool was covered by a roughly polygonal flagstone pierced in the center. The stair ascended along the east wall on arches sprung from rubblework piers which formed deep niches beneath the stair. The first five steps, of which the bottom three were protected on the court side by a sloping parapet 0.34 m. high, rested on a solid fill and remained intact. With an average tread of 0.31 m. and riser of 0.24 m. the stair probably rose some 4.50 m. to the roof of room L2.

### L2, Diwan

The doorway from the north side of the court had double doors. About the room ran a rubblework bench, 0.17 m. high, on which beside the east reveal of the doorway rested a rubblework fireplace. It was deeply firemarked and screened on three sides by a parapet, 0.28 m. high. The floor was of rammed earth.

### L3, Chamber

The doorway from room L2 was an arched opening roughly converted with rubblework to take a single door. In the northwest corner of the room was a rubblework platform, 0.12 m. high. The floor was of rammed earth.

### L4, Women's Chamber (?)

The doorway from the court was fitted with double doors. A stair, of which the three bottom steps remain, ascended along the east wall on an arch sprung from a rubblework pier. The extant steps have treads of 0.29 m. and risers of 0.25 m. The stair probably reached a low loft or attic in seven or eight steps. In the southeast corner of the room an oval terra cotta basin was set in the rammed earth floor and secured with plaster.

## 2. East Central Portion, Houses D, H, and J

### (Figs. 78, 79, 81, 82; Pl. V, 2)

### a. History

Houses J and H occupied the area of the four two-room shops of the north row and the three of the south row of the Seleucid shop building west of Shops S1–S5 and House K. It was in this area that the destruction of the original stone socles was most complete, and that subsequent building and rebuilding were most sweeping and thorough. The excavated remains fail to present any clear picture of the earliest steps by which the two houses came into being.

At the earliest stage revealed by excavation each house occupied the area of three of the original two-room shops. The area later taken up by rooms J8, H1, H2, and H2[1] was not part of the houses, but still functioned as an independent two-room shop, like K5–K6 under similar circumstances.[8] It clearly retained its stone Seleucid socles with their openings. The central longitudinal partition of the shop building con-

[8] Above, p. 69.

tinued to serve as the dividing wall of the early Houses J and H, as is indicated by the basin built against it in the early court of House H. Both houses were likewise bounded on the west by the original shop walls.

House J at this stage consisted of seven rooms, J1–J7, of which J1 was a small court with a cesspool and J3 a shop. The remains of the socles of this stage, where they are preserved beneath later floors (original walls J1–J5 and J1–J2) or as foundations for a rebuilt superstructure (J2–J3, J3–J4, J1–J6, J6–J7, and the exterior wall) show the early type of rubblework familiar from Houses M and K with its large pieces of broken Seleucid blocks laid in mud. None of the surviving door trim appears to belong to this stage.

An approximate date is furnished by the earliest doorsill levels of the street entrances to J1 and J3 and by the lowest layers of deposit in the cesspool of J1. The level of Street H along Block G3 rose 1.80 m. to 2.20 m. in roughly five hundred fifty years, an average of between 0.003 m. and 0.004 m. per annum. The earliest street doorsill of J1 was some 0.615 m., that of J3 some 0.735 m., above the Seleucid sill level. A date about the turn of the second and first centuries B.C. is indicated, and this evidence is confirmed by the potsherds from the cesspool.

The contemporary House H is clear only in outline. Of the interior structure only socle H9–D8 and its continuation beneath the floor of the later H8 can be assigned with certainty to this period. Its rubblework of large pieces of gypsum laid in mud is of a piece with the socle of wall H9–K5, D8–K6 in which several unbroken Seleucid blocks were used. It is apparent that the original entrance to the house was from the market place to the south. Probably D8 together with the portion of H8 south of the early socle was the vestibule. All else is of later construction.

The material for dating provided by the early House H is confined to the construction of the remaining original socles and the ceramic content of the lowest layers of deposit in the cesspool. Neither is conclusive, though the date implied would seem to be about the same as that of House J. In any case, a terminus ante quem is furnished by the erection of House D, which is placed about the middle of the first century B.C. by its synchronism with House L.[9]

House D from the time it was built underwent no important change in plan, save for the addition of room D8. Consequently its principal

[9] Above, pp. 70 f.

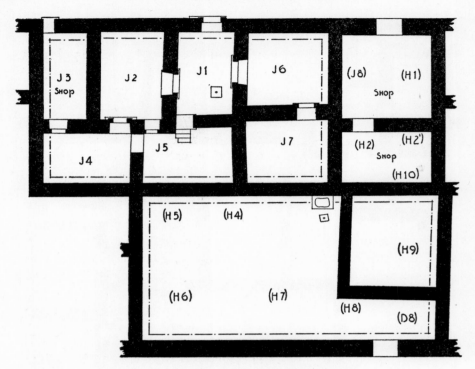

Fig. 27. G3, D–H–J. Early State. Restored Plan

features, the brick paving of the court, the stairs, the doorways D1–D2, D2–D6, D2–D4, and D2–D7, were part of the original construction. All the socles, including the exceptionally thick party wall with House H, were of rubblework of large pieces of gypsum laid in mud. In this case they were pointed with plaster and rendered with a thick coat of mud, over which plaster was later applied. The four original doorways were of a simple intermediate type, without splay and with stone thresholds which projected on the interior (Fig. 12a). The jambs were monolithic and not molded, but cut on the ends of slabs which revetted about half the depth of the reveals. There were no capitals, and the flat lintels projected slightly beyond the jambs. The stratified deposit in the cesspool of court D2 extended well back into the first century B.C.

The construction of House D initiated a series of changes which gave House H the plan it was to retain throughout its history. The obstruction of its façade on the market place deprived it of communication with

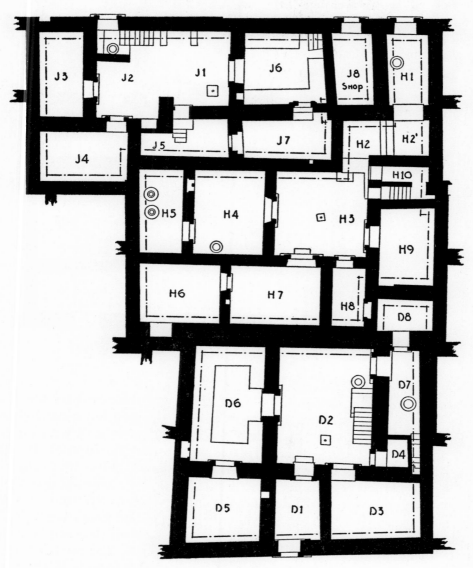

Fig. 28. G3, D–H–J. Final State. Restored Plan

the exterior, and a new entrance was contrived from Street 4. This was effected by the suppression of the original two-room shop in area J8, H1, H2, H2¹, which was acquired jointly by Houses H and J. The reorientation of House H brought with it a complete rebuilding of the interior walls which left scant traces of the old plan. It also involved the demolition of the old Seleucid party wall with House J and its reconstitution 1.40 m.–1.60 m. north of its former position. The resultant loss to House J was in part compensated by the addition of room J8.

With the exception of the socle of wall H9–D8, which was retained from the preceding period, all the new interior socles were, like those of House D, of rubblework of large pieces of gypsum laid in mud and carefully pointed with plaster. If there was an original rendering of mud, it has everywhere disappeared. There is abundant evidence that almost all the socles were at various times repaired, repointed, and rendered with plaster. The doorways offer a puzzling problem, since most of them appear to have been from time to time rebuilt and fitted with new trim or with new capitals and lintels on the old jambs and sills. Only doorways H4–H5 and H3–H8 seem to have kept their original form unchanged. They appear to have been similar to the doorways of House D, though they lack stone thresholds. The original doorsill of the street entrance to H1 was laid at some 0.94 m. above the level of the Seleucid shop sills, 0.82 m. higher than the level of the court. The transition was effected by four steps: at the doorway itself, at the stone sill of the arched opening between H1 and H2¹, and in the vestibule where two rubblework steps across the passage divide it into H2 and H2¹.

The building of House H had narrowed rooms J5 and J7 of House J and had added room J8 as a chamber behind J6. No other direct results can be detected, though it seems likely that doorways J2–J5 and J6–J7 received their lasting form at about this time. Both were without splay and had rubblework thresholds and trim of the same sort as that described in House D.[10] After a considerable lapse of time, sixty to one hundred years to judge from the rise in street level, J3 ceased to be used as a shop. It was converted to a room of the house, accessible only through room J4. Its narrow street doorway had been raised 0.47 m. before it was blocked up.

Many years later, probably, to judge again from the rise in street level, only shortly before the end of the city, House J was drastically remodelled. Court J1 and room J2 were thrown together to form a single large

[10] Above, p. 82.

court. The original street entrance to J1 was walled up, and a new one was cut at the northwest corner. At the same time room J8 was converted to a shop with a low cellar beneath. The old street entrance to J1 had been raised a total of 0.90 m. in two or more stages before its suppression, and the new entrance sill was laid 1.86 m. above the original Seleucid sill level. In addition to these major changes, rooms J5 and J3 were reoriented to suit the new arrangement. Doorway J5–J4 was walled up, and doorway J2–J5 was closed with a screen of mud brick which left a deep niche on the court side. Partition J5–J1 was rebuilt 0.52 m. north of its original position, and the new room J5 was made to communicate with the court and room J7. Room J3 was similarly made directly accessible from the court by means of a new doorway, J2–J3, and old doorway J4–J3 was blocked up.

In consequence of these operations the new court was regraded above the foundations of wall J1–J2 and brought to a level some 0.30 m. above the old. The floors of rooms J3, J4, and J6 were raised to correspond. Since the new court level was still some 0.95 m. below the level of the street and the entrance threshold, three steps led down to it from the doorway. The floor of room J5, which had previously lain some 0.55 m. below the old court level and was reached by three steps, remained the same, and its old doorsill served as a new top step. Room J7 also kept its former level. The conversion of room J8 was made possible by the rise in the level of the street. The doorsill of the new shop lay 1.89 m. above the Seleucid sill level. The cellar beneath was excavated almost to bed rock and reached by three steps descending 0.75 m. from room J6. Its height from floor to ceiling was only 1.56 m. During the work, partition J6–J8 and with it the portion of partition J6–J7 east of doorway J6–J7 was completely rebuilt.

With the exception of doorways J2–J5 and J6–J7, all the doorways of House J date from this final reconstruction. All were of the latest type in which the stone trim is merely a facing for rubblework and plaster sills and jambs (Fig. 12a). Even doorway J6–J7 was raised 0.23 m. and fitted with new jambs, but these were simply applied against the old.

Meanwhile Houses H and D had experienced little change. The street entrance of H1 was thrice raised to a final level of 1.88 m. above the Seleucid sill level, and the floor of H1 was treated as a ramp sloping sharply down to the sill of opening H1–H2.[1] At some intermediate time room D8 was ceded to House D. Doorway H8–D8 was closed with a screen of rubblework to form a deep cupboard in H8, and a new doorway was broken through from D7. At various times doorways H3–H4, H3–H9, H3–H7, and H7–H6 were rebuilt. In House D the entrance from Alley G3 was raised a total of 0.89 m. in at least two stages, and finally rebuilt with new trim. Within, doorway D1–D5 was walled up, and doorways D2–D3 and D6–D5 were rebuilt with new trim.

## b. Description. House J. Eight Rooms

### J1–J2, Court

The street entrance, which was fitted with double doors, opened on a covered landing closed on the south by a screen wall. Along the west wall of this vestibule ran a narrow bench, 0.47 m. high, and before its south wall stood a "cooler." Two steps led down to the rammed earth paving of the court. The mouth of the cesspool was covered by a square pierced gypsum lid. From the landing the stair ascended along the north wall on three arches sprung from rubblework piers. The first seven steps remain in place with an average tread of 0.30 m. and riser of 0.21 m. The stair originally consisted of twenty-three or twenty-four steps, and reached the roof of room J6 at approximately 5.50 m. above the level of the court. In the northeast corner beneath the stair stood a small thymiaterion of chalky white limestone. Its bowl was deeply charred, and it bore on one face the image of a deity in graffito.[11]

### J6, Diwan

The doorway from the east side of the court probably had double doors. In the northeast corner of the room steps led down to cellar J8. About the walls ran a broad rubblework bench, 0.16 m. high. Above it in the west wall just south of the doorway was a niche, and on the south wall at 1.28 m. from the floor an applied plaster shrine for private worship.[12] The floor was of rammed earth. On the east and south walls were scattered graffiti.[13]

### J8, Cellar

The doorway from room J6 had no threshold but was fitted with a single door, which swung in a socket set in a block of the Seleucid footing course. In the walls on either side of the southeast corner were niches.

### J8, Shop

The doorway from the street had a single door with a bar socket. The walls of the shop stood only some 0.75 m. high above the floor, which was no longer in place.

### J7, Chamber

The doorways from rooms J6 and J5 were fitted with single doors. Before the former a step led down to the rammed earth floor of the chamber. The latter had stepped re-

[11] Below, pp. 161 f.; Fig. 86.          [12] Below, pp. 162 f.
[13] Below, p. 168.

veals and was provided with a bar socket. In the north and south walls were small niches.

## J5

The doorway from the court had a single door with a bar socket and four steps leading down to the rammed earth floor within. Along the north wall the old foundation was left projecting to form a bench.

### J4, Women's Chamber ( ? )

The doorway from the court was hung with double doors, and the floor was of rammed earth.

### J3, Storeroom ( ? )

The doorway from the court was hung with double doors, and the floor was of rammed earth.

## House H. Ten Rooms

### H1, Vestibule

The street entrance was fitted with a single door with a bar socket. On the sloping rammed earth floor rested a "cooler."

### H2–H2¹, Passage

The arched openings at either end had stone thresholds. The rammed earth floor was divided into two levels by the rubblework steps across the middle of the passage.

### H3, Court (Pl. V, 2)

The paving was of rammed earth. The opening of the cesspool was covered by a square pierced gypsum slab. Before the threshold of the entrance a rectangular basin lined with upright gypsum slabs was let into the paving.

### H10, Stair Unit

The arched opening to the stair lay at the right, that to the space beneath the stair at the left. The latter had a narrow stone sill and was fitted with a single door. The stair ascended counter-clockwise about a newel wall. The five bottom steps of the first flight remain in place. The imprint of the sixth step of the first flight and both steps of the second flight is preserved on the newel and side walls. A stump of the first two steps of the third flight was found attached to the newel. With an average tread of 0.245 m. and riser of 0.18 m. the stair in all probability reached the roof in two full turns of eight flights at about 5.70 m. above the level of the court. In one of the walls of the stair was set a bas-relief of a goddess in military dress.[14]

[14] Below, p. 163.

### H7, Diwan

The doorway from the south side of the court had a stone step before it and double doors. About the room ran a broad rubblework bench, 0.22 m. high. Above it in the west wall was a small niche. The floor was of rammed earth.

### H6, Chamber

The doorway from room H7 was fitted with a single door with a bar socket. In the south wall was a deep niche cupboard. The floor was of rammed earth.

### H4, Diwan

The doorway from the west side of the court had double doors. In the west wall was a deep niche cupboard with a double arched opening and a shelf. On the rammed earth floor before the south wall stood a "cooler." See below, pp. 186–202.

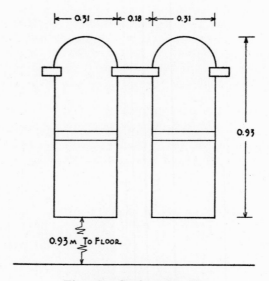

Fig. 28a. Cupboard in H4

### H5, Women's Chamber (?)

The doorway from room H4 was fitted with a single door with a bar socket. The room was floored with rammed earth and contained two large dolia. See below, pp. 163 f.

### H9

The doorway from the court was hung with double doors. The floor was of rammed earth.

### H8, Storeroom (?)

The doorway from the court had a single door with a bar socket. In the east wall a niche cupboard with three shelves was formed by the old door frame. The floor was of rammed earth.

## House D. Eight Rooms[15]

### D1, Vestibule

The street entrance had double doors with a bar socket, the doorway to the court a single door with a bar socket, stone threshold, and stone step. The floor was of rammed earth.

### D2, Court

In the paving of bricks, 0.30 m.–0.31 m. square, was set the square pierced gypsum lid of the cesspool. Along the east wall the stair ascended on three arches sprung from rubblework piers, of which the first, carrying seven steps, remains in place. The average tread was 0.29 m., the average riser 0.235 m. The stair is best restored as rising 4.25 m. in eighteen steps to a landing whence the roof of room D7 was gained, some 4.65 m. above the court. The space beneath the second arch of the stair was paved with plaster; beneath the third stood a "cooler."

### D6, Diwan

The doorway from the west side of the court had a stone threshold and was fitted with a single door with a bar socket. About the room ran a broad rubblework bench, 0.22 m. high. At the south end of the west wall was a deep niche cupboard similar to that in room H4, with a double arched opening and a shelf. The floor was of rammed earth.

### D5, Chamber

The doorway from room D6 had a single door. The floor was of rammed earth. In the east wall a niche was contrived in the walled-up doorway to D1.

### D3, Women's Chamber (?)

The doorway from the court had a single door with a bar socket. The floor was of rammed earth. Into the southeast corner was built the plaster casing, 2.28 m. high, of several sections of terra cotta pipe.

### D4, Closet

The low doorway from the court was only 1.24 m. from sill to lintel. It had a stone threshold and was fitted with a single door with a bar socket. The closet was floored with rammed earth.

[15] Cf. *Rep. V*, p. 67.

### D7, Storeroom (?)

The doorway from the court beneath the north arch of the stair had a stone threshold and was fitted with double doors. From the south end of the room a narrow stair ascended to a low loft over rooms D4 and D7. Seven steps with a total rise of 2.41 m. are preserved, and it is clear that not more than one step is missing. On the rammed earth floor of the room stood a "cooler."

### D8, Storeroom (?)

The doorway from D7 had a single door with a bar socket. The floor was of rammed earth.

## 3.  West Central Portion. Houses B, C, and G

## (Figs. 78, 79, 81, 82; Pls. IV, 2, V, 1)

### a.  History

Houses B6–11 and G occupied the area of the three two-room Seleucid shops in either row west of Houses H and J. As nearly as may be judged, they were contemporaneous. In the original construction of both houses the utmost use was made of the existing shop walls, and the dwelling rooms were fitted into the framework already provided, with as little change as possible. In both cases the exterior socle on Street 4 was rebuilt in rubblework on the old foundations, and with it the northern portion of their party wall, B9–G1, was rebuilt 0.45 m.–0.50 m. east of the Seleucid line, but partly on the Seleucid footing course. Within House G the only change was the rebuilding of wall G1–G6 in rubblework on the earlier foundation. Within House B two shop walls were razed in B7, and the walls of room B8 were erected new. For the rest the Seleucid socles and in large part the Seleucid openings continued to serve. Both houses were planned to extend through the entire width of the shop building with entrances on Street 4 and two-room shops on the market place.

House B consisted of six rooms, of which B10 and B11 were the original shop on the market place with a doorway broken through from court B7. Room B6 had its doorway from the market place walled up, and served as diwan. The original rubblework socles were built of large pieces of gypsum laid in mud mortar with much use of material from the Seleucid socles. Of the doorways only B7–B6 belongs to this early period. It was made by enlarging the Seleucid shop doorway at this point and fitting it with new stone trim: flat projecting jambs cut on the ends of sectional reveal slabs, capitals and lintel molded with the cavetto and Lesbian cyma. The doorway was thus of exactly the same type as doorway L1–L2 of House L and was presumably roughly contemporary.[16] The sill of the original street entrance to B9 was laid 0.875 m. above the Seleucid sills at a level which, to judge from the normal rate of rise, the street had reached about the middle of the first century B.C. This combined evidence is confirmed by the exceptionally rich ceramic series from the cesspool of B7.

House G likewise consisted of six rooms, of which G4 and G3 were the original shop on the market place communicating with the house by a new doorway, G6–G3. Former Shop G2 lost its street entrance and served as diwan. The new exterior socle and socle G1–G6 were built of rubblework of large pieces of gypsum, mainly broken Seleucid blocks. These were laid in mud mortar and, as in Houses D and H, carefully pointed with plaster. Of the doorways only G6–G3 remained unchanged. It was fitted into a breach in the Seleucid socle and trimmed with plain monolithic jambs cut on the ends of reveal slabs but without projection beyond the face of the wall. They had no capitals and carried a flat lintel block, also set flush with the wall face. The sill of the original street entrance was only 0.02 m. higher than that of House B6–B11, 0.895 m. above the Seleucid sill level.

A long lapse of time was followed by the erection of Houses C and B1–B5. They too were closely contemporary, and from their relation to courtyard A1 to the west and House A of Block G1 opposite were probably built in the twenties or thirties of the second century of our era. The construction of House A of Block G1 had been attended by a grading of the new western portion of Alley G3, sloped to the approximate contemporary level of the older eastern portion, 0.55 m.–0.70 m. above the level of the market place. The street entrances of Houses C and B1–B5 were built to this new level, which remained practically constant from this time forward. None of the scanty ceramic material from the cesspool of House B1–B5 is older than the first century after Christ.

The two houses, built to communicate by opening B5–C6, were constructionally in every respect the same. Their socles were of a developed form of rubblework with small pieces of both gypsum and red limestone laid solid through the wall in plaster mortar. The doorways were of the normal third type with monolithic jambs of gypsum and rubblework reveals. In most cases they had capitals and lintels with developed ca-

[16] Above, pp. 71 f.

vetto-fillet moldings. At the time of the building of House C, the original west exterior wall of House D was extensively rebuilt to serve as a party wall. Later changes in both houses were few and unimportant.

Since the new houses completely masked the old south façades of Houses G and B6–B11, a rearrangement of the adjacent portions of the latter was necessary. The Seleucid shop doorways of G4 and B10 were walled up with the rubblework of the new socles, and in C2 this was laid in one piece with the pier of the stair arch. The Seleucid partitions G4–B6 and B6–B10 were consequently demolished, and the area of the three Seleucid shop rooms was divided into four by new partitions. In the process, room G5 of House G gained a strip of about 1.00 m. from original room B6 of House B6–B11. The three new socles were of plaster rubblework similar to that in Houses C and B1–B5. At the same time Seleucid doorway G3–G4 was walled up with rubblework of a piece with that of partition G4–G5, and a new doorway was broken through the Seleucid socle to the west. The reveals were of rubblework; the trim was of plain monolithic jambs and lintel set flush with the wall face. Seleucid doorway B11–B10, which had meanwhile been provided with simple jambs flush with the wall, was similarly walled up. Its place was taken by a doorway in partition B6–B10, trimmed like doorway G3–G4. As part of the same remodelling, Seleucid partition B7–B11 was razed and replaced by a wall on a rubblework socle about 1.00 m. to the east. The doorway at its northern end was similar to doorway B6–B10.

About the turn of the second and third centuries, to judge from the progressive rise in Street 4, Houses B6–B11 and B1–B5 were combined to form a single dwelling. The original entrance to House B6–B11 from Street 4 was abolished. The doorway, which had been raised a total of 0.875 m. in three stages during the previous history of the house, was blocked up with its sill at 1.75 m. above the Seleucid sill level. The opening of vestibule B9 on the court was closed with a wall of mud brick, and B9 became a back room entered from B8 by a narrow makeshift opening. The union of the two houses was simply achieved by reopening the Seleucid entrance to B6. Opening B5–C6 was closed with mud brick.

House G apparently remained unchanged until very near the end of the city's history. At that time the northern portion was extensively remodelled. As elsewhere this remodelling was closely related to the cumulative rise in the level of the adjacent street. In House G its essential feature was the rearrangement of rooms G2 and G7 and the creation of cellar rooms beneath (Pl. IV, 2). Original partition G2–G7 was removed, and a new one was built 1.40 m. to the south, lengthening G2 at the expense of G7. At the same time partition G2–G1, G7–G6 was thoroughly rebuilt above its foundations. Within the new G2 the bed rock was dug away to a depth of 0.39 m. and within G7 to 0.24 m. to give head room in the cellars, whose ceilings were 1.94 m. from the floor. The cellar of G2 was vaulted on the west with three transverse barrel vaults, 1.50 m., 1.62 m., and 1.82 m. in span. They were sprung from rubblework counter walls 0.50 m. and 0.24 m. thick at either end and from rubblework partitions 0.71 m. and 0.58 m. thick at a uniform height of 1.20 m. from the floor. Only the narrowest vault at the north was therefore semicircular, the others being more or less segmental. The vaults themselves were each built with seven rubblework ribs, 0.17 m. wide and 0.09 m. thick, each of which was cast in two sections before being put in place. They were set 0.50 m.–0.60 m. apart, and the spaces between were filled with a shell of rubblework, behind which the haunches were filled with loose rubble. The plaster mortar floor of room G2 above rested directly on the ribs. On the east the three vaulted spaces were connected by a corridor with arched openings 0.88 m. wide at the eastern ends of the partitions. The arches sprang, like the vaults, 1.20 m. from the floor and were thus 1.64 m. to the crown. To avoid an intersection of vaults the space above was roofed flat on beams. An arched opening like the others gave access from the cellar of G7. The latter was simply roofed with beams carrying the floor of room G7 above, and its entry from room G6 constituted the sole access to the cellars.

The new floor of room G2 lay some 1.06 m. above the old court level, while in the course of time the street entrance had been progressively raised until its sill lay 1.41 m. above it. At the same time the new arrangement required that room G6 remain at its old level so as to afford access to the cellars. As a result the court level was raised 1.01 m. by a fill of earth and debris, while doorway G1–G6 was correspondingly raised, rebuilt, and provided with a step down to G6. The street entrance was raised another 0.31 m. to lie 2.085 m. above the Seleucid sill level. To the new court level were built a covered interior porch with a screen wall and single rubblework column and a new stair. The mouth of the cesspool was built up to the new paving. The difference of 0.70 m. between the entrance doorsill and the court was taken up in the doorway itself and by a step of 0.30 m. at the porch.

The new and rebuilt socles were of the latest type of plaster rubblework with carefully laid faces of small red limestone rubble heavily pointed and rendered and a looser interior filler. Doorways G1–G2 and G2–G7 were new. The jambs and lintel of G2–G7 were carried out entirely in rubblework. The trim of G1–G2 was similar save that the rubblework jambs were faced with thin slabs of gypsum. Its massive lintel with soffit moldings is illustrated in Fig. 29. In doorway G1–G6 the old stone trim with plain jambs and lintel set flush with the face of the wall was reused.

Fig. 29. G3, G1–G2. Lintel Profile

### b. Description. House B. Eleven Rooms[17]

#### B1, Vestibule

The street entrance had double doors, and the opening to the court was probably arched. Two steps led down to the interior floor of rammed earth.

#### B2, Court (Pl. V, 1)

The paving was of rammed earth. The mouth of the cesspool was covered with a square pierced gypsum lid, and before the north wall stood a "cooler." The stair ascended along the east wall on three arches springing from rubblework piers. The first arch remains in place, bearing the eight bottom steps which had treads of 0.30 m. and risers of 0.21 m. The stair reached the roof of room B5 probably in twenty steps at some 4.20 m. above the court. At the level of the fifth step there was a horizontal platform three steps wide, and in the second and third arches beneath the stair stood terra cotta ovens.

#### B3, Diwan

The doorway from the west side of the court was fitted with double doors, and the room was floored with rammed earth.

#### B4, Diwan

The doorway from the west side of the court had double doors, and its reveals projected on the interior. On the rammed earth floor in the southeast corner of the room stood a large dolium.

[17] Cf. *Rep. V*, p. 67.

### B5, Passage

Opening B2–B5 was a low arch, only 1.43 m. to the crown, beneath the third arch of the stair. Opening B4–B5 had a single door, while opening B5–B6 was presumably arched. The floor was of rammed earth.

### B6, Women's Chamber (?)

The doorway from the south side of court B7 had a stone threshold and reveals projecting on the interior. It was hung with double doors. The floor was of rammed earth.

### B10, Women's Chamber

The doorway from room B6 had a stone threshold and double doors. In the north and south walls were shallow niche cupboards within the frames of former doorways B10–C2 and B10–B11. The floor was of rammed earth.

### B7, Court

The court was paved with rammed earth. Its northern portion was an interior porch, the roof of which was supported by a single rubblework column standing on a rough stylobate, 0.54 m. high. The latter terminated 1.20 m. from the west wall to permit free access. Within the porch stood two "coolers." The mouth of the cesspool in the open court was covered with a square pierced gypsum lid. In the southwest corner was a stepped masonry table with a terra cotta basin set in the top. The stair ascended along the south wall on two arches sprung from rubblework piers. Portions of all first five steps are preserved and show an average tread of 0.32 m. and riser of 0.24 m. The total rise of the stair and the manner in which it gained the roof of room B11 could not be determined.

### B11

The doorway from the court was fitted with double doors. The floor was of rammed earth.

### B8, Storeroom (?)

The doorway from the porch of court B7 had a single door with a bar socket. The floor was of rammed earth.

### B9, Storeroom (?)

The narrow opening from B8 was not fitted with doors. The floor was of rammed earth.

## House C. Six Rooms[18]

### C1, Vestibule

The street entrance had double doors and two steps leading down to the rammed earth floor of the interior.

[18] Cf. *Rep. V*, p. 67.

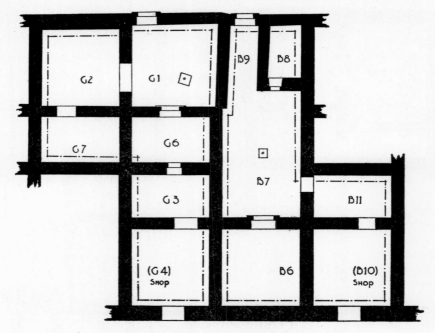

Fig. 30. G3, B–C–G. Early State. Restored Plan

## C2, Court

The doorway from vestibule C1 was fitted with a single door. The paving was of rammed earth and there was no cesspool. In the paving against the west wall before the stair was sunk a plaster basin. The stair ascended along the north wall from a landing approached by a flight of four steps from the court. It was supported on two arches sprung from rubblework piers. The first flight, the landing, and the two bottom steps of the second flight remain in place. With an average tread of 0.27 m. and riser of 0.23 m. the stair probably rose in nineteen steps from the landing to the roof of room C7 at some 5.30 m. above the court.

## C6, Alcove

A single rubblework column with a pilaster respond against the north wall supported the roof of the side open to the court. The floor was of rammed earth.

## C3, Diwan

The doorway from the south side of the court had a stone threshold, and its reveals projected on the interior. It was hung with double doors. The room was floored with rammed earth.

Fig. 31. G3, B–C–G. Final State. Restored Plan

### C5, Chamber

The doors of the doorway from the court have left no traces; the doorway from room C3 had a stone threshold and double doors. The floor was of rammed earth.

### C7, Women's Chamber (?)

The doors of the doorway from the court have left no certain traces. The floor was of rammed earth.

## House G. Nine Rooms[19]

### G1, Court

The street entrance was fitted with double doors and had a single step before it. It opened behind a screen wall into the interior porch of one column across the north end of the court. Both porch and open court were paved with rammed earth, and the step of 0.30 m. between was faced with plaster. Within the porch were two "coolers," and two more stood in the court. The mouth of the cesspool was covered with a square pierced gypsum lid. The stair ascended from the porch along the east wall on three arches springing from rubblework piers. The broad bottom step and portions of the five following remain in place. The latter had treads of 0.30 m. and risers of 0.24 m., and the stair probably rose in seventeen steps to the roof of room G6 at some 4.40 m. above the court. In one of the walls of the court was set a bas-relief of Hercules.[20]

### G2, Diwan (Pl. IV, 2)

The wide doorway from the west side of the court had double doors and a stone threshold. The floor was of plaster mortar, and along the west and south walls ran broad benches of rubblework, 0.14 m. high.

### G2, Cellar

Described above, p. 93.

### G7, Chamber

The doorway from room G2 was fitted with double doors. The floor was of plaster mortar.

### G7, Cellar

Described above, p. 93.

### G6, Diwan

The doorway from the south side of the court had double doors. The room was floored with rammed earth.

### G3, Women's Chamber (?)

The doorway from G6 was hung with double doors. The floor was of rammed earth.

### G4, Work- or Storeroom (?)

The doors of doorway G3–G4 have left no certain traces. Opening G4–G5 was arched. The floor was of rammed earth.

[19] Cf. *Rep. V*, p. 67.          [20] *Rep. V*, p. 68.

G5, Storeroom (?)

On the rammed earth floor in the southeast corner stood a "cooler."

## 4. Western Portion. House F and Building A

### (Figs. 78, 79, 81, 82; Pls. III, IV, 1)

### a. History

The history of Building A, the public record office, has been dis-cussed above.[21] House F occupied the area of the western pair of Seleu-cid two-room shops in the north row. Here the rear room at least of the westernmost shop had for a time before the creation of the house formed part of the record office complex. The walling up of opening A4–F2 was probably coincident with the making over of the shops to form House F. In this process the Seleucid socles were retained as party walls on the south and east. The exterior socles on the north and west were largely replaced by rubblework founded on their lower courses. Within the house area the Seleucid socles were all but completely razed. The area was redivided into four by walls on socles of an early type of plaster rubblework in which the caementa were mostly broken Seleucid blocks.

Of the four original rooms, F2 was a shop with a doorway on Street F. The street entrance of the house and doorway F4–F3 were subsequently rebuilt, but doorways F4–F1, F1–F2, and F3–F2 kept their original form unchanged. They were simple open-ings with rubblework reveals set without splay and trimmed with projecting monolithic jambs. Their jamb capitals and lintels bore the flattened ovolo molding (Fig. 32).[22] The sill of the street entrance to Shop F2 was laid on the Seleucid base header course, 0.41 m. above the higher sill level of the south, east, and west sides of the Seleucid building. The original sill of the street entrance to the court lay 0.975 m. above the lower Seleucid sill level of the north side of the building, at about the same level as that of F2.

Fig. 32. G3, F1–F2. Jamb Capital Profile

[21] Pp. 28–32.                    [22] Cf. above, p. 73.

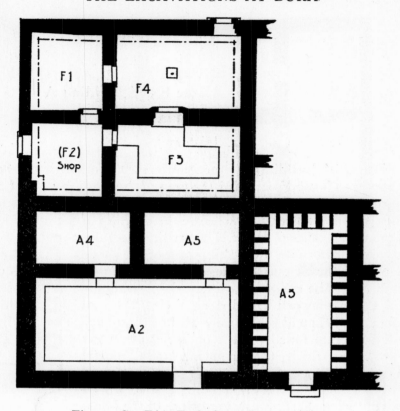

Fig. 33. G3, F–A. Early State. Restored Plan

The estimated rate of rise of Street 4 to this level goes with the constructional features and the door trim to suggest a date in the last quarter of the first century B.C. for the origin of the house.

Later years saw few essential changes. The street entrance of Shop F2 was walled up, apparently before it had been found necessary to raise its sill, and F2 became an ordinary room of the house. Doorway F4–F3 was rebuilt with irregularly splayed reveals and jambs largely carried out in rubblework. The type is late and is probably to be associated with the final stage of court F4. Here the street entrance had, as the street level rose, been raised 0.81 m. in at least two stages. The final level of its doorsill, 1.785 m. above the Seleucid sill level, was presumably reached early in the third century. The court now lay 1.10 m. below the doorsill. The transition was effected by means of a broad covered land-

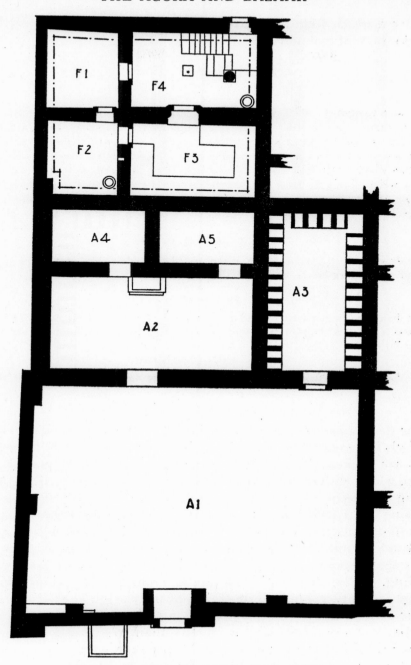

Fig. 34. G3, F–A. Final State. Restored Plan

ing, from which four steps led down to the court and from which the
stair to the roof took off.

## b. Description. House F. Four Rooms[23]

### F4, Court

The street entrance, which was fitted with double doors, opened onto a landing beneath an interior porch across the east end of the court. A single column of rubblework
supported its roof. The court was paved with rammed earth, and the mouth of the cesspool was covered with a square pierced gypsum slab. In the southeast corner beneath
the porch stood a "cooler." The stair ascended along the north wall from the landing
on two arches springing from rubblework piers. Its eight bottom steps are preserved
in whole or part. Their treads average 0.31 m., their risers 0.23 m., and the complete
stair probably reached the roof of room F1 in eighteen steps at some 4.85 m. above the
court.

### F3, Diwan (Pl. IV, 1)

The doorway from the south side of the court had double doors. About the room ran
a broad rubblework bench, 0.14 m. high. The floor was of rammed earth.

### F2, Chamber

The doorways from rooms F3 and F1 contained no trace of their doors. In the east
wall was a small niche. On the rammed earth floor in the southeast corner stood a
"cooler."

### F1, Women's Chamber ( ? )

The doorway from the court was hung with double doors. The floor was of rammed
earth.

## B. Blocks G7 and G5 (Pl. XIII, 1)

The development of the series of houses, H to A, in these two blocks
parallels in a general way that of the houses of Block G3, but the differences are obvious. Houses H to A formed a strikingly homogeneous
group, which with the exception of House H changed very little in plan
during the course of its existence. They were the result of a far more
sweeping destruction of the Seleucid shop building whose area they
came to occupy, and all appear to have been laid down within a relatively much shorter space of time, scarcely more than a generation. As a
result they ignored to a far greater degree the lines of the Seleucid
building, while their walls, constantly repaired and rebuilt without
change in position, retained much less of their original character.

The excavated stretch of Street 4 along the north side of Blocks G7
and G5 rose somewhat more gradually than the stretch along Block
G3, at a rate of some 0.003 m.–0.0035 m. per year.

[23] Cf. *Rep. V*, p. 67.

## 1. G7, House H (Figs. 78, 83)

### a. History

The earliest remains of dwellings on the site of House H are a number of fragmentary foundations of rubblework beneath the floor levels of the later house. They consist of large pieces of broken gypsum blocks laid in mud mortar, and are found in the later rooms H4, H3, H9, and in court H1. In room H3 the upper surface of these foundations was flush with the plaster floor and was accordingly heavily rendered with plaster. In room H9 the rubblework foundations were supplemented by a section in which Seleucid socle blocks were reused as a sort of rough masonry mortared with mud, and the bedding of a doorway is preserved. The traces indicate that it was a doorway of the early transitional type with a raised sill but without projecting jambs. With these foundations are associated two cesspools. One was the cesspool later used in House H, the lowest layers of whose stratified deposit go back to the end of the second century. The other was a cesspool over the mouth of which partition H10–H4 was later built. Its small but sealed and representative deposit extends from the end of the second century B.C. to about the beginning of our era. Beside the first a fire pit was sunk 0.65 m. into bed rock. It was subsequently filled in and covered over by the rammed earth floor of the early court. These remains are unfortunately insufficient to permit a restoration of the plan of the two houses.

These early houses were demolished about the beginning of our era to make way for House H in its original form. The approximate date is furnished by the end of the deposit in the cesspool beneath partition H4–H10 and by the earliest level of the street entrance to H10, which lay almost exactly 1.00 m. above the original street level.

As originally planned the house consisted of a vestibule, H10, and a court, H1, on which gave two diwans, H2 and H3, and two rooms, H9 and H7. Diwan H2 had a dependent chamber, H8, Diwan H3 three dependent chambers, H5, H6, and H4, the latter also accessible from the vestibule. In the court the south pilaster respond of the interior porch was built of a piece with the north wall of H2, and the north pilaster respond with the south wall of the stair unit. Both were thus part of the original scheme, but the stair unit was so imperfectly designed that when constructed its front wall considerably overlapped the east jamb of doorway H1–H9.

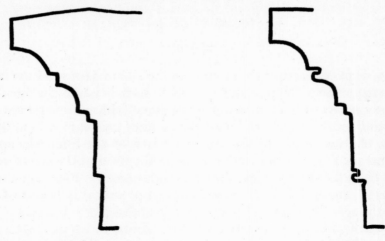

Fig. 35. G7, H1–H2.
Lintel Profile

Fig. 36. G7, H2–
H8. Lintel Profile

All the socles were of plaster rubblework of a relatively early type with caementa of both gypsum and red limestone laid solid through the wall. They were well pointed with plaster but rendered only above floor level. All the doorways of the final period, save H1–H5, H2–H6, and H7–H8, were of the original construction. They were of the normal third type with slightly splayed reveals, rubblework thresholds, and monolithic projecting stone jambs. With one exception they carried capitals and lintels with an early form of the regular cavetto-fillet molding (Fig. 35). The exception was doorway H2–H8 whose jamb capitals and lintel were of the earlier type with the Lesbian cyma (Type II; Fig. 12a) and represent the same stage of development as those of doorway L1–L2 in Block G3 (Fig. 36).[24] The reveals of doorways H1–H2, H1–H3, and H1–H9 projected slightly on the interior. Those of H1–H2 and H1–H3 were revetted with stone. Rooms H2 and H3 were floored with plaster mortar.

To produce the gypsum plaster required for the construction a kiln was built on the site in the angle of the early foundations beneath room H3. It was a simple trench, 0.90 m. deep, lined with mud brick which was laid flat along the sides and on end at the ends. The bricks were found with their surfaces in a vitrified condition.

At a later date the interior arrangements were reorganized by the

[24] Cf. above, pp. 71 f.

simple expedient of closing old doorways and opening new ones. Doorways H10–H4, H3–H5, H5–H6, and H2–H8 were walled up with
rubblework, the latter with its jambs and lintel still in place. Doorways
H1–H5, H2–H6, and H7–H8 were cut to replace them. As a result H8
became a dependence of H7, H6 became the chamber of diwan H2, and
H5 became a room off the court, leaving H4 the chamber of diwan H3.
The new doorways had the simplest of stone trim, plain narrow jambs,
and lintels set flush with the wall face without capitals or moldings.

These changes were probably associated with the final raising of the
street entrance, which from its relation to the level of the street probably
took place in the third quarter of the second century. The new threshold
was 0.52 m. above the original one and had presumably been raised once
before, though all traces of this step are obliterated. There was now a
difference of some 0.60 m. between the entrance and court levels. It was
taken up without steps by pitching the floor of vestibule H10, which was
now lightly paved with plaster at its lower end. This grading of the
vestibule floor was clearly related to the blocking up of doorway H10–
H4, which, if not done before, would have become necessary at this time.
Probably as part of the same program the court was repaved with plaster
mortar.

Somewhat later, to judge from the street levels, a large kiln was built
in Street 4 close by the house wall and opposite the intersection of Street
E. It consisted of a well-preserved fire box of mud brick set in a pit dug
1.17 m. below the street surface. Above it there was originally an oven
of which no traces remain. The rectangular fire box was covered by
four mud brick arches springing from low side walls some 0.40 m. high
and separated by intervals of 0.18 m.–0.22 m., through which the heat
passed to the oven above. It had a semicircular fire door at its east end.
The relation, if any, of the kiln to House H is obscure. Perhaps it was
used to calcine gypsum for construction in the houses farther to the east
or in the Roman camp to the north. In any case it soon served its purpose. The oven was demolished; the fire box and its pit in the street filled
in and paved over.

Later periods have left no traces save for the usual evidence of repair
and replastering of the walls. The only witness to the fact that the house
during the thirties or forties of the third century had come into the possession of Aurelia Appia, widow of Julius Terentius, tribune of the
Twentieth Palmyrene Cohort of the Roman garrison, was the epitaph
of her husband.[25]

[25] Below, pp. 176–185.

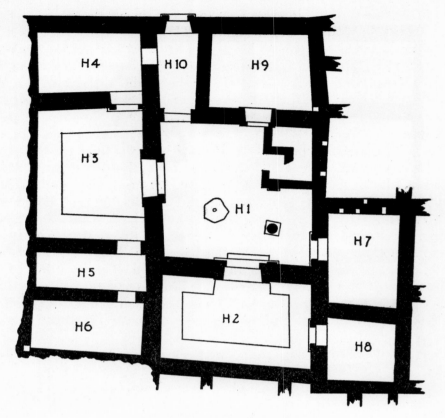

Fig. 37. G7, H. Early State. Restored Plan

## b. Description. Ten Rooms

### H10, Vestibule

The street entrance was fitted with double doors. The rammed earth floor was covered with a coat of plaster before the arched opening to the court. In the west wall was a niche cupboard left in the blocked opening of doorway H10–H4.

### H1, Court (Fig. 40)

Set in the plaster mortar paving was a large pierced polygonal lid of gypsum covering the mouth of the cesspool. Before the north wall stood a "cooler," and thrust into the paving beside the west jamb of doorway H1–H2 was a heavy iron shoe for a

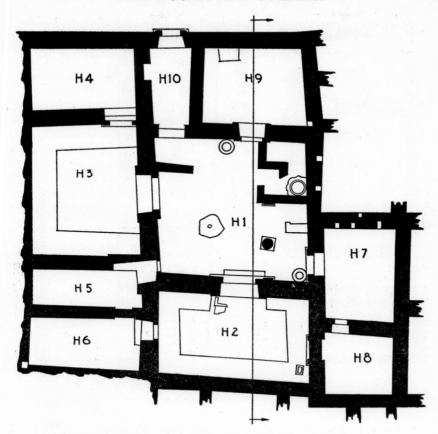

Fig. 38. G7, H. Final State. Restored Plan

wooden staff or mast of about 0.40 m. diameter. Traces of wood remained in the socket. In the northeast corner was the stair unit. The stair ascended to the left of the arched entrance, clockwise about a central newel wall. Side and newel walls bore the imprint of the three steps of the first flight, the first landing, and the three steps of the second flight. The treads averaged 0.29 m., the risers 0.21 m. The stair is best restored as rising thirteen steps in four full flights with an additional fifth flight of six to a height of some 4.15 m. above the court. The opening to the space beneath the stair was within the stair unit, beneath the fourth flight and third landing. In the northeast corner beneath the second landing stood a table of rubblework, 0.90 m. high, and in the southeast corner beneath the third landing a terra cotta oven heavily insulated with mud. The space south of the stair unit was filled by an interior porch whose roof was supported by a single column of rubblework. It was 0.55 m. in lower and 0.46 m. in upper diameter, and rested on a square gypsum base worked with a quarter round torus. Its gypsum

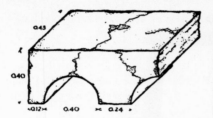

Fig. 39. G7, H1. Arch Fragment

Doric capital of the late local form carried a reinforced rubblework epistyle with a projecting fascia across the center. Beneath the porch was a masonry bench or table, 0.49 m. high, and a "cooler." Room H7, with an inadequate source of light from doorway H1–H7 beneath the porch, was apparently lit in addition by five arched openings above its roof. The cast rubblework arches were found in fragments amid the elements of the porch in the southeast corner of the court. Of the fragments which comprise parts of five arches, the largest is illustrated in Fig. 39. They exactly fit the requisite space of 3.20 m. The epitaph of Julius Terentius, which was found amid the same debris, was probably set into the epistyle or above doorway H1–H7.

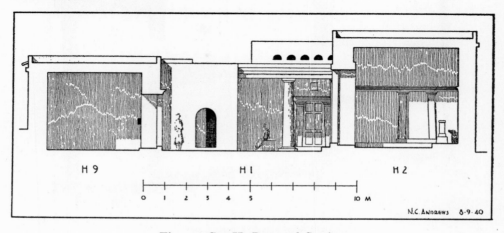

Fig. 40. G7, H. Restored Section

### H2, Diwan

The doorway from the south side of the court had a rubblework step before it and double doors. The room was floored with plaster mortar, and about the walls ran a broad bench, 0.21 m. high. Before the west side of the door were the remains of a rubblework hearth with an L-shaped shield. On the bench in the southeast corner stood the stepped base of a rectangular stele or altar consisting of two steps with inclined faces, 0.27 m. and 0.15 m. high, and a corner fragment of the die. Behind it the frame of blocked doorway H2–H8 formed a panel, and at the height of its lintel a plaster cornice with the cavetto-fillet molding ran about the walls of the room.

### H6, Chamber

The doorway from the court had a single door with a bar socket and a rubblework step down to the rammed earth floor within. In the angle of the southwest corner was a niche with a narrow opening. About the walls ran a plaster cornice of the "Orthono-bazus" type.[26]

### H3, Diwan

The doorway from the west side of the court was fitted with double doors. The floor was of plaster mortar. About the walls ran a broad rubblework bench, 0.21 m. high, and above it a plaster cavetto-fillet cornice like that of room H2.

### H4, Women's Chamber (?)

The doorway from room H3 had double doors and a step within the reveals. The floor was of rammed earth.

### H9, Dining Room (?)

The doorway from the court was hung with double doors. The floor was of rammed earth. Against the north wall was a rubblework bench or table 0.53 m. high, and in the southeast corner a small niche.

### H5, Workroom

The narrow doorway from the court had double doors. In a line across the middle of the rammed earth floor were found six basalt hand mills of the rectangular grinder type.

### H7, Storeroom (?)

The doorway from the court was fitted with double doors. The floor was of rammed earth. In the north wall were three small niches. In the wall beside or above the court doorway was set a plaster bas-relief of Hercules.[27]

### H8, Slave's Room (?)

The doorway from room H7 had double doors. The floor was of rammed earth. In the west wall a shallow niche or panel was formed by the blocked opening of doorway H2–H8.

## 2. G5, House E (Figs. 78, 83)

### a. History

The original level of its street entrance indicates that House E was laid down at approximately the same time as the early houses which preceded House H, i.e., about the turn of the first and second centuries B.C. The essential features of its plan remained unchanged throughout its

---

[26] Cumont, *Fouilles*, pp. 226–238.     [27] Below, p. 164.

history, though its fabric was subject to repeated rebuilding. The original fabric remains most clearly in evidence in the socles of rooms E2, E7, and of the party wall with House F. They were of rubblework of large pieces of gypsum, in large part broken Seleucid blocks, laid in mud mortar. Elsewhere the socles were found to have been rebuilt in plaster rubblework of various types above the foundations, and all were given a uniform appearance by frequently renewed coats of plaster.

None of the doorways retained its original trim or dimensions, but abundant evidence of their character during the first century B.C. is furnished by a series of reused jamb capitals and lintels. The late trim of doorway E1–E3 was completed by a pair of early jamb capitals of the ovolo type, which carried a lintel of the Lesbian cyma type (Fig. 41). The core of the rubblework plinth of the column in court E1 was formed by a jamb capital of the Lesbian cyma type, while a fragmentary lintel of the same variety was found imbedded in the rebuilt western portion of socle E1–E2 (Fig. 41). The cesspool of the court had apparently been cleared out shortly before the end of the city.

The street entrance was raised a total of 0.96 m. in three separate stages, the last one of about the beginning of the third century of our era. The resultant difference of some 0.80 m. between the entrance threshold and court levels was adjusted in vestibule E6. A rubblework foundation was thrown across the passage to retain a filled landing in-

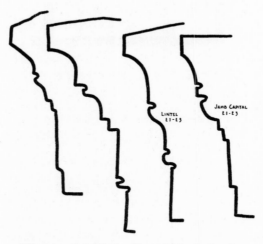

Fig. 41. G5, E. Profiles of Early Jamb
Capitals and Lintels

side the entrance. It formed a step from which the floor sloped down to a rough stone sill before opening E6–E1. Opening E6–E2 was fitted with a pair of steps.

Still later, very near the end of the city, room E4–E5, originally the chamber of diwans E2 and E3, was converted to a pair of cellar rooms with a large shop above. The rise in the level of Street 4 had made it possible by excavating the floor of E4–E5 to bed rock to obtain the meager head room of 1.76 m. for cellars. Here partition E4–E5 was erected and provided with an arched opening, while the west wall of room E2 was completely rebuilt. Cellar E5 was entered by a narrow doorway from room E2. The threshold of the shop entrance above was laid 1.92 m. above the cellar floors, 1.45 m. above the Seleucid street level. The shop itself was floored with plaster mortar and entered from the house by a doorway from room E3 and three or more steps, all trace of which has disappeared. Both doorways were of the simplest construction with narrow plain stone jambs and lintels set flush with the face of the wall. The other doorways of the house are late but cannot be precisely dated.

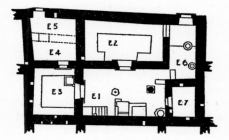

Fig. 42. G5, E. Restored Plan

## b. Description. Eight Rooms

### E6, Vestibule

The street entrance was fitted with a single door. On the sloping rammed earth floor stood two "coolers."

### E1, Court

The entrance from vestibule E6 was through a covered interior porch across the east end of the court. Its roof was supported by a single rubblework column, 0.68 m. in lower diameter, which rested on a square gypsum base capping a low rubblework plinth. The flat stone capital was roughly cut, and its Doric profile was carried out in plaster.

Beneath the porch stood a rubblework bench or table, 0.46 m. high, and in its southeast corner an oven of terra cotta insulated with mud. The court was paved with rammed earth, and the mouth of its cesspool was covered with a roughly circular pierced lid of gypsum. The stair ascended along the south wall on two arches springing from rubble-work piers and a section of supporting wall. The bottom landing and five steps are preserved with treads of 0.29 m. and risers of 0.20 m. The stair when complete prob-ably rose in eighteen steps to the roof of the porch at some 3.80 m. above the court. Against the wall on the second and third steps there remained the lower portion of a small plaster stele. Beneath the stair were kitchen and stable. In the second arch was a fireplace of burnt brick with a brick-faced rubblework pot ledge and an L-shaped shield about the northwest corner. Behind the supporting wall of the upper portion of the stair was a cobbled area large enough for a single donkey.

### E2, Diwan

The doorway from the north side of the court had double doors and its reveals pro-jected on the interior. The doorway to cellar E5 had a single door with a bar socket. About the room ran a broad rubblework bench, 0.19 m. high. In the southwest corner was a niche. The floor was of rammed earth.

### E3, Diwan

The doorway from the west side of the court had double doors, that to Shop E4–E5 a single door. About three sides of the room ran a broad rubblework bench, 0.22 m. high. On the rammed earth floor at the north side of the doorway was a hearth with a rubblework parapet, 0.37 m. high. The parapet ended on each side against square plinths, each 0.43 m. high, with shallow charred sinkings in the top, which probably served as thymiateria. There was a niche in the south wall, and a pair of niches in the west wall. Between the latter, 1.20 m. above the bench, about half of a crudely daubed icon for private worship was preserved. When complete, it was apparently closely simi-lar to that in room J6 of Block G3.[28] Here four copies could be distinguished on suc-cessive thin coats of plaster.

### E7, Storeroom (?)

The doorway from the court retained no certain traces of its doors. There was a niche in each of the north, south, and west walls. The floor was of rammed earth.

### E4–E5, Shop

The street entrance retained no certain traces of its doors. The floor was of plaster mortar, and in the north wall was a niche.

### E4 and E5, Cellars

Described above, p. 111.

[28] Above, p. 86; below, pp. 162 f.

### 3. G5, House F (Figs. 78, 83)

### a. History

No such convenient measuring stick as the progressive rise in the level of Street 4 can be applied to House F, but its close relationship with Houses E and H is sufficient indication of their original contemporaneity. The socles of House F, moreover, with the exception of its party walls with Houses H and D, remained very much as built beneath their accumulated coats of plaster. They were of mud-mortared rubblework with caementa of broken Seleucid blocks. The party wall with House H was completely rebuilt when that house was erected. The party wall with House D was built as part of the fabric of that house. It is possible that during the short time before the erection of House D the Seleucid shop wall served as the east wall of House F. This evidence is borne out by the meager deposit in the cesspool of court F1. It contained no sherds which can be dated earlier than the last half of the second century B.C.

The original entrance to the house was from the open market place to the south, and its sill remains in place, 0.26 m. below the later rubblework threshold. When the development of houses before the early east façade of Block G7 necessitated the building of corridor F5, the original entrance was replaced by an arch, 0.26 m. higher. At the same time the level of the court within was raised some 0.40 m. by a fill of earth and debris, and the interior porch and stair were constructed. The new level of the court covered the original step before doorway F1–F2 and caused the raising of doorway F1–F3, both of which were fitted with new stone trim. These changes have been approximately dated early in the second century of our era from their place in the general evolution of the bazaar area.[29] This date is confirmed in a general way by the ceramic material found in the fill in the court, and by the jamb capitals and lintel of doorway F1–F2, which were of the developed normal cavetto-fillet type (Fig. 43).

Fig. 43. G5, F1–F2. Jamb Capital and Lintel Profiles

[29] Above, pp. 59 f.

The exterior doorway of corridor F5 was subsequently raised 0.51 m. in two stages owing to the rapid rise in the level of the area before it after the erection of Shops S1–S5. The addition of a bench in diwan F2 necessitated the raising of doorway F2–F4.

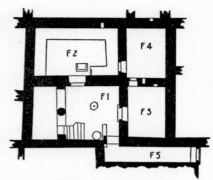

Fig. 44. G5, F. Restored Plan

## b. Description. Five Rooms

### F5, Corridor

The street entrance retained no certain traces of its doors. The floor was of rammed earth.

### F1, Court

The court was paved with rammed earth, and the mouth of the cesspool was covered with a roughly circular pierced gypsum lid. Across the west end was an interior porch, the roof of which was supported by a single column of rubblework with pilaster responds against either wall. The column, 0.68 m. in lower diameter, rested directly on a rubblework stylobate 0.23 m. high above the court paving. The stair ascended from the stylobate along the south wall on three arches springing from rubblework piers. The lowest arch with the six steps which it carried remains in place. With an average tread of 0.28 m. and riser of 0.20 m. the stair probably rose in eighteen steps to the roof of room F3 some 3.83 m. above the court. Beneath the stair arches lay the kitchen. In the lowest arch was a brick fireplace, and in the second a terra cotta oven.

### F2, Diwan

The doorway from the north side of the court was fitted with double doors. About the room ran a broad rubblework bench, 0.24 m. high. On the rammed earth floor before the doorway was a hearth of brick with a rubblework parapet 0.29 m. high. In the wall above the north bench was a niche. A plaster cavetto-fillet cornice ran about the walls at 1.90 m. from the floor.

### F4, Chamber

The doorways from room F2 and to room F3 had single doors. The floor was of rammed earth. In the south wall was a deep niche, and in one of the walls was set a bas-relief of an unidentified divinity.[30]

### F3, Women's Chamber (?)

The doorway from the court was fitted with a single door. The floor was of rammed earth. There was a niche in the north wall.

## 4. G5, Houses C and A (Figs. 78, 83)

### a. History

Houses C and A appear to have been laid down together. The socle of their party wall together with the adjacent portions of socles C1–C2, A2–A3, and the north exterior socle bear every evidence of having been built in a single operation, and remained essentially unchanged. Their construction was similar to that of the other early socles in the block. The exterior socles on the north and east were footed on the remains of the Hellenistic socle, which stood in part three courses high. It is possible that at the outset the central longitudinal partition of the Seleucid shop building formed the south wall of the two houses. The original street entrance doorsill of House C was laid 0.25 m.–0.30 m. higher than that of House E, indicating perhaps that the houses were erected toward the end of the first quarter of the first century B.C. The corresponding doorsill of House A was laid some 0.13 m. higher, on the base header course of the Seleucid socle. The cesspools in this case furnish no useful evidence, and all of the original doorways were replaced from time to time in the history of the houses. The oldest piece of stone trim appears to be the lintel of door-

Fig. 45. G5, A1–A2.
Lintel Profile

[30] Below, pp. 165 f.

way A1–A2, which shows the earliest form of the cavetto-fillet type. It was probably carved about the beginning of our era (Fig. 45).

The history of House C can be read only in the evidence of the repair, rebuilding, and replastering of its walls, in the mounting level of its street entrance, and in the measures taken to adjust the levels of court and threshold. The street entrance was raised a total of 0.91 m. in three stages. At the time of the second stage, probably some time in the first half of the second century, it became necessary to introduce three steps leading down to the court level. A century later, when the third stage had increased the difference by some 0.30 m., it was found expedient to raise the general level of the court by an equivalent amount. This was accomplished by a fill of earth and debris, and was accompanied by other far-reaching changes. The steps to the threshold themselves were heightened 0.23 m.–0.27 m. with new rubblework treads, and doorway C1–C2 with the adjacent portions of the socle was completely rebuilt to the new level. The floors of rooms C2 and C3 were raised to correspond, and doorways C2–C3 and C4–C3 were raised and rebuilt. All the interior features of court and diwan thus date from this final period.

Just before the end of its existence room C4 underwent the same metamorphosis as room E4–E5 and became a cellar with a shop above. Its floor was excavated to bed rock to provide head room of 1.72 m.; doorway C1–C4 was sunk and cut down to serve as the cellar entry; and doorway C4–C3 was walled up. The shop above had a narrow entrance from Street 4 but no direct communication with the house.

This final period saw House C, or at any rate room C2, become the headquarters of a guild of entertainers and prostitutes.[31] This phenomenon and the reappearance at this late date of a series of shops, E4–E5, C4, and A4 of Block G5, J8 of Block G3, opening on Street 4 or near it, were probably due to the proximity of this side of the bazaar quarter to the Roman camp.

The history of House A was parallel. Its street entrance was raised in five successive stages, 1.04 m. in all. The final stage, well into the third century to judge from the street levels, was accompanied by a general renovation of the interior and raising of its floor level 0.24 m.–0.28 m. Doorways A1–A2, A2–A3, with the adjoining socles were rebuilt to the new level. Room A4 became a shop with an entrance from Street F, and doorway A1–A4 was replaced by an arched opening.

[31] Below, pp. 203–265.

## b. Description. House C. Five Rooms

### C1, Court

The street entrance had double doors and three steps down to the court level beneath an interior porch. The roof of the porch was supported by a single column of rubblework, 0.58 m. in lower diameter, which rested on a square gypsum base worked with a quarter round torus. The mouth of the cesspool was covered with a square pierced gypsum lid. On the rammed earth paving stood a "cooler." The stair ascended from the steps of the entrance along the north wall on three arches springing from rubblework piers. The bottom five steps and the entire first arch remain in place. The average tread was 0.26 m., the average riser 0.215 m. The stair, when complete, probably rose in twenty steps to the roof of Shop C4 some 4.80 m. above the court. Beneath the stair the kitchen was installed. In the first arch was a flagged fireplace, in the third a terra cotta oven insulated with mud. In the wall opposite was a shallow smoke-blackened lamp niche.

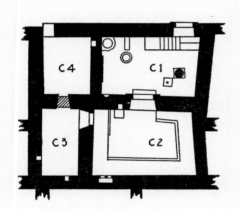

Fig. 46. G5, C. Restored Plan

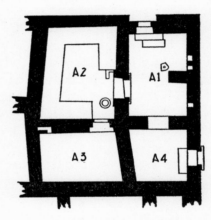

Fig. 47. G5, A. Restored Plan

### C2, Diwan

The doorway from the south side of the court had a step before it and was fitted with double doors with a bar socket. The floor was of rammed earth. About the room ran a broad rubblework bench, 0.26 m. high, with a narrow step along the edge. Probably at the height of the lintel of doorway C2–C3 a plaster cavetto-fillet cornice circled the walls. In the north wall beside the doorway and 1.17 m. from the floor was a niche with a fire-blackened bipedal set in the floor before it. In the south wall was an elaborate niche cupboard of four compartments in two tiers with arched openings ornamented with applied colonettes. A plaster relief plaque of Aphrodite was probably set in the west wall and surrounded with painted decoration.[32] On the other walls were painted the inscriptions of a guild of entertainers and prostitutes.[33]

[32] Below, pp. 166 f.                    [33] Below, pp. 203–265.

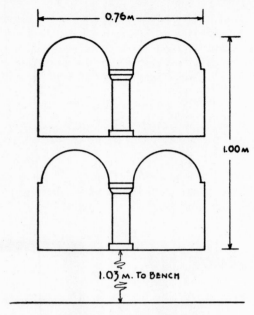

Fig. 47a. Cupboard in C2

### C3, Chamber

The doorway from room C2 retained no certain traces of its doors. In the south and west walls were niches, and the blocked opening of doorway C4–C3 left a shallow panel in the north wall. The floor was of rammed earth.

### C4, Shop

The street entrance was a narrow opening without sill or jambs. The floor was of plaster mortar. In the east wall was a niche.

### C4, Cellar

The doorway from room C1 retained no certain traces of its doors. Against the north wall stood a rubblework bench or table, 0.54 m. high. The blocked opening of doorway C4–C3 left a shallow panel in the south wall.

## House A. Four Rooms

### A1, Court

The street entrance had a single door and three steps down to the rammed earth paving of the court. The cesspool was covered by a roughly circular pierced lid of gypsum. The western portion of the court was divided in two by a screen wall of mud brick. In the west wall were three niches.

### A2, Diwan

The doorway from the west side of the court had double doors, and its reveals projected on the interior. About the room ran a rubblework bench, 0.18 m. high, and on the rammed earth floor stood a "cooler." Within the north side of the doorway was a rubblework hearth with an L-shaped screen, 0.37 m. high.

### A3, Chamber

The doorway from room A2 was fitted with a single door with a bar socket. At the west end of the north wall was a deep elbow niche only 0.31 m. from the rammed earth floor.

### A4, Shop

The street entrance had a single door and two steps down to the rammed earth floor of the interior. The opening from court A1 was arched.

## 5. Houses D and B (Figs. 78, 83; Pl. XIII, 2)

### a. History

Houses D and B, like Houses C and A, were evidently erected together. Their party wall was built of a piece with their common party wall with Houses C and A and with walls D2–D1 and B2–B1. The original socles, when their later plaster renderings are stripped off, show the familiar early mud-mortared rubblework of large pieces of broken gypsum blocks. It is clear that D and B were later than both F and C–A, since the original east wall of F and south wall of C–A were replaced by the corresponding walls of D–B. The socles of these walls, however, are of the same early rubblework construction, and the difference in time cannot have been great. The possibility that until the construction of D and B the original Seleucid socles had served for the east wall of House F and the south wall of Houses C and A has already been suggested. The Seleucid exterior socle remained in use as the socle of the west exterior wall of House B. The south exterior socle of both houses from a point 3.36 m. west of the southeast corner was of rubblework on the lower courses of the Seleucid socle.

From these considerations we may probably date Houses D and B in the second quarter of the first century B.C. The exterior doorway levels, unfortunately, provide no convenient check. The entrance to House D is missing. The section of wall which contained it was found to have collapsed outward from the foundations carrying the doorway with it. The total rise of 0.71 m. in the entrance of House B is irrelevant, since it is clear that the level of the area on which the house faced began to mount rapidly only after the erection of Shops S1–S5. Of the interior doorways none preserved its original dimensions or trim, while the meager deposits in the cesspools were worthless for dating.

Even without the evidence of its exterior doorway, it is apparent that the history of House D was much the same as that of the other similar small houses in the block. At a relatively late date it was found expedient to counter the increasing disparity between the exterior and interior levels by a general heightening of the interior floor level. In House D this amounted to some 0.26 m. in the court and 0.21 m. in the surrounding rooms. As a result all the doorways, with the exception of D2–D4 which was walled up, were rebuilt to the new level and fitted with new trim. In the court the stair was left unchanged, its bottom step covered by the new paving.

In House B no change in the interior floor level occurred, and a broad step was laid inside the street entrance. When the difference in level increased to some 0.60 m., another step was necessary, and the stair was rebuilt to take off from it. Late in the history of the house the doorway B1–B2 was remodelled with jambs of rubblework veneered with slabs of gypsum.

### b. Description. House D. Four Rooms

#### D1, Court

The street entrance is missing. Before it on the rammed earth floor stood a "cooler." The mouth of the cesspool was covered with a roughly circular pierced gypsum lid. The northeast corner of the court was screened off by a partition of mud brick. The stair ascended in a flight of three steps along the west wall to a landing in the southwest corner, thence along the south wall over the street entrance. The first flight and landing and the rubblework pier of the first supporting arch along the south wall are preserved. The upper landing was probably in part supported by the parallel mud brick screen wall, and the stair with its risers of 0.22 m. reached the roof of the enclosed portion of the court in eighteen or nineteen steps at a height of some 4.20 m.–4.40 m.

#### D2, Diwan

The doorway from the north side of the court had double doors. In the south wall on either side was a niche. In the west wall the blocked opening of doorway D2–D4 left a shallow panel. The floor was of rammed earth.

#### D3, Diwan

The doorway from the west side of the court was fitted with double doors. The floor was of rammed earth. In the southwest corner was buried a small hoard of 48 third century bronze coins.[34]

### D4, Women's Chamber (?)

The doorway from room D3 had a single door. The floor was of rammed earth.

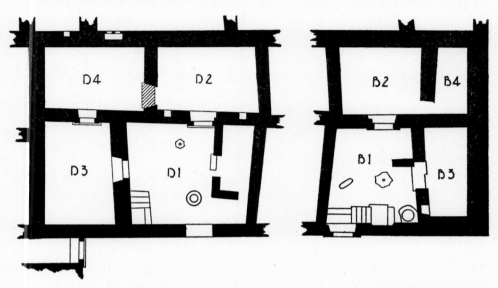

Fig. 48. G5, D. Restored Plan          Fig. 49. G5, B. Restored Plan

## House B. Four Rooms

### B1, Court

The street entrance had double doors and three steps down to the rammed earth paving of the court. A short screen of mud brick shut off the northeast corner. The mouth of the cesspool was covered with a roughly circular pierced gypsum lid. Near it was a small oval fire pit. The stair ascended from the steps of the entrance along the south wall on two arches sprung from rubblework piers. The stumps of the first three steps are preserved with treads of 0.26 m. and risers of 0.23 m. When complete, the stair probably rose in sixteen steps to the roof of room B3 some 4.08 m. above the court. The kitchen was beneath the stair. In the first arch was a rubblework fireplace edged with brick, and in the second an oven of terra cotta insulated with mud.

### B2, Diwan

The doorway from the north side of the court had double doors. The floor was of rammed earth. On the south wall east of the doorway at 1.26 m. from the floor was a

[34] Hoard XI, *Rep. VII–VIII*, pp. 422 f. Below, pp. 259 f.

fragment of a painted icon for domestic worship. The remaining traces suggest that it was similar to the icon of room G3–J6.[35]

### B4, Chamber

The opening from room B2 was without trim or doors. The floor was of rammed earth.

### B3, Women's Chamber (?)

The doorway from the court had a stone threshold but neither jambs nor lintel. It was hung with double doors. At the south end of the west wall was a niche. Set in one of the walls was an alabaster relief of a nude goddess.[36] The floor was of rammed earth.

## 6. G5, Shops S1–S5 (Figs. 78, 83)

### a. History

Three clearly marked periods are to be distinguished. The earliest can be dated only as later than the house against whose façade the shops were built, probably in the first half of the second century of our era.

The original building (Fig. 50) consisted of three small shops laid down as a unit. Its north and east socles were retained in the following periods. Its south socle is represented by the stumps of its foundations beneath the later floors of S1, S2, and S3. One interior socle was retained in partition S2–S3; the other was superseded by partition S1–S2 of the following period. Of the openings, which were in the south façade, no vestige remains. The socles were of fully developed plaster rubble-work laid in courses with tight faces and a well packed filler of smaller stones and mortar. They were pointed and rendered with plaster on the faces and across the top of each course. Of the interior arrangements nothing remains, save an oval terra cotta tub sunk in the floor in the northeast corner of the west shop and secured with a collar of plaster mortar.

The second period (Fig. 51) saw the razing of the earlier south façade, the construction of a new one on an oblique line 1.90 m.–2.80 m. to the south, and the rebuilding of partition S1–S2, moved 0.17 m. to the east on the old foundation. The resultant trapezoidal rooms showed little if any change in level from the preceding period. The new socles were closely similar to the old. The openings of the south façade were entirely replaced by those of the following period with the exception of

[35] Below, pp. 162 f.                    [36] Below, p. 167.

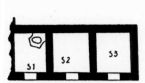

Fig. 50. G5, S1–S5.
Restored Plan
Period I.

Fig. 51. G5, S1–S5.
Restored Plan
Period II.

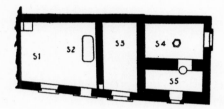

Fig. 52. G5, S1–S5. Final State.
Restored Plan

the doorsill of S2 which was removed to the new doorway and reused some 0.87 m. above its former level.

The final period (Fig. 52) saw the razing of partition S1–S2, the addition of rooms S4 and S5 to the east, and a general remodelling of the whole unit. The floor level of the older shops was raised 0.25 m.–0.30 m. to the level at which the new shops were built. The entrance to S3 was rebuilt to the new level. The old entrance to S2 was replaced by a sort of window or wicket, 0.61 m. above floor level, and a new entrance to the enlarged Shop S1–S2 was cut, partially overlapping the foundation of earlier partition S1–S2. Late in the period S4, which had been built as the rear room of S5, was provided with an exterior doorway at a level some 0.08 m. higher than the others. The new socles of rooms S4 and S5 were of plaster rubblework of the most advanced type. They were built in courses averaging 0.62 m. high with carefully laid faces of large pieces of red limestone and a loose filler of the same material scantily mortared with a sort of plaster grout. The faces were pointed with plaster, and the plaster rendering extended over the top of each course. Save for sills and jamb facings of stone, the new doorways were carried out entirely in rubblework, even to the molded capitals and lintels.

## b. Description

### Shop 1–2

The street entrance retained no certain traces of its doors. In the same wall was the window or wicket noted above. The floor was of rammed earth, and in the northwest corner stood a stepped rubblework counter. Beside the east wall was a fire pit, 0.62 m. deep with fire-hardened sides of earth. It was found half filled with wood ashes.

### Shop 3

The street entrance was fitted with double doors. The floor was of rammed earth.

### Shop 5

The street entrance retained no certain traces of its doors. Sunk partly in the rammed earth floor and partly in the threshold of arched opening S5–S4 was the lower portion of a large dolium.

### Shop 4

The street entrance was fitted with double doors. In the center of the rammed earth floor was a small fire pit lined with six burnt bricks.

## C. Block G1

### 1. Northeastern Portion. Shops S110–S112, S114–S118, Houses F and G

### (Figs. 78, 80, 82; Pls. IX, 1, X, XI)

### a. History

The eastern half of this area was originally occupied by nine shops of the east Seleucid shop building. Toward the end of the second century B.C., at the same time as the development of the houses in area 70–71[1], 83–102, 126 to the south, these were gradually replaced by a series of smaller shops, probably with work, store, or dwelling rooms in the rear.[37] Disconnected and fragmentary remains of these shops were found beneath the later rooms S116, S118, S115, and G103 (Pl. X, 1). The rooms in the rear are represented by a section of foundation beneath S117. In Fig. 53 these scanty vestiges are shown superimposed on the outline of the Seleucid shop foundations. There was possibly a similar row of shops facing on the open square to the west.

[37] Above, pp. 46 f.

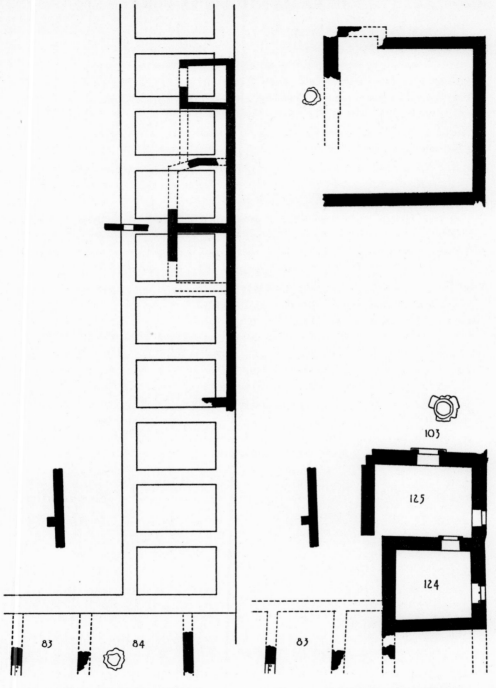

Fig. 53. G1, Northeastern Portion.
Early Shops

Fig. 54. G1, Northeastern Portion.
Early Houses

The shop foundations beneath S116, S118, S115, and G103 were built of coarse masonry or rubblework of broken gypsum blocks from the Seleucid socles mortared with mud. The exterior wall along Street H was less than half the width of the Seleucid socle. It was founded on the outer row of the Seleucid footing course, the inner row of which was torn out. Subsequent building obliterated all trace of the doorways on Street H. The rammed earth floors within lay some 0.20 m.–0.25 m. higher than the Seleucid floors. The foundation beneath S117 was of similar construction, but stood about 0.20 m. higher and retained traces of the bedding for a doorsill. On the south the shops adjoined the houses of area 70–71[1], 83–102, 126, and the foundation beneath later room F123 is all that remains of the house on the interior corner.

Most or all of these shops were soon superseded by more substantial houses. For these the evidence is restricted to the north and south ends of the area, owing to the thoroughgoing demolition of earlier structures which attended the building of House F at a still later date.

The house at the north end (Fig. 54; Pls. IX, 1, X) occupied approximately the area of the later Shops S111, S111[1], S114, S116, and S118. The foundations of its east wall on Street H and of the eastern portions of its north and south walls remain in place as the foundations for the later north socle of S116, east socle of S116 and S118, and south socle of S118. A fragment of the north wall of a projecting bay was preserved beneath the paving of Alley G3, and within later Shop S111 was a segment of main interior foundation. Near the latter was the cesspool of the original court. These foundations were of rubblework of large broken Seleucid blocks and smaller pieces of gypsum mortared with mud. Originally they were presumably also rendered with mud. The interior plan cannot be recovered. The interior foundation beneath S111 shows one end of the foundation of a doorway, presumably that from the court to the diwan, with a threshold projecting on the interior. The level of the court as indicated by the mouth of the cesspool was some 0.32 m. above bed rock and approximately the same as that of the earlier shops. The cesspool itself was filled in at the beginning of the next period. Beneath the fill, it contained a small but homogeneous deposit apparently dating from shortly before the middle of the first century B.C. to the first quarter of the first century of our era.

The house at the south end was House G in its original form (Fig. 54; Pl. XI, 1). The socles of rooms G125 and S124 came down essentially unchanged beneath later coats of plaster save for the southwest

corner of G125. The west, north, and east socles of court
G103 were completely rebuilt at the time of the construction of House F. The original limits of the house
cannot be precisely determined, although its cesspool
was of the original construction. The original socles
were of rubblework of large pieces of gypsum mortared
with mud and pointed with plaster. Along Street H the
socle was carried down to bed rock, since the Seleucid
footing course had been removed south of the later entrance to G103. The street entrances to rooms G125 and
S124 remained at their original level: 0.68 m.–0.72 m.
above the Seleucid sill level, though both were later rebuilt with new trim. Doorway G125–S124, however, despite its subsequent conversion to a cellar door, retained
the upper part of its original trim. It had projecting
jambs cut on the ends of sectional slabs which revetted
about half the depth of the reveal. Other slabs covered
the rest. The jambs carried capitals of the ovolo type

Fig. 55. G1,
G125–S124.
Jamb Capital
Profile

(Fig. 55). The lintel is missing. Doorway G103–G125 was similar in
form. The cesspool of court G103 was abandoned and filled in at the
time of the construction of House F. Its meager deposit beneath the fill
afforded no material for dating, but the evidence of construction and of
doorway G125–S124 suggests a date somewhat later than that of the
northern house, perhaps in the third quarter of the first century B.C.

The erection of House F (Fig. 56; Pls. IX, 1, X, XI, 2) brought
sweeping changes in the central and northern portions of the area. The
earlier structures disappeared, and their place was taken by the house
itself with three single and two double shops. Within the limits of House
F no vestiges of earlier buildings were left, since the paving of its court
was only some 0.17 m. above bed rock. Within the limits of the shops to
the north only scattered foundations were left beneath the higher floor
levels, save where the socles of the earlier northern house were retained
as foundations. House F and the seven shop rooms were built at the same
time and as a single project, presumably under a single ownership. So
much is evident from the constructional identity of the socles, their lack
of unbonded vertical joints, and the original uniformity of the exterior
doorways in dimensions and level.

The socles were of plaster rubblework with caementa of relatively small and uniform chunks of gypsum and red limestone laid solid through the wall. They were pointed and above ground level rendered with plaster. The original exterior openings were uniformly 4 feet (1.41 m.) wide. They were without splay and had stone thresholds and projecting monolithic jambs, which carried similar capitals and lintels with cavetto-fillet moldings of an early form. Their sills were laid at a uniform level of 0.89 m.–0.92 m. above the Seleucid sill level. The street entrances of Shops S111, S116, and S118 were subsequently rebuilt at a higher level.

Within the shops a uniform floor level of 0.45 m.–0.55 m. above the preceding one was established by means of a fill of earth and debris. Partitions S111–S111$^1$ and S110–S112 and all the interior features of the shops are of later construction.

House F in its original form consisted of a vestibule, a court with a stair unit and an interior porch, two rooms, and a closet. It had a uniform floor level some 0.80 m. lower than that of the shops, and the floor of vestibule F104 was pitched down from the street entrance.

Only the court of House G was affected by the new constructions (Pl. XI, 1). Its west and north sides were now bounded by socles F109–G103 and F104–G103 of House F, and its east wall was rebuilt to conform. The street entrance was accordingly rebuilt to the new uniform level. The cesspool was covered by a new paving 0.20 m. above the old, and doorway G103–G125 was provided with a new sill resting on the old one. The west end of the court was made an interior porch with one column.

The use for dating of the rise in the level of Street H along Block G1 is complicated by the fact that unlike the rise of Street 4 along Blocks G3 and G5 it was far from uniform. It rose gradually in three steps or stages from south to north, and at the end of its history there was a difference in level between the north and south ends of the block of some 0.85 m. This difference, however, was not the result of a constantly variable rate of rise. It came about because from time to time most of the doorways established along Street H succeeded in fixing the level of the adjacent portion of the street, which thereafter remained the same. Thus the street entrances to rooms G125 and S124 of House G were laid at 0.68 m.–0.72 m. above the Seleucid sill level and never raised. That the street itself remained at this level is shown by the sills of the doorways on the opposite side. Similarly the doorsills of the street entrances to G103, F104, S110, and S115 in the following period were laid at 0.89

m.–0.92 m. above the Seleucid sill level and remained without alteration. North of Shop S115 the street level continued to rise, and the street
entrances to Shops S118 and S116 were ultimately raised to 1.53 m.–
1.56 m. above the Seleucid sill level.

The latter figure may therefore with due reserve be taken as representing the total rise of Street H along Block G1, and from it an annual
rate of approximately 0.0028 m. may be computed. When this is applied
to the sill levels of House F and its dependences, a date toward the end
of the first quarter of the first century of our era is obtained. This date is
subject to control by the end of the deposit in the cesspool beneath S111,
by the beginning of the deposit in the cesspool in court F109, and by the
fill under the floors of Shops S110–S112, S114–S118. In each case the
ceramic evidence is confirmatory.

About a century later the extensive demolition necessitated by the
erection of House A[38] made it possible for the owner of House F to add
the area immediately west of rooms G125 and S124 to his holding. This
space was cleared, and on it three additional rooms, F123, F121, and
F122, were erected (Fig. 57). The old south socle of the house was
pierced with a large archway, F109–F123. At the same time Shop S124
of House G was attached to House F. An opening was made from F122
which had been designed as a passage to communicate between F123
and S124. With this change is associated the cellar beneath S124. By its
construction the shop was divorced from direct connection with House
G, while the cellar was accessible only from G125. The cellar was excavated out of the bed rock to a depth of 1.57 m., and at either side a pier
of rubblework 1.90 m. high was erected to take a beam carrying the floor
of the shop above. The headroom was approximately 2.15 m. From the
level of room G125 a crude flight of steps was excavated through the
opening of doorway G125–S124 and coated with plaster. The doorway
itself was sunk into the opening, so that the bottom of its lintel stood
only some 0.55 m. above the floor of G125, while its sill lay 1.40 m.
below it.

Opening F122–S124 was later walled up again, and S124 became an
independent shop, F122 a sort of closet.

The last half century before the end of the city saw a thorough renovation of the five shops belonging to House F. The floors of the four
northern rooms were raised in accord with their new doorsill levels,

[38] Above, pp. 57 f.; below, pp. 136 f.

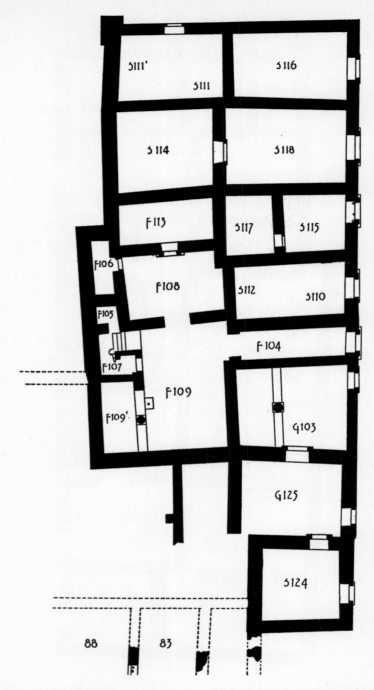

Fig. 56. G1, F–G–S110–112–S114–118. Early State. Restored Plan

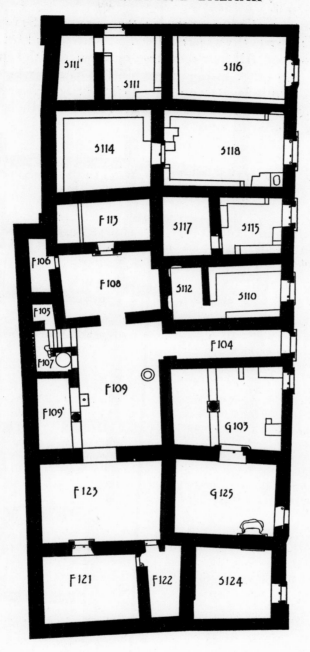

Fig. 57. G1, F–G–S110–112–S114–118. Final State. Restored Plan

S111–S111$^1$ 0.43 m., S116 0.34 m., S118 0.33 m., and S114 0.59 m. The west end of S111–S111$^1$ was partitioned off with a mud brick wall resting on the new floor. All four rooms were provided with benches, and in S118 a niche and other fittings were built. The other three rooms remained unchanged in level, but the west end of S110–S112 was screened off by a mud brick partition and fitted with niches, while both S110 and S115 received similar benches.

## b. Description. Shops S110–S112, S114–S118

### Shop S111–S111$^1$ (Pl. IX, 1)

The street entrance had a stone threshold and was fitted with a single door. The floor was of rammed earth. Against three walls of S111 were narrow benches of packed mud thinly coated with plaster and 0.45 m. high. They were built in three sections with raised "arms" at the free ends. The opening to S111$^1$ was not trimmed or hung with doors.

### Shop S116 (Pl. IX, 1, X, 1)

The street entrance had a stone threshold and double doors. The floor was of rammed earth. Along the west and south walls ran narrow benches of packed mud thinly coated with plaster and 0.46 m. high.

### Shop S118 (Pl. X, 2)

The street entrance had a stone threshold and double doors. The floor was of rammed earth. Along three walls ran narrow benches of packed mud reinforced on top with large sherds from broken dolia and thinly plastered. They were 0.42 m. high and built in three sections with raised "arms" at the free ends. In the southeast corner stood a basin made of eight Roman bath tubuli set upright and plastered. Beside it was a low platform of rubblework. Before the north jamb of doorway S118–S114 was a rubble-work hearth with a table or counter of plaster-coated mud, 0.67 m. high, beside it. In the northeast corner was a shallow niche.

### Shop S114

The doorway from Shop S118 had a threshold of plaster-covered brick and was hung with double doors. The floor was of rammed earth. Along three walls ran a narrow bench of packed mud thinly coated with plaster and 0.39 m. high.

### Shop S115

The street entrance had a plaster-covered stone threshold and double doors. The floor was of rammed earth. About the walls were benches of packed mud thinly coated with plaster and 0.37 m. high. They were built in four sections with raised "arms" at two free ends and at the angles.

## Shop S117

The doorway from Shop S115 had a single jamb, single door, and bar socket. The floor was of rammed earth.

## Shop S110–S112

The street entrance had a plaster-covered stone threshold and double doors. The floor was of rammed earth. Along three walls ran a narrow bench of packed mud, 0.42 m. high, reinforced on top with pieces of broken wall plaster and thinly plastered. The opening to S112 was not trimmed or provided with doors. In the west wall and north-west corner of the latter were shallow niches.

# House F. Ten Rooms

## F104, Vestibule

The street entrance had a plaster-covered stone threshold. The doors have left no certain traces. The rammed earth floor sloped down to the arched opening to court F109.

## F109, Court (Pl. XI, 2)

On the rammed earth paving beside the opening from the vestibule stood a "cooler." The mouth of the cesspool was covered with a pierced rectangular slab of gypsum. In the southwest angle was an interior porch, the roof of which was supported by a single column on a square gypsum base resting on a rubblework stylobate 0.40 m. high above the paving. The column, which was found fallen complete, was 0.58 m. in lower and 0.50 in upper diameter. It consisted of five rubblework drums, 0.70 m., 0.62 m., 0.70 m., 0.70 m., and 0.40 m. high from bottom to top, and had a gypsum Doric capital of the local quarter round type (Fig. 58). The stair unit, F107, occupied the angle north of the porch. To the right was the arched opening to the stair, to the left that to the space beneath. The stair ascended counter-clockwise about a central newel wall. Three steps of the first flight of four and the stumps of two of the second flight of four remain in place, showing treads of 0.26 m. and risers of 0.23 m. When complete the stair probably had eighteen steps in five flights, reaching the roof of the porch at some 4.25 m. above the court. In the space beneath the third flight and landing stood a large terra cotta oven. From the first flight opened a small closet, F105.

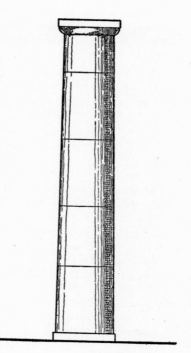

Fig. 58. G1, F109. Doric Column

### F123, Diwan

The wide opening from the south side of the court was arched. The floor was of rammed earth. In the north wall was a small niche.

### F121, Chamber

The doorway from room F123 had a stone threshold and double doors. The floor was of rammed earth.

### F122, Closet

The doorway from room F123 was without stone trim but was hung with a single door. That from room F121 had simple trim and a single door. The floor was of rammed earth.

### F108, Diwan

The opening from the north side of the court was arched. The floor was of rammed earth.

### F113, Women's Chamber and Storeroom

The doorway from room F108 was fitted with a single door and a bar socket. The floor was of rammed earth. The west end of the room was walled off as a large storage bin by a thin parapet of rubblework 0.70 m. high.

### F106, Closet

The doorway from room F108 was fitted with a single door and a bar socket. The floor was of rammed earth.

## House G. Three Rooms

### G103, Court (Pl. XI, 1)

The street entrance had a stone threshold and was fitted with double doors. The paving was of rammed earth. Against the east wall stood a rough masonry table, 0.56 m. high. Across the west end of the court was an interior porch, the roof of which was supported by a single column of rubblework, 0.50 m. in lower and 0.43 m. in upper diameter. The column was founded below floor level on a square plinth of rubblework, on either side of which was a rough retaining wall of small stones set in mud. It had a gypsum base and capital of similar size and quarter round profile, save that the lower part of the Doric echinus was carried out in plaster. The stair ascended along the north wall from a narrow rubblework platform just inside the entrance. It was supported by a narrow rubblework pier. No traces of the steps remain, but the total rise was probably some 3.50 m. to the roof of the porch.

### G125, Diwan

The doorway from the south side of the court had a stone threshold and double doors. The street entrance was fitted with a single door. The floor was of rammed earth. From the southeast corner of the room descended the steps to the cellar beneath S124.

### S124, Cellar

The doorway over the steps from room G125 was fitted with double doors. The floor was the bed rock.

### S124, Shop

The street entrance had a stone threshold and double doors. The floor was apparently of planking covered with rammed earth.

## 2. House D (Figs. 78, 80)

### a. History

The excavated northern half of the house has been cleared only to the level of the final period. None of the doorways of this period appears to have retained its original form or trim. Despite this circumstance the evidence clearly indicates that House D in its original form was one of the earliest houses of Block G1, approximately contemporary with the houses of area 70–71[1], 83–102, 126.

The north party wall with House C was long a free façade on the market place, as is shown by its complete lack of bond with the abutting walls of C. This north exterior wall had been replastered at least four times before the walls of C were made to abut against it. Similarly the east wall shows no bond with the late partitions S6–S126 and S100–S99. The north wall, the east wall north of partition S100–S99, and partition D77–D78, when stripped of their accumulated plaster renderings, were found to be of the same early rubblework construction of

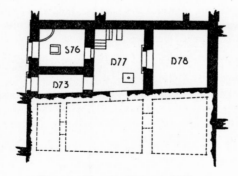

Fig. 59. G1, D. Restored Plan

broken gypsum blocks and mud mortar as the houses of area 70–71[1], 83–102, 126. The other walls had been more or less completely rebuilt. Finally, the cesspool contained a stratified deposit, the lowest layers of which probably go back to the early first century B.C.

## b. Description. Seven Rooms ( ? )[39]

### D73, Vestibule

The street entrance had double doors, and the opening to court D77 was arched. The floor was of rammed earth.

### D77, Court

The paving was of rammed earth. A pierced square slab of gypsum covered the mouth of the cesspool. The stair, carried on two arches sprung from a rubblework pier, ascended along the north wall from a landing in the northwest corner, reached by a flight of four steps. This bottom flight, the landing, and two fragmentary steps remain in place. With treads of 0.25 m. and riser of 0.23 m. the stair probably reached the roof of room D78 in seventeen steps at a height of some 3.90 m. above the court.

### D78, Women's Chamber ( ? )

The doorway from the court was hung with double doors. The floor was of rammed earth.

## 3. House A

### (Figs. 78, 80, 81, 82; Pls. IX, 2, XII)

### a. History

A number of lines of evidence converge to place the building of House A early in the second century of our era. A considerable lapse of time is indicated by the unbonded abutment of its walls against the original west façade of House F and Shop S111[1]. This façade had been twice replastered and was somewhat weathered when the walls of A were built against it. The earlier buildings within the southern portion of the area of the house were demolished to the last vestige. The northern portion of the area was at the time of building part of the open market place. The floors of the house were laid on a fill of earth and debris varying from 0.30 m. to 0.80 m. in thickness. A careful examination of the contents of this fill and of the lowest layers of deposit in the two cesspools in A10 and A39 showed a distribution of potsherds typical of the first quarter of the second century.

[39] Cf. *Rep. V*, p. 58.

This evidence is confirmed in a general way by the construction of socles and doorways. The former were all of plaster rubblework laid in courses 0.71 m. high. They were built course by course with carefully laid and pointed faces of large pieces of gypsum and red limestone and a well grouted filler of smaller stones. The rendering was carried just over the upper edges of each course. This technique precedes that of the late second and early third centuries with a loose or slightly grouted filler and fully rendered top surface. The doorways were of the normal third type, without splay and with monolithic stone jambs carrying capitals and lintels of a fully developed but not decadent cavetto-fillet profile (Fig. 12a). Figure 60 shows the profile of the lintel of doorway A10–A3, which is typical for the house. The reveals of important doorways such as A10–A3, A3–A20, and A39–A12 were revetted with stone.

Fig. 60. G1, A10–A3. Lintel Profile

House A and its dependences were built as a unit and remained without essential change during the course of their history. At indeterminable dates House B was made to communicate by means of doorway B21–A13, and room A34 was created in the southwest angle of court A39.

### b. Description. Twenty-four Rooms[40]

#### A25, Entry and Vestibule

The street entrance and the court doorway were fitted with double doors. An arch divided the L-shaped space into two sections. The floor was of brick.

#### A10, Court

The paving was of brick. The mouth of the cesspool was covered with a square pierced slab of gypsum. Before doorway A10–A3 stood a "cooler."

#### A43, Stair Unit

To the right was the entrance to the stair, fitted with double doors, to the left that to the space beneath the stair, whose doors have left no certain traces. The stair ascended

[40] Cf. *Rep. V*, pp. 49 f.

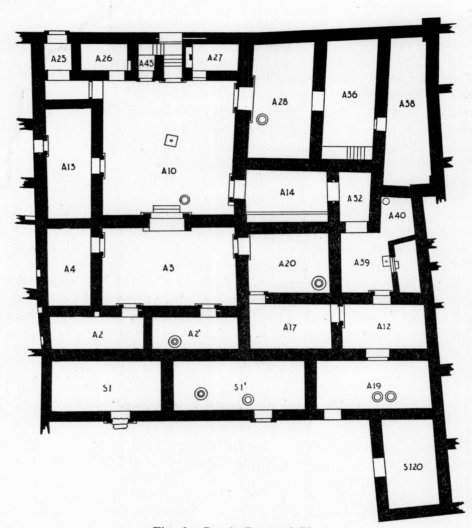

Fig. 61. G1, A. Restored Plan

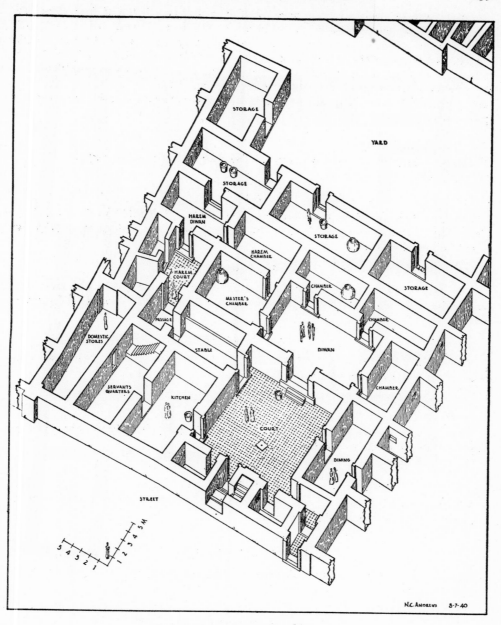

Fig. 62. G1, A. Restored Isometric

counter-clockwise about a central newel wall. The first two flights of four steps each and the first two landings were found in place. The average tread was 0.30 m., the average riser 0.17 m. When complete the stair probably made two full turns of eight flights, twenty-nine steps in all (4+4+3+4+3+4+3+4) and reached the roof at some 4.90 m. above the court. From the first landing a wide bay, which could be closed by a heavy bar, opened on the exterior some 0.60 m. above the street level. Its probable purpose was to facilitate the unloading of heavy goods and supplies from carts or pack animals.

### A26

The opening from the court was arched. The floor was of rammed earth.

### A27

The arched opening from the court was fitted with a sill of rubblework and a single door. The floor was of rammed earth. In the west wall was a deep niche with two simple arched openings.

### A3, Diwan

The wide doorway from the south side of the court was preceded by two stone steps and had double doors. Its reveals projected on the interior. The floor was of rammed earth.

### A4, Chamber

The doorway from room A3 had double doors. In the rammed earth floor just within was set the lower portion of a pointed amphora.

### A2, Chamber

The doorway from room A3 was fitted with a single door, and a bar socket. The floor was of rammed earth. In the north wall was a niche.

### A2¹, Chamber

The doorway from room A3 was fitted with a single door and a bar socket. On the rammed earth floor stood a large dolium.

### A20, Master's Chamber

The doorway from room A3 had double doors, and its reveals projected on the interior. On the rammed earth floor in the southeast corner stood a "cooler."

### A17, Women's Chamber

The doorways from chamber A20 and women's diwan A12 were fitted with single doors and bar sockets. The floor was of rammed earth.

### A13, Dining Room (?)

The doorway from the court had double doors, that to room B21 a single door with a bar socket. The floor was of rammed earth.

### A28, Kitchen (?)

The doorway from the court had double doors, and its reveals projected on the interior. On the rammed earth floor stood a "cooler."

### A36, Servants' Quarters (?)

The opening from room A28 was arched. The floor was of rammed earth. Along the south wall a stair ascended on a solid substructure of coarse rubblework. The bottom landing and six steps remain in place with treads of 0.27 m. and risers of 0.18 m., and the space allows for a total of twelve steps with a landing of 0.55 m. at the top. This indicates a total rise of some 2.16 m., probably to a low loft over room A36.[41]

### A38, Storeroom (?)

The narrow doorway from room A36 had a stone threshold and a single door. The floor was of rammed earth.

### A14, Stable

The doorway from the court was fitted with double doors. It was presumably in the wall above this doorway that the bas-relief head of a divinity described in *Rep. V*, pp. 50 f., was set.[42] Along the south wall was a manger of rubblework with a parapet 1.32 m. high from the floor and a trough 0.38 m. deep. The earthen floor for a width of some 2.50 m. before it was roughly flagged with irregular slabs of gypsum.

### A32, Passage

The open archway from stable A14 was provided with sockets for a cross bar 1.18 m. above the sill. The opening to court A39 was also arched. The floor was of rammed earth.

### A39, Women's Court

The paving was of brick. The mouth of the cesspool was covered with a square pierced gypsum slab. Alcove A40 was probably roofed. In its rammed earth floor was set the bottom portion of a pointed amphora.

[41] For the finds in this room, see *Rep. V*, p. 49.

[42] This opportunity is taken to correct in one particular the description of the head given in *Rep. V*. The object which appears to the right of the god's head is not a distorted hand holding a lance or a snake but the upper portion of a bow of the composite reflex type. The long reinforced ear and the curve of the flexible upper arm of the strung bow are clearly visible. For this type of bow, see *Annales de l'Institut Kondakov*, IX (1937), pp. 1–10. Here the bow may be taken to characterize the god as the protector of the hunt or of the caravan, and the position of the relief at the entrance to the stable becomes significant.

### A34

The opening from the court had a rough sill but was not fitted with doors. The northern half of the floor was the brick of the court paving, the southern half a raised platform of plaster mortar, 0.08 m. high.

### A12, Women's Diwan

The doorway from the south side of the court had a stone threshold and double doors. The doorway from room A19 was also fitted with double doors. The floor was of rammed earth. In the west wall was the doorway to chamber A17; in the southwest corner the rubblework socket for a mast or staff.

### A19, Storeroom (?)

The opening from the open yard to the south was arched. On the rammed earth floor stood two "coolers."

### S120, Warehouse

The opening from the yard was arched. The floor was of rammed earth.

### S1¹, Warehouse

The doorway from the yard was fitted with double doors. On the rammed earth floor stood a large dolium and a "cooler."

### S1, Warehouse

The doorway from the yard had double doors. On its sill a rough stone step had been fitted, and a stone step had been introduced before it. The floor was of rammed earth.

## 4. House B (Figs. 78, 80; Pl. XII)

### a. History

House B was built after, but not long after, House A, probably about the middle of the second century of our era. The west socle of House A, where the unbonded socles of House B abutted against it, had not been replastered and showed only slight signs of weathering. No earlier buildings had occupied the site in the open market place, and the socles of House B, which were carried down to bed rock, were similar in construction to those of House A. The doorways were also of the same general type. The moldings of their jamb capitals and lintels compare very closely with those of House A. Figure 63 shows the profile of the lintel of diwan doorway B18–B8. The scanty contents of the two cesspools afforded insufficient material for dating.

House B in its original state was an extremely compact example of a functionally complete Dura house. It had its main court, men's diwan and dependent chambers, stable, servants' and store rooms. In this scheme B37 was the women's court with its own cesspool and B29 the women's diwan (Fig. 64). In this area alone the original plan was later radically altered. Court B37 was roofed and cut off from direct communication with the main court. It became a domestic work room with a low loft or gallery across its northern end, accessible only through room B29. To effect this change the southern end of the original court was partitioned off and divided into a closet and corridor. The corridor, at

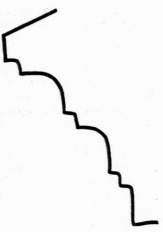

Fig. 63. G1, B18–B8. Lintel Profile

either end of which a new door was cut, provided communication between the main court and room B29. The closet contained the original court cesspool and was entered by the original court doorway. The only other appreciable change in the house was its attachment to House A by means of doorway A13–B21.

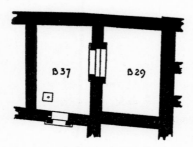

Fig. 64. G1, B29–B37–B105. Original State

## b. Description. Fourteen Rooms[43]

### B31, Vestibule

The entrance from the market place had double doors and two steps down to the interior floor of plaster mortar. An archway with two more steps before it gave on the court.

### B18, Court

The paving was of rammed earth. Along the west wall and the south wall west of doorway B18–B8 ran a narrow bench of rubblework, 0.27 m. high. Across the east side of the court was an interior porch, the roof of which was supported by two columns on square rubblework plinths 0.41 m. high above the paving. The columns, which were built up of rubblework drums, were 0.60 m. in lower and 0.52 m. in upper diameter. They had gypsum Doric capitals with the local quarter round echinus, and identical members reversed as bases. In the northern half of the porch stood a "cooler." The southern half served as a stable. Between the southern column and its pilaster respond a rubblework manger was inserted. It stood 1.38 m. high from the paving, and consisted of a trough 0.28 m. deep supported by two arches springing from a central pier.[44] It would comfortably accommodate one horse.

### B30, Stair Unit

The doorways to the stair at the right and to the space beneath at the left were fitted with single doors. The stair ascended counter-clockwise about a central newel wall, probably in three flights of twenty steps (8+4+8) to the roof. The first flight of eight steps and a segment of the first landing remain in place. The average tread was 0.23 m., the average riser 0.21 m., and the total rise some 4.30 m. In the corner beneath the first landing was a cesspool with a square pierced lid of gypsum.

### B8, Diwan

The doorway from the south side of the court was preceded by two stone steps. It was hung with double doors, and its reveals projected on the interior. About the room ran a broad rubblework bench, 0.19 m. high. The floor was of rammed earth.

### B23, Chamber

The doorway from room B8 had a single door with a bar socket. A rubblework step led down to the rammed earth floor. The doorway from passage B24 was also fitted with a single door.

### B24, Passage

The doorway from the court had a single door. The floor was of rammed earth.

[43] Cf. *Rep. V*, p. 53.

[44] Not a kneading trough, as suggested in *Rep. V*, p. 53, for which its height is unsuitable.

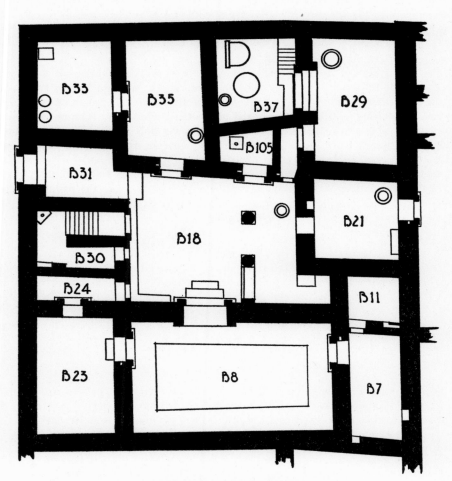

Fig. 65. G1, B. Restored Plan

### B7, Chamber

The doorway from room B8 had a single door with a bar socket. The floor was of rammed earth. In the east wall and at the west end of the south wall were niches.

### B11, Closet

The narrow doorway from room B7 was hung with a single door. At the east end of the south wall was a deep "elbow" niche.

### B21

The arched opening from the court had no doors. The doorway from room A13 had a single door with a bar socket. In the west wall was a niche, and against the east wall stood a rubblework bench or table 0.52 m. high. On the rammed earth floor stood a "cooler."

### B29, Women's Chamber

The doorway from the court to the entry passage had a single door with a bar socket. The doorways from the passage and room B37 had double doors. The reveals of the latter projected on the interior. On the rammed earth floor stood a "cooler."

### B37, Workroom

In the center of the rammed earth floor was a wide circular depression some 0.17 m. deep. Beside it stood a "cooler." From the north wall a low rubblework parapet projected, and before it was a U-shaped depression. From a step and landing 0.19 m. high the stair ascended along the east wall. It was found intact together with fragments of its supporting timbers. It rose 1.82 m. in seven steps to a landing, at the level of which a gallery or loft must have lain.

### B105, Closet

The doorway from the court had a single door with a bar socket. The mouth of the cesspool was covered with a square pierced slab of gypsum. The floor was of rammed earth.

### B35, Servant's Quarters (?)

The doorway from the court was fitted with a single door with a bar socket. On the rammed earth floor stood a "cooler."

### B33, Storeroom (?)

The doorway from room B35 was fitted with a single door and a bar socket. Sunk in the rammed earth floor beside the west wall were the lower portions of two pointed amphorae. In the northwest corner was a large basalt grinding stone.

## 5. House C (Figs. 78, 80)

### a. History

House C occupied the vacant space between
Houses B and D, and was the latest to be built in
the block. It followed soon after House B, for the
original rendering of the latter's south façade was
fresh and unweathered behind the unbonded abutment of wall C9–C5. The socles and doorways of
C are closely similar to those of House B, with the
exception of doorway C9–C15. This opening without sill or jambs was spanned by a lintel of exceptional profile, which was probably the work of a
Roman stonecutter (Fig. 66). The contents of the
cesspool furnished a ceramic series typical of the
last century of the city's existence.

Fig. 66. G1, C9–C15.
Lintel Profile

### b. Description. Five Rooms[45]

#### C107, Vestibule

The entrance from the market place had double doors. Two steps led down to a floor
of plaster mortar which terminated in a third step 0.90 m. before the arched opening
to the court.

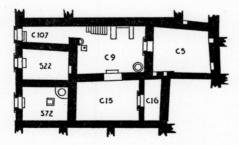

Fig. 67. G1, C. Restored Plan

[45] Cf. *Rep. V*, p. 55.

### C9, Court

The paving was of rammed earth. The mouth of the cesspool was covered with a small square lid of gypsum. In the southeast corner stood a "cooler." The stair ascended along the north wall on three arches springing from rubblework piers. A section of the lowest arch carrying the nine bottom steps remained in place. With treads of 0.23 m. and risers of 0.17 m. the stair probably reached the roof of room C5 in twenty-five steps at a height of some 4.60 m. above the court.

### C15, Diwan

The doorway from the south side of the court was not fitted with doors. The floor was of rammed earth.

### C16, Chamber

The doorway from room C15 had double doors. The floor was of rammed earth.

### C5, Women's Chamber (?)

The doorway from the court had a single door. The floor was of rammed earth. There were two niches in the east and two in the south wall.

## D. Block G2

### 1. Northern Section. Houses B and C

### (Figs. 78, 84; Pl. XIV, 1)

### a. History

Fig. 68. G2, C43–C23. Lintel Profile

Houses B and C were built at the same time and relatively late in the city's history, probably during the second half of the second century of our era. The evidence is furnished by the socles and doorways, since neither house had a cesspool. The southwest corner, the south and east exterior socles, and socles B42–C43 and C43–C23 were built in one piece without vertical joints. The construction was plaster rubblework of the latest type in courses 0.61 m. high. The faces were carefully laid and pointed, the interior filler loose and scantily grouted. The rendering was carried over the top of each course. The new interior socles of House B, which are of exactly the same type, represent a separate stage in the same program of construction. The three exterior doorways were never rebuilt or changed from their original level.

In the trim of the street entrance to C23 a lintel of developed cavetto-fillet profile was reused as the central block of the sill. The jambs of all the new doorways were carried out in rubblework with a mere facing of gypsum slabs. The late and angular form of the lintel moldings is well illustrated by the lintel of doorway C43–C23 (Fig. 68). Doorway C43–C44 was a remodelled earlier shop entrance.

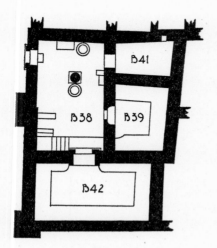

Fig. 69. G2, B. Restored Plan

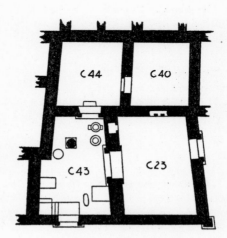

Fig. 70. G2, C. Restored Plan

## b. Description. House B. Four Rooms[46]

### B38, Court

The street entrance had a single door with a bar socket, and opened into an interior porch across the north end of the court. The roof of the porch was supported by a single rubblework column 0.62 m. in lower diameter, resting on a square gypsum base with a quarter round torus. The base was founded on a low rubblework plinth flush with the rammed earth paving. Against the north wall beneath the porch were a "cooler" and a rubblework bench or table 0.57 m. high. Before the column stood a second "cooler," and against the east wall on the axis of the column a second seat or table. The stair rose from a low step 0.08 m. high before doorway B38–B42. It had a bottom flight of five steps along the south wall and continued from a landing along the west wall on an arch and supporting timbers resting on a rubblework pier. The bottom flight and land-

[46] Cf. *Rep. V*, p. 65.

ing are preserved with treads of 0.26 m. and risers of 0.20 m. When complete the stair probably reached the roof of the porch in twenty steps at some 4.08 m. above the court.

### B42, Diwan

The doorway from the south side of the court was hung with double doors, and its reveals projected on the interior. The floor was of rammed earth. About the room ran a broad rubblework bench 0.23 m. high.

### B39, Diwan

The doorway from the court had double doors. The floor was of rammed earth. About three sides of the room ran a broad rubblework bench 0.18 m. high.

### B41

The opening from the porch of the court was an arch without doors. The floor was of rammed earth. In the north wall was a niche.

It is likely that the porch and room B41 served as the owner's place of business.

## House C. Four Rooms[47]

### C43, Court

The street entrance was fitted with double doors and opened onto a broad rubblework step, 0.08 m. high. The paving was of rammed earth. Across the north end of the court was an interior porch, the roof of which was supported by a single column of rubblework 0.62 m. in lower diameter. It was founded on a low rubblework plinth flush with the paving and capped with a square gypsum base with a quarter round torus. Beneath the porch stood a mill of "hourglass" type and a "cooler." Against the east wall beside doorway C43–C23 was a large rubblework table 0.61 m. high. In the paving before it was dug a small oval fire pit. The stair took off from the step within the entrance with a flight of three steps along the south wall and a landing. Its continuation along the west wall was carried on two arches sprung from a heavy rubblework pier. The bottom flight and landing, which remain in place, have treads of 0.23 m. and risers of 0.20 m. When complete the stair probably rose to the roof of the porch in twenty steps at some 4.08 m. above the court, precisely the same rise as the stair of House B. Beneath the upper portion of the stair was a terra cotta oven.

### C23, Diwan

Both the doorway from the east side of the court and the street entrance had double doors. The reveals of the former projected on the interior. The floor was of rammed earth. In the north wall a large niche cupboard with a triple arched opening and two shelves was constructed in the doorway opening to former shop C40. In the west wall was a deep niche.

Room C23 probably served as the owner's shop as well as diwan.

[47] Cf. *Rep. V*, p. 65.

### C44, Diwan

The doorway from the court had double doors and a rubblework step on the interior. The floor was of rammed earth.

### C40, Women's Chamber (?)

The doorway from room C44 was fitted with a single door and a bar socket. Near the southeast corner an oval fire pit was dug in the rammed earth floor.

## E. Block G4

### 1. Northern Portion. Houses A and B

### (Figs. 78, 84)

### a. History

The excavated portion of the block has been cleared only to the floor levels of the final period. Evidence for earlier stages of the plan is therefore lacking, though the general history of Houses A and B is clear. The cesspool of House A contained a stratified deposit, the lowest layers of which probably go back to about the middle of the first century of our era. A trench carried to bed rock along the façades of the block gave evidence of the rise in street level and of the raising of the doorways along Market Street and Street G an average of 0.56 m. to meet it. Most of the exterior doorways appear to have been at one time or other remodelled, often with new trim. In the entrance to Shop S49 a section of the original lintel was used to piece out a new jamb. It shows an early form of the fully developed cavetto-fillet profile. The trench also revealed that the original socles were of uncoursed plaster rubblework with caementa laid solid through the wall. It was likewise clear that House A had at one time been thoroughly renovated with a general raising of the floor level of some 0.27 m. The renovation included the repair and in many places the replacement of the existing socles and the rebuilding of all the doorways. House B, apparently, remained essentially unchanged.

### b. Description. House A. Five Rooms[48]

#### A61, Vestibule

Both the street entrance and the doorway from the court had double doors. The floor was of rammed earth.

[48] Cf. *Rep. V*, p. 69.

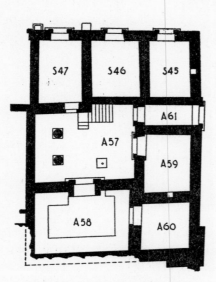

Fig. 71. G4, A. Restored Plan

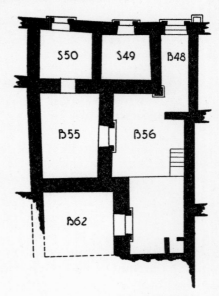

Fig. 72. G4, B. Restored Plan

### A57, Court

The doorway from the vestibule opened beneath the stair arch. The paving was of rammed earth. The mouth of the cesspool was covered with a square pierced slab of gypsum. Across the west end of the court was an interior porch, the roof of which was supported by two columns of rubblework 0.60 m. in lower diameter. They rested on square gypsum bases with quarter round tori which capped low plinths of rubblework beneath the paving level. In the north wall beside the porch a doorway fitted with a single door and a bar socket gave entrance to Shop 47. The stair ascended steeply along the north wall from a landing gained by three steps from the court. It was carried on two arches sprung from a rubblework pier. The bottom flight, the landing, and most of the first arch carrying seven steps of the stair remain in place. With treads of 0.25 m. and risers of 0.23 m. the stair probably reached the roof of the vestibule in seventeen steps at some 3.95 m. above the court. The space beneath the first arch was screened off with a rubblework parapet to serve as a sort of bin.

### A58, Diwan

The doorway from the south side of the court had double doors, and its reveals projected on the interior. The floor was of rammed earth. About the room ran a broad rubblework bench 0.17 m. high.

### A60, Chamber

The doorway from room A58 was hung with double doors. The floor was of rammed earth.

### A59, Women's Chamber (?)

The doorway from the court had double doors. The floor was of rammed earth. In the south wall was a niche.

## House B. Four Rooms[49]

### B48, Vestibule

The street entrance was fitted with double doors and had a step between the reveals. The sloping floor was of rammed earth. The opening to the court behind a screen wall apparently had the full height of the vestibule. It was marked by a shallow pilaster on the west side.

### B56, Court

The court proper was paved with rammed earth. A deep covered alcove to the south was paved with plaster mortar. In the southeast corner of the latter a large bin was formed by parapets of rubblework. The stair ascended along the east wall from a landing 0.22 m. high, and was carried on two arches and a short span of timbering. The bottom landing and portions of four steps are preserved. The treads measured 0.28 m.–0.29 m., the risers 0.22 m. When complete the stair probably reached the vestibule roof in sixteen steps at a height of some 3.75 m. above the court.

### B55, Diwan

The doorway from the west side of the court had double doors. The floor was of rammed earth. An arched opening in the north wall communicated with Shop S50. In one of the walls was set a bas-relief of Hercules.[50]

### B62, Women's Chamber (?)

The doorway from the alcove of the court had double doors. The floor was of rammed earth.

## F. Block G6

### 1. Northern Section. House C (Fig. 78; Pl. XIV, 2)

### a. History

The rich deposit in the cesspool of court C10 probably goes back to about the end of the first quarter of the first century of our era. The socles of plaster rubblework with the caementa laid solid through the

---

[49] Cf. *Rep. V*, p. 69.    [50] *Rep. V*, pp. 69 f.

Fig. 73. G6, C10–C11. Jamb Capital and Lintel Profiles

wall and the fine early form of the cavetto-fillet profiles of the original door trim point to the same time. The latter was particularly well made with undercutting of the fillets and fasciae of the lintel (Fig. 73). The excavations disclosed no earlier buildings on the site.

In its original form House C was designed to combine the owner's habitation and place of business in the closest possible manner. The eight units of the complex included vestibule (C9), passage (C6–C3), court (C10), diwan (C11), chamber (C5), shops (S7 and C8), and storeroom (C4). The single chamber communicated with both a shop and the storeroom. The passage united the court, the other shop, and the storeroom, and one half of it was itself used for storage. Even the court contained a large vat. The storeroom besides its communication with the chamber and the passage had two doors on the exterior.

The house long remained practically unchanged. Only the rise in the level of the narrow street along its south façade necessitated the raising of the entrances to S7 and C4 0.35 m. in the course of time. The slow rise in the level of the market place was insufficient to affect the exterior doorways.

The construction of the Roman market square, however, brought a number of alterations. The east façade of room C4 was masked by the new Shops S1–S3, and its doorway was walled up leaving a deep niche on the interior. Similarly Shop S7 was severed from the house by the walling up of doorway S7–C5. The Roman grading and paving of the market place with red sand necessitated the raising of the entrances to C9 and C8 and the introduction of steps on the interior. In its final form the house had but one shop, C8, and its storeroom but one exterior doorway, beneath the portico of the Roman square.

## b. Description. Seven Rooms[51]

### C9, Vestibule

The street entrance was fitted with a single door and a bar socket. A step led down to the rammed earth floor of the interior. The opening to passage C6 was arched.

### C6–C3, Passage

The opening to the court was arched. That to room C4 was hung with double doors. Across the middle of the passage on a line with partition C10–C11 was a sill and door frame without doors. South of this opening a row of three round terra cotta tubs was sunk in the rammed earth floor.

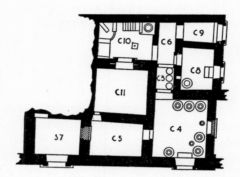

Fig. 74. G6, C. Restored Plan

### C10, Court

The paving was of brick. The mouth of the cesspool was covered with a square pierced slab of gypsum. In the northeast corner was a circular vat of terra cotta sunk in a rubblework table 0.64 m. high, which was screened on the west by a high parapet. The stair ascended along the north and west walls on two arches sprung from rubblework piers. The landing was supported by a separate angle pier. The bottom landing and four steps with treads of 0.23 m. and risers of 0.20 m. are preserved. The complete stair probably reached the roof of the diwan in twenty-four steps at a height of some 4.84 m. above the court. The space beneath the corner landing, enclosed by the piers of the arches and bisected by the angle pier, was screened off with a quadrant parapet of rubblework 0.58 m. high to form a large double bin. The space beneath the second arch was floored with four bipedals to form a fireplace.

### C11, Diwan

The doorway from the south side of the court had double doors and deep bar sockets.

[51] Cf. *Rep. V*, p. 70.

The floor was of rammed earth. About the walls at the height of the top of the door-way ran a plaster Bacchic mask cornice.

### C5, Chamber

The doorways from rooms C11 and C4 had single doors. The floor was of rammed earth. In the west wall was a shallow panel in the opening of former doorway S7–C5.

### C4, Storeroom

The entrance from the Roman square had double doors, a step between the reveals, and another on the interior. On the rammed earth floor stood six large dolia, and in it were sunk to half their depth two pointed amphorae.

### C8, Shop

Both the street entrance and the doorway from passage C6 were fitted with single doors and bar sockets. The former had two rubblework steps on the interior. On the rammed earth floor stood a large dolium. In the west wall was a niche.

## 2. Southern Section. House D (Fig. 78)[52]

### a. History

The lower portions of the socles, wherever they have been studied, were found to be of an early type of plaster rubblework with large pieces of gypsum laid solid through the wall. Above ground they had been extensively rebuilt and repaired. Amid the material used to wall up doorway D1–D6 was found a large fragment of the original lintel, which had the Lesbian cyma profile (Fig. 75). This combined evidence points to the last half of the first century B.C. as the date of the building of the house. The cesspool, unfortunately, affords no confirmation, since its contents were removed in Cumont's excavations.

This early date, however, is borne out in a general way by the number of times it was found necessary to adjust the exterior doorways to the progressive rise in the level of the adjacent streets. The entrance from Street E was raised three times, a total of 1.46 m.

[52] Cf. Cumont, *Fouilles*, pp. 241–250. The excavation of the house was completed during the season of 1931/32. The superficial character of Cumont's excavation, which was left unfinished, led him to a number of misapprehensions as to the plan of this house, particularly with reference to the number and kind of openings, the levels of the various rooms, and the supposed existence of a cellar. This last arose from a failure to take account of the difference between the interior level of the house and that of Shop S22 and Main Street to the south. The reader by referring back to the original publication will be able to make the necessary corrections.

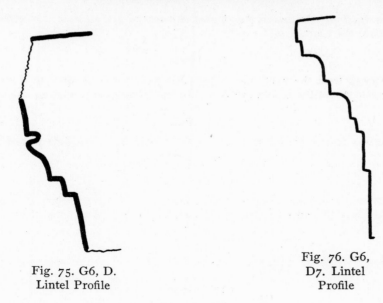

Fig. 75. G6, D.
Lintel Profile

Fig. 76. G6,
D7. Lintel
Profile

The plan of the house changed very little in the course of time, though most of its walls and doorways were at one time or other rebuilt. Probably at the time of its last raising the entrance from Street E received the late trim of which the profile is shown in Fig. 76. Equally late in its history doorway D2–D3 received the exceptional foliate capitals and lintel described by Cumont.[53] At an undetermined date doorways D1–D6 and D1–D4 were walled up. Though the floor level of the house remained the same, that of Shop S22 kept step with the rising street and doorsill.

### b. Description. Seven Rooms

#### D7, Vestibule

The street entrance had double doors, a step between the reveals, and another on the interior. The floor was of rammed earth.

#### D1, Court

The paving was of rammed earth. The mouth of the cesspool was covered with a square pierced slab of gypsum. The stair unit opened off the northeast corner. The stair ascended counter-clockwise about a central newel wall. The first flight of seven steps with treads of 0.30 m. and risers of 0.18 m. remains in place. The whole is best

[53] *Fouilles*, pp. 247–249.

restored as reaching the roof in five flights of twenty-three steps at a height of some 4.30 m. above the court.

### D2, Diwan

The doorway from the west side of the court had double doors. The floor was of rammed earth. About the room ran a broad bench of rubblework 0.21 m. high.

### D3, Chamber

The doorway from room D2 was fitted with a single door. The floor was of rammed earth.

### D4, Chamber

The doorway from room D3 had double doors, and the inner edges of the reveals had a wide rabbet for an inner frame of wood. The floor was of rammed earth.

### D5

The doorway from the court had a single door. The floor was of rammed earth.

### D6, Closet

The doorway from the vestibule had a single door. The floor was of rammed earth. Against the north wall before former doorway D6–D1 was a bench or table of rubblework 0.54 m. high.

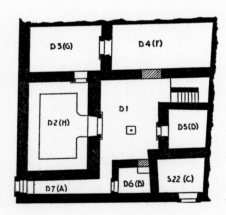

Fig. 77. G6, D. Restored Plan

# V

## SCULPTURE AND PAINTING

THE objects described below come from the hitherto unpublished portions of Block G3 and from Blocks G7 and G5. For the sculpture from the other portions of Section G, see *Rep. V*, pp. 49–70, 79–82, 86–90.

### A. *Block G3*

#### 1. House M

##### a. Diwan M2 (Pl. XV, 1)

Relief cut from an irregular slab of gypsum, 0.306 m. × 0.224 m. in greatest length and breadth and 0.07 m.–0.08 m. thick. There are abundant traces on the back and about the edges of the plaster of the wall in which it was set. The upper right hand corner was pieced out with plaster.

The subject is Hercules slaying the Nemean lion. In the center Hercules standing left grasps the lion by the forelock with his left hand and with his right raises his club to strike. To his right is a small horned altar. The hero is represented nude with a short beard and bushy locks. His brow is crowned by a circular medallion.[1]

The composition is a variant of the ancient oriental lion-slaying hero. The conception is stiff and conceptual in the extreme. The hero's head and torso are frontal, his arms and legs in profile. The execution is crude and schematic. The relief is cut back almost at right angles to the surface plane. This plane is practically flat, and modelling, save for the protruding eyes, beard, and right hand, is achieved by incision. Parallel incisions indicate hair and beard. The breasts, navel, and medallion, the lion's mane, and the texture of the wooden club are indicated by concentric circles struck with a compass of radii 0.0035 and 0.0065 m.

##### b. Chamber M4 (Pl. XV, 2)

Relief cut from a rectangular slab of soft, fine-grained limestone, 0.21 m. × 0.29 m. The background is 0.031 m. thick, the relief 0.042 m. at

[1] Cf. *Rep. I*, pp. 75–77; *Rep. III*, pp. 88–91.

its highest point. On the back are traces of the plaster of the wall in which it was set. In the center of the top and along the bottom the projecting surface is broken away.

The field of the relief had a simple raised border, 0.014 m. in width, interrupted at the top by the head. The subject is Hercules bibax. Hercules stands facing in repose, weight on left leg, right leg slightly flexed. His knotted club rests on the ground and leans against his thigh, where it is grasped by the right hand. The left arm is bent, and in the left hand is the cantherus held before the abdomen. The hind paws of the hero's lion skin are knotted over his chest. The skin hung down behind and was brought forward, so that the head, mane, and front paws hung over the bent left arm. The head, right hand, and feet are missing.

The relief is high, and the figure is almost free from the background. The carving of the massive forms is bold and summary, but reflects skill, facility, and thorough acquaintance with western models and techniques.

## 2. House L

### a. Chamber L3 (Cf. above, p. 72) (Pl. XVI)

Pair of bronze statuettes representing a syrinx player and a piper. The former, which is complete, is 0.103 m. high. The latter, whose feet are missing, measures 0.096 m. The statuettes were found in excellent preservation with only a slight oxidation. The lower portion of the syrinx had been bent inward. The projecting ends of the pipes had been broken away.

Both figures stand with the weight on the right leg, left leg slightly advanced. The arms are bent at the elbows, both hands holding the instruments to the mouth. The heads are turned slightly to the right. Both figures are clad in long, short-sleeved, ungirdled tunics which fit close to the forms of the body. Their heads are bare, the short-cropped hair blocked in as a mass of curls. The syrinx player is μονοσάνδαλος, his right foot shod with a sandal with a heavy overlapping tongue, his left foot bare. His syrinx is an enormous one of nine pipes, represented as square or rectangular in section.

The modelling is fluent and fully plastic. It is simplified into large unbroken forms. Both figures were cast solid and left just as they came from the mold. Surface imperfections due to casting are numerous. There are no signs of cold working or chasing. The easy grace and mastery of the figures, their simple flowing lines, the treatment of hair and features all suggest work of the late fourth or early third centuries. No exact parallels have come to my attention, though syrinx players and pipers are not infrequently represented in Hellenistic terra cottas. The syrinx player, at any rate, if we may judge from his single sandal, may have been conceived as a cult musician.[2]

### 3. House J

#### a. Court J1 (Fig. 86)

Small altar of chalky white limestone, 0.155 m. high and 0.09 m. square at base and top. The base and crowning moldings consist of a series of five stepped fillets. The top has truncated horns and a circular

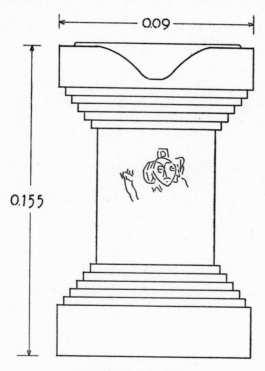

Fig. 86. G3, J1. Altar

[2] For the significance of the unshod foot, see W. Amelung, *Diss. della Pontif. Accad. Romana di Arch.*, Ser. II, IX (1907), pp. 115–135; cf. Sir James G. Frazer, *The Golden Bough*[3] (1935), III, pp. 311–313.

bowl much blackened by fire. The die bears on one face a representation in graffito of the head, shoulders, and one arm of a god. The right hand is upraised in benediction. The hair is dressed in the tripartite Parthian fashion and crowned with a polos.

### b. Court J1 (Pl. XVII, 2)

Lower half of a small gypsum statuette, 0.156 m. high, standing on a base 0.014 m. thick. It represents the body from the waist down of a nude female figure with the left hand covering the pudenda. At the left and rear is a support covered with drapery. There are traces of pink pigment in the navel and in the folds of the drapery. The pose is evidently intended to be that of the Cnidian Aphrodite with the action reversed. The work is extremely clumsy and perfunctory, evidently local.

### c. Diwan J6 (Fig. 87)

Plaster wall shrine, 0.40 m. $\times$ 0.28 m. It consisted of a heavy, roughly semicircular frame, 0.05 m.–0.08 m. wide and some 0.02 m. thick, enclosing a panel. The whole was covered with six coats of very thin plaster, on each of which save the last the same scene was reproduced in red and black pigment. The frame was decorated with interlacing chevrons in red, the field with a cult image.

Within an arched aedicula supported by two columns a divinity is represented on a stepped plinth. He is about to be crowned by a Victory advancing from his left. He is shown facing, and, apparently, only from the waist up, holding in his right hand a lance or scepter, his left extended down and to the side. He is dressed in a sleeved jacket with two stripes down the front and has a bracelet on his left wrist. His hair is black, and he probably had a black moustache. On the front of the plinth was a representation no longer clear. At either side were indistinguishable objects, perhaps thymiateria. The Victory is also facing and holds a garland in her outstretched right hand. Her left is crossed over her body and holds a palm branch. She is dressed in a peplos, probably thought of as a girdled upper garment and a skirt.[8] The edges of the field about the figures and the frame were sprinkled with large red and black dots. Thirty-four is the largest number visible on any single coat of plaster.

[8] Cf. *Rep. II*, p. 189; *Rep. VI*, pp. 64 f.

Fig. 87. G3, J6. Plaster Wall Shrine

Fig. 88. G7, H1. Antefix

The representations were merely crude sketches or copies. The dots have the look of having been added from time to time until the shrine was covered, when a new coat of plaster was applied and the process began anew. Perhaps they formed a record of observances performed. There is no clue to the identity of the household god, though his worship in a similar fashion was widespread in the city as shown by the occurrence of similar shrines.[4]

### 4. House H

### a. Stair Unit H10 (Pl. XVII, 1)

Relief cut from a roughly rectangular slab of gypsum, 0.328 m. × 0.152 m. in greatest length and breadth and 0.03 m.–0.04 m. thick. The relief was found in two pieces. The upper right and lower left hand portions are missing. The back bears traces of the plaster of the wall in which it was fixed.

The subject is a goddess (Athena-Allath?) armed with lance and shield. The figure stands facing, holding a lance close beneath the head with upraised right hand. The left hand presumably supported the oval shield which rests on the ground at the left. The features are much worn. The most prominent element is the large eyes outlined with black pigment. The body is clothed in a single long garment which reached from beneath the arms to the ground and is represented by five heavy vertical folds. It leaves the chest and shoulders bare. It is not clear whether the head was thought of as crowned by a polos or a crested helmet.

The work is crude and schematic in the extreme. Although the edges are rounded off to the background, the relief is cut back from a single plane, and the details are rendered by deep incisions. Local craftsmanship.

### b. Diwan H4 (Pl. XXII)

A bronze plaque, described in Appendix I, pp. 186–202.

### c. Chamber H5 (Pl. XVII, 3)

Plaster relief plaque, 0.175 m. × 0.14 m. in greatest height and

[4] *Rep. IV*, p. 35; *Rep. V*, pp. 36, 41; *Rep. VI*, p. 118; above, pp. 86, 112, 121 f. In most cases the image of the deity was not represented and the shrine consisted simply of a plaque of plaster covered haphazard with dots and frequently replastered.

width. The back was made concave for application to some rounded surface. The plaque is broken away along the right edge and at the bottom, though the bottom edge is preserved in at least two places.

The plaque represents a mask of the neck and head of a goddess. The face is a long oval with schematically modelled features: deeply sunk mouth corners, long nose, heavily accented brows which overhang the protruding eyes and project beyond them at the sides. The hair is dressed in the tripartite Parthian fashion with a high chignon in the center. It is represented by rows of round knobs. There are no ornaments, but these were probably represented in paint, for traces of red pigment remain on the lips and left cheek. Closely following the outline of the hair along the preserved left side runs a raised border, the aureole which proclaims a divinity.

The plaque was cast in a mold and worked over in places with a knife, as is clearly apparent in the sharp cutting of the brows. In style it is closely similar to the heads of the cast plaster Victories from the temple of Artemis-Nannaia published by Cumont.[5]

## B. Block G7

### 1. House H

### a. Room H7 (Pl. XVIII, 2)

Plaster relief figure, 0.36 m. high. The relief had a flat background of which segments remain at the right. The figure is broken away at the bottom and both sides, and the head is badly damaged.

The subject was the nude Hercules at rest leaning on his club. The figure stood facing, weight on the left leg, right leg slightly bent, head turned slightly to the left. The club rested on the ground and its butt was propped beneath the right armpit, where a fragment of it may be seen. The left arm as in other examples of the type was probably crossed behind the back. Little remains of the hair or features, but it is clear that the face was bearded.

The type is that of the Hercules Farnese with the action reversed. The relief was cast in a mold, probably of western origin. The bold and accurate musculature is typically Hellenistic or Roman.

---

[5] *Fouilles*, pp. 220–222, Pl. LXXXIV; cf. *Rep. VII–VIII*, p. 267 f., Pl. XXXVI, 3.

### b. Court H1. Cf. above, p. 11 (Fig. 88; Pl. XVIII, 1)

Terra cotta antefix with female mask, 0.168 m. wide and 0.152 m. high. The tip of the nose and the lower left hand border are broken away.

The face has a simple angular structure with prominent cheekbones. The preserved left ear is a rudimentary indication on a level with the eyes. The latter have protruding eyeballs. The lashes and eyebrows are indicated by incised hatching. The lips are compressed and pouting. On the forehead is a pair of projecting knobs (vestigial locks of hair?). The face is framed by a wide border of three ridges, the outermost of which is scalloped.

The features show pronounced archaic characteristics, and the type is perhaps a descendant from the north Greek facial antefixes. Perhaps the tradition was preserved in Macedonia. In any case the Dura antefix was made from local clay, presumably in an imported mold.

## C. Block G5

### 1. House F

### a. Chamber F4 (Pl. XVIII, 3)

Lower portion of a relief cut from a slab of soft fine-grained limestone, 0.136 m. wide and 0.118 m. in greatest preserved height. The background is 0.043 m. thick, and the relief 0.031 m. at its highest point. The upper portion is missing, and the bottom edge is broken away at the left.

The field of the relief had a plain raised border, 0.01 m. wide. The subject, a goddess, stands on a little semicircular projection of the bottom border, facing, weight apparently on the right leg with the left leg brought slightly forward. The pose has evidently been misunderstood, and the action of the hips is contrary to that of the legs. To the right is the shaft of a lance or sceptre held in the missing right hand. The left arm is bent at the elbow, and the left hand will have held some object, now missing, level with the breast. The figure was fully clothed in a long, sleeved tunic which falls to the ground between the legs, lying in heavy folds over the feet. About the hips is draped a himation, the end of which, probably thrown over the left arm, hangs down at the left. The feet were shod, and the left wrist bore a bracelet. The character of the garments leaves little doubt as to the sex of the divinity represented.

The relief is high, and the edges are cut vertically back from the surface planes. The drapery is highly stylized. The workmanship is sharp, formulaic, and insensitive.

## 2. House C

### a. Diwan C2 (Pl. XIX)

Plaster relief plaque, 0.53 m. × 0.28 m. The plaque was found in eight pieces. Two large fragments are missing from the left side and two small fragments from the right. The surface is rubbed and pitted. When found, the red and black pigment of the decoration and details was well preserved.

The subject, framed in an aedicula, is Venus Anadyomene. The aedicula consists of two slender columns supporting an arch. The columns rest on conical bases painted with three red bands separated by black lines to represent tori. The bottom 0.18 m. of the columns was painted with a pattern of interlacing chevrons, black and red with dots in the interstices. Above a black band at this point they were solid red to the capitals. Both capitals are missing, but the black inner contour of the right hand one indicates that they were tall and bellshaped. The arch is a rounded member of the same thickness as the columns, painted black for a space of 0.06 m. above the capitals, and beyond this covered with the same pattern as the lower part of the columns.

Beneath the aedicula stands the nude goddess, her weight on her right leg, her left knee bent coquettishly forward and inward. In her left hand she holds a round mirror, turning her head to the left to gaze into it. With her right hand she grasps the tresses of the right side of her head. Those of the left side fall on her shoulder. The contour of the body against the background was outlined in red. Of the forms within the breasts, abdomen, belly, and mons veneris were outlined with red, the nipples were picked out with red dots, and the navel with a black dot and red outline. The hair was black within a red outline, the eyebrows and irises black, the cornea red. The mouth was red with black dots at the corners. The mirror had a black outline with a red circle within it. Low slippers, bracelets on the right wrist and left upper arm, and a necklace with a crescent pendant were also indicated by red outlines.

The plaque was cast in a mold which was much used and worn, since the definition of the forms is everywhere blurred and indistinct. Similar plaques but of different dimensions have been published in Cumont, *Fouilles*, p. 226, pl. LXXXV, and *Rep. IV*, p. 243, pl. VIII.

When set in place in the wall the plaque was surrounded by a frame of painted decoration, apparently representing a trellised arbor. Several small fragments showing bits of trellis-work and tendrils were found nearby in the room, and two clusters of grapes appear on the upper right hand margin of the plaque. There can be little doubt that the Venus of the plaque was the tutelary divinity of the guild of entertainers and prostitutes who made House C their headquarters.

### 3. House B

#### a. Room B3 (Pl. XVIII, 4)

Lower half of an alabaster statuette, 0.127 m. wide and 0.193 m. in greatest preserved height. The statuette had a plain border of slight projection across the bottom, which was returned at least part way up the right side and broadened at 0.041 m. from the bottom, perhaps to represent an altar.

The preserved portion represents the legs of a nude female figure in relief from the thighs down against a background of schematized drapery (or water?). The figure appears to stand upon a roughly indicated diminutive figure prone at her feet. The attitude of this figure is evidently intended to be that of swimming, and one should probably see in the statuette a goddess surmounting an aquatic deity—Aphrodite (?), Goddess of the Euphrates (?), Tyche of Dura (?).

# VI

## INSCRIPTIONS

The inscriptions published below come with the exception of no. 410 from the hitherto unpublished portions of Block G3 and from Blocks G7 and G5. For the inscriptions from other portions of Section G, see *Rep. V*, pp. 53 f., 66, 69–71, 93–97.

### A. *Block G3*

#### 1. House J

##### a. Diwan J6

934. Graffito. On the south wall of the room. Letters average 0.006 m.

Τίτος Φρόντων

935. Graffito. On the east wall of the room. Letters average 0.006 m.

'Απολλώνιος 'Αρχελάου

ΑΒΓΔΕΖΗ ΘΙΚΛΜΝ Ξ ΟΠΡ ΣΤΥ ΦΧΨΩΑΩΒ ΥΓ

#### 2. Building A

##### a. Room A2

936. Dipinto (Fig. 89). On the surface of the north bench beside doorway A2–A5. Letters average 0.011 m. Abecedarium.

ΑΒΓΔΕΖΗΘΙΚΛΜΝΞΟΠΡΣΤΥΦΧΨΩΑΩΒΨΓ[

937. Graffito (Fig. 89). In front of no. 936. Letters average 0.017 m. Carefully incised in double outline within a rectangular frame of two lines. Μνησ | θῆ Πολύ | μηλος | Διοκλέο | υς τοῦ Δ | ανύμου

Diocles, son of Danymus, is known from

Fig. 89. Inscriptions from G3, A2

two seats in the temple of Azzanathkona inscribed by his wife, Timo-
nassa, in 62–63 A.D.[1] He was dead in 87 A.D. His son's connection with
the record office is unknown but not strange considering the prominence
of the family.[2]

### b. Room A3

938. Stamped amphora handle. Cf. above, p. 20. Letters average
0.005 m. (Pl. XX, 1).

Θασίων

(Vine stalk with leaves and three grape clusters)

Πρηξίπολι(ς)

Cf. E. Pridik, *Inventory-Catalogue of the Stamps on Handles and
Necks of Amphorae and on Bricks, of the Hermitage Collection* (1917)
(in Russian) nos. 375–378.

410. Graffito. This inscription was published by Hopkins in *Rep. V*,
pp. 82–84. A fresh examination of the portions which remained in situ
and of the detached fragments which could be located has made it possible to offer improved readings in many cases (a, b, f, g, k, l, n). These
texts are republished herewith together with a general discussion of the
character of the inscription and the light it sheds on the date and destination of the installation with which it was connected.

The numerals which make up the inscription were inscribed in large
and careful letters on the plaster surface of the junctions of the diago-
nals of the framework of the bins or compartments built about the west,
north, and east sides of the room. They were arranged seriatim in
groups which, within the range of the extant material, comprise from
thirteen to three numerals. The portions which remain in situ indicate
that the groups were inscribed to the left of the compartments to which
they had reference, and that the lowest row of compartments was without numbers. The separate fragments are here given in the order established by Hopkins so as to facilitate reference to the earlier publication.
(Fig. 90; Pls. II, 2, III.)

(a) In situ left of the eleventh compartment of the third row of the
west side. Letters 0.021–0.03 m. (Pl. XX, 2). Thirteen years, 458–470
S.E. = A.D. 146/7–158/9.

[1] *Rep. V*, nos. 523, 525.
[2] *Rep. VI*, pp. 420 f.; *Zeitschr. der Savigny-Stiftung*, LVI (1936), pp. 99–135.

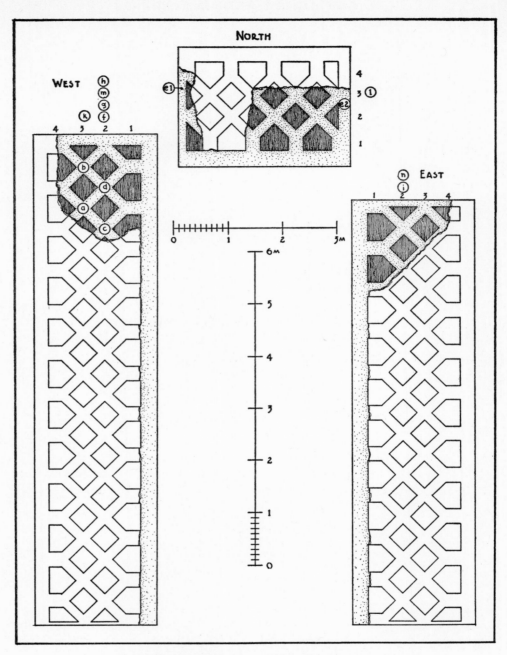

Fig. 90. Compartments and Graffiti from G3, A3

HNY    ΘNY    ΞY

AXY    BΞY    ΓΞY

ΔΞY    EΞY    FΞY

ZΞY    HΞY    ΘΞY

OY     T KAI  ⚹

(b) In situ left of the twelfth (end) compartment of the third row of the west side. Letters 0.021–0.03 m. Ten years, 471–480 S.E. = A.D. 159/60–168/9.

AOY    BOY

ΓOY    ΔOY

EOY    FOY

ZOY    HOY    ΘOY

ΠY     ⳨      KAI ⚹[8]

(c) In situ left of the eleventh compartment of the second row of the west side. Letters average 0.05 m. (Pl. XX, 2). Three years, 266–268 S.E. = 47/6–45/4 B.C.

[F]ΞΣ KAI

[Z]ΞΣ KAI

HΞΣ

] ⚹

(d) In situ left of the twelfth (end) compartment of the second row of the west side. Letters average 0.05 m. (Pl. XX, 3). Three years, 269–271 S.E. = 44/3–42/1 B.C.

ΘΞΣ K[AI]

OΣ KAI

AOΣ

A KAI ⚹

(e) Two fragments: (1) in situ left of the first compartment of the third row of the north side; letters average 0.024 m. (2) in situ right

[8] Col. 3 published by Hopkins as a separate fragment, 410 (j). It belongs below and to the right of (b). The last lines of cols. 1 and 2 were not published by Hopkins.

of the fourth (end) compartment of the second row of the north side; letters 0.062 m. (Pl. XX, 4). Six years, 481–486 S.E. = A.D. 169/70–174/5.

(1)    ΑΠΥ  ΒΠ[Υ  ΓΠΥ]
       Δ[ΠΥ  ΕΠΥ   FΠΥ]

(2)    ⚹[4]

       ☧

(f) Detached fragment. Letters average 0.031 m. 188–190 S.E. = 125/4–123/2 B.C.

       ΗΠΡ  Θ[ΠΡ]
       Ϙ[Ρ]

(g) Detached fragment. Letters average 0.032 m. Between 191–199 S.E. = 122/1 and 114/3 B.C.

       .]ϘΡ
       .]ϘΡ
       . . .

(h) Detached fragment. Letters average 0.05 m. About 260–265 S.E. = 53/2–48/7 B.C.

       ]Σ  Κ[ΑΙ]
       ]ΞΣ  [ΚΑΙ]
       ]Σ

(i) Detached fragment. Letters average 0.045 m. 319–320 S.E. = A.D. 7/8–8/9.

       ΘΙΤ  ΚΑΙ
       Κ]Τ  ΚΑΙ

(k) Detached fragment. Letters average 0.035 m. 408–409 S.E. = A.D. 96/7–97/8.

       ΗΥ  ΘΥ
       ΚΑΙ
       ☧

[4] The two texts are probably not related. The monograms are larger than elsewhere and are exceptional in being written to the right of the compartment.

(1) Detached fragment. Letters 0.02–0.03 m. 505–509 s.e. = a.d. 193/4–197/8.

Ε]Φ   Φ[Φ   ΖΦ]

ΗΦ   Κ[ΑΙ]

ΘΦ

(m) Detached fragment, copy only. 213–214 s.e. = 100/99–99/8 b.c.

Γ]ΙΣ   ΔΙ[Σ

KAI

(n) Detached fragment. Letters average 0.04 m. 378–380 s.e. = a.d. 66/7–68/9.

ΗΟ[Τ][5]

ΘΟ[Τ]

Π[Τ]

The letters of the fragments differ considerably in form as well as size. The following characteristic forms may be noted: (m), 213 and 214, has the four-bar sigma; (h), in the 260's, has the four-bar sigma and three bar xi; (c) and (d), 266–271, have the four-bar sigma, three-bar xi, oval theta, and square omicron; (i), 319 and 320, has the square theta; (n), probably 378–380, has the square theta and omicron, (k), 408 and 409, has the square theta; (a) and (b), 458–480, have the four-bar xi, oval theta, round omicron; (l), 505–509, has again the square theta and square phi. The letters of (f), (g), (m), (h), (c), and (d) were ornamented with serifs.

It is plain from this that the inscriptions were made at different times, and that the numerical series rose chronologically, since the ascending numbers follow the evolution of the alphabet at Dura. At the same time within any given fragment or group of numbers the letter forms are uniform. The conclusion that the numbers were inscribed from time to time in groups is made certain by the fact that each complete group is carefully composed within the available space however many numbers it may contain.

[5] The numeral for 300 is restored because of the uniformly square form of the letters, whereas in the 70's of the sigma series the theta is rounded as in (d), and because the appropriate numbers of the upsilon series occur on (b) and (j).

Each group of numbers, as we have seen, had reference to the compartment to the right of it, or rather to the contents of that compartment. The nature of these contents is betrayed by the monogram ☧, which follows the list of numbers on five fragments (c, d, k, a, b) and appears below another monogram on a sixth (e). It is the familiar abbreviation for Χρ(εοφύλαξ), Χρ(εοφυλάκειον), Χρ(εοφυλακικός).[6] Since the chreophylax was the official charged with the registration and filing of documents, the numbered contents of the compartments, to the list of which he has appended the monogram of his office, cannot have been other than the documents in his charge.

The numbers of the contents filed in each compartment are too few in any given group to have reference to individual documents. Neither can they refer to collections of uniform numbers of documents numbered serially, as is shown by the great difference in the number of collections filed in different compartments. Dura, then, must have followed the regular practice of ancient secretariats and filed by annual collections, which might vary in size from year to year according to the number of documents registered.

In this case the numbers in each group must be dates, and we may envisage the procedure somewhat as follows. On the analogy of Egyptian practice, we may expect to find that the registrar kept copies of all documents drawn up for registration in his office, and combined them in the form of an expanding roll, attaching the sheets of parchment or (after the arrival of the Romans in the sixties of the second century, which does not seem to mark a change in the procedure) papyrus together edge to edge by stitching or gluing. This τόμος συγκολλήσιμος, to give it its Egyptian name (L. Mitteis, *Chrestomathie der Papyruskunde*, 1912, no. 183; A. Segrè, *Aegyptus*, VII, 1920, pp. 97–107; A. E. R. Boak, *Papyri from Tebtunis*, I, 1933, p. 2), may have been kept locally, but more probably was sent up after a set period to a central office at Antioch, Ctesiphon, or wherever it may have been at different periods. The individual contracting parties, or their delegated representatives, kept the originals or duplicate originals folded into a little packet and sealed. These are represented among the Dura documents by *D.Pg.* 10, 13, 20–23, 26, 32, and 40, and *D.P.* 73, 74, and 90 (*Rep. II*, pp. 201–216; *Rep. VI*, pp. 419–438; *Rep. VII–VIII*, pp. 426–441). For office record, the *chreophylakion* or *chrematisterion* kept a roll of abstracts, the so-called εἰρόμενα (*D.Pg.* 2 and 28; cf. *Münchener Beit-*

---

[6] The other regular pre-Christian resolution of this monogram, i.e., ἑκατοντάρχης, ἑκατονταρχία, χ(ιλιά)ρ(χης) is obviously unsuited to this context.

*räge*, XIX, 1934, p. 397), and probably also a journal or finding list or "register," the ἀναγραφή. These last may then have been accumulated in the next free pigeonhole over a period of several years, until such time as the roll or rolls became large enough to occupy it completely. Thus in the case of those compartments for which we have complete dates, it is possible to gauge the volume of business in the community and surrounding territory. It is interesting to note that the records of three years occupied a full compartment at the time of Dura's recovery in the First Century B.C., 47–44 (c above) and 44–41 (d), whereas in the years of the Roman threat and occupation in the Second Century, A.D. 146–175, thirteen years were required to fill a whole compartment (a), and ten (b) and six (e) years to fill a half compartment.

This offers an interpretation of the precise significance of the monogram ℞, i.e., χρ(εοφυλακικὸς τόμος). In fragment (d) the complete subscription to the numbers reads, A καὶ ℞, in fragment (a), T καὶ ℞, in (b), ⸶ καὶ ℞ and in (e) we have the monogram ⸶ with ℞. Here the abbreviations A, T, TA may perhaps be taken to signify the second type of roll deposited with the roll of summaries, and resolved ἀ(γορανομικὸς τόμος) and τα(μιευτικὸς τόμος).[7]

It is not difficult to restore the approximate disposition of the dated files about the room. Each complete row contained twenty-five compartments, eleven and one-half on the west side, three and one-half on the north side, and ten on the east. Fragments (c), (d), and (a), (b) in situ at the north end of the second and third rows of the west side give the terminal dates, 272 and 480, of one complete circuit of the room consisting of the second row of the north and east sides and the third of the west. The difference of 208 years gives an average of 8.3 years for each compartment, and indicates that the numbering began at the south end of the west side. The same fragments then show that the complete first row together with the west side of the second row contained the years numbered through 271. The filing of documents may be assumed to have begun with the organization of the city's administration about 300 B.C.

---

[7] Or is *alpha* the first letter of ἀναγραφή in some form, and is the χρεοφυλακικὸς τόμος the εἰρόμενα of Egypt?

For the rôle of the Alexandrian *tamiai* in property transfers cf. *P. Hal.* 1, 245, as restored by E. Schönbauer (*Beiträge zur Geschichte des Liegenschaftrechtes im Altertum* [1924], p. 13) on the basis of *BGU* 1213; cf. most recently A. Segrè, *An Essay on the Nature of Real Property in the Classical World* (Paul Bassinor, New York, 1943), with full bibliography. The Dura archives were, perhaps, under *agoranomoi* in the 1st cent. B.C., under Royal Judges in the first Christian century (*D.Pg.* 21 and 40), and under *tamiai* in the second.

Since the dates must be those of the Seleucid era, we may further assume that the numbering of documents began not with 1 but with about 12. It follows that the complete first row and the west side of the second contained the documents not of 271 but of about 259 years, an average of some 7.1 years for each compartment.

To determine the approximate date of the end of the first row and beginning of the second we may employ this figure and reach year 189 or 190 (7.1 × 25 + 12). If, however, we reckon back from the north end of the second row using the average of 8.3, we reach year 175 or 176 (271 — 8.3 × 11.5). Striking an average we may assume that the dates of the first row ran from 12 to about 183, and that the numbering of the second row began about 184. We have seen, moreover, that no numbers were inscribed against the compartments of the first row, and that the compartments themselves on archaeological evidence were built toward the end of the second century B.C. The connection of these dates is obvious. Sel. 184 is 128–9 B.C. Prior to about this time the filed documents of Dura were kept in some other place. When the new chreophylakeion was built, the earlier annual files were simply docketed and placed in the lowest row of compartments. The inscription of dates beside the compartments began with the new office. The earliest date among the extant material is that of (f), 125–121 B.C.

The west side of the second row on this evidence covered some 88 years, 184–271. The north and east sides at the average of 8.3 years per compartment covered some 112 years, a total of 200 years dated approximately 184–384. By the same reckoning the west side of the third row covered some 96 years, 384–480, the north side at the same average some 29 years, 481–510. The east side would have contained approximately years 511–593 had not the fall of the city about 568 intervened. The latest date among the extant material is that of (1), 193–198 A.D. The fourth row above remained unused.

### B. Block G7

#### 1. House H

##### a. Court H1

939. Inscription (Pl. XXI). For the circumstances of finding, see above, p. 108. The inscription has been published with full commentary and notes in *The Harvard Theological Review*, XXIV (1941), pp. 79–109. The reader is referred for details to that publication of which the following is an abridgment.

The text is partly incised, partly painted in red (beginning with the E of ΘΕΑΙ in 1.8), on an irregularly shaped piece of local alabaster, 0.29 m. × 0.34 m. in maximum dimensions, and varying in thickness from 0.019 m. at the top to 0.011 m. at the bottom. The stone had been left unsquared in order that none of its surface area might be lost. The face was carefully smoothed, but the back was left rough, and traces of plaster indicate that the stone had been attached to or let into a wall. Seven fragments were recovered, apparently only one, forming the upper right corner, being missing. See further below, note 14.

The script is a well-executed example of the oval alphabet of the second and third centuries, with cursive tendencies.[8] The letters are progressively smaller and more crowded, the height varying from 0.03–0.25 m. in the first three lines to 0.025–0.02 m. in lines four and five and 0.021–0.016 m. in lines six to nine. The language is the conventional "epic" or "hexameter" language of the funerary epigrams. Only ΕΙ for I in ΧΕΙΛΙΑΡΧΟΝ, the confusion of *tau* for *theta* in ΣΤΕΝΑΡΟΝ and probably of ΑΙ for Ε in ΔΕΞΑΣΘΑΙ, all common enough at Dura as elsewhere, need be noted. A medial dot punctuation is used irregularly.

> Ἰούλιον [Τε-]
> ρέντιον χει-
> λίαρχον Σπείρ(ης) κ' Παλμ(υρηνῶν).
> Τὸν θρασὺν ἐν στρατιαῖς,
> στεναρὸν πολέμοισι, θανόντα,
> μνήμης ἄξιον ἄνδρα, Αὐρηλία
> Ἀρρία θάψε πόσιν φίλιον, ὃν ψυ-
> χαὶ δέξασθαι θεαί, ἐλαφρὰ
> καλύψαι τε γαῖα.

The final six lines may be considered first. They consist of a cento, more or less metrical in form, more or less conventional in character, rather difficult to punctuate satisfactorily, composed simply by juxtaposition of phrases.[9]

The first metrical unit is a dactylic hexameter, to be translated "The

[8] The type is common. Cf., for example, the instances collected at Jerash, C. H. Kraeling, *Gerasa, City of the Decapolis* (1938), p. 363, Fig. 12.

[9] This style of composition has been often noted in the Latin epitaphs; cf. R. Cagnat, "Sur les Manuels Professionnels des Graveurs d'Inscriptions Romaines," *Rev. de Phil.* N.S. XIII (1889), pp. 51–65; J. Tolkiehn, *Neue Jahrb. f. d. kl. Altertum*, VII (1901), p. 184; H. Focillon in F. Plessis, *Poésie Latine, Epitaphes* (1905), pp. xvii, xxix; E.

brave in campaigns, mighty in wars, dead." A somewhat extensive survey of the field produces no adequate parallel to this combination of locutions, by which the author wished to indicate that the man honored, a valiant and powerful fighter, had died in battle. Similar groups of adjectives are, however, not uncommon, though they are ordinarily better combined.

The next unit includes most of the next two lines, and consists of a hexameter and a little more. The final syllables of the proper names Αὐρηλία and Ἀρρία had to be shortened if they were to fit into dactyls, and this the Greeks regularly did, doubtless influenced in part by the fact that these vowels were short in Latin. The section consists, then, of three dactylic elements, μνήμης ἄξιον ἄνδρα, Αὐρηλία Ἀρρία θάψε, and θάψε πόσιν φίλιον. The first two of these make up a hexameter, either if the final alpha of ἄνδρα is elided or if the first syllable of Αὐρηλία is regarded as short. Both devices are readily paralleled in the epigrams of Imperial times, where in general proper names are roughly handled. I have come upon no exact verbal parallels to these phrases, but they are, of course, commonplace.

The remainder of the inscription, the last two and a quarter lines, is likewise dactylic. It consists of two metrical elements joined to form a line one foot too long for a hexameter, the final AI of both δέξασθαι and καλύψαι being scanned as short, while the same element is treated as long in ψυχαί and θεαί. The word ἐλαφρά is anapaestic ($\cup \cup -$), and the first syllable of καλύψαι is lengthened in the usual manner. The syntax of the clause admits of varying interpretations. I prefer to take ΔΕΞΑΣΘΑΙ as the aorist imperative (= δέξασθε), and ΚΑΛΥΨΑΙ as the aorist optative; this mood occurs regularly in such formulae.[10]

The second of these two phrases is, of course, the universal Latin *sit tibi terra levis.*

The other phrase has likewise a formulaic aspect. "Receiving" of the

Galletier, *Étude sur la Poésie Funéraire Romaine d'après les Inscriptions* (1922), 225–235.

[10] It seems less likely that ΔΕΞΑΣΘΑΙ and ΚΑΛΥΨΑΙ are aorist indicatives without the augment (= ἐδέξασθε and ἐκάλυψε), because in this case the change in person is less accountable, and the meaning of the second cliché becomes quite distorted. It would, in addition, be possible also to take both ΔΕΞΑΣΘΑΙ and ΚΑΛΥΨΑΙ as aorist infinitives used as imperatives, or to combine ΚΑΛΥΨΑΙ and ΤΕ as the aorist optative with the subject θεαί, ΕΛΑΦΡΑ ΓΑΙΑ being then an instrumental dative with the *iota adscriptum* omitted. That would, however, involve the sacrifice of the connective, which is necessary even if misplaced *metri causa.*

dead in various ways and by various agencies is a sentiment which occurs not infrequently in epitaphs, also "keeping" or "releasing."

The evidence would suggest that the ψυχαὶ θεαί of the Dura text, a term for which no direct parallels have been found, should be the deities of the Lower World in some conception. It rested with them to receive the soul of the dead to the positive delights or at least to the comparative rest and security of their realm, or to reject it, and compel it to wander endlessly, on the earth or elsewhere, subject especially to the beck and call of wizards and magicians who might want merely to know the future, but who might also desire to effect any kind of mischief.[11] There would seem to be no reason, antecedently, why ψυχαὶ θεαί should not be a translation of Di Manes. The Thesaurus Linguae Latinae, II, 72, contains numerous instances of the use of animae in the sense of Manes (that is, of the souls of the dead), and ψυχαὶ θεαί would be a literal translation of Di (or Deae) Animae.

There are, however, certain considerations which make against this assumption, for which an inherent probability is furnished by the following Roman formula. Not only is Di Manes translated into Greek by other formulae. No Latin dedications to the Deae Animae occur, so far as my investigation goes, and no appeals to the Deae Animae to receive the soul of a relative or friend, and this need not be accidental. To a Greek, moreover, the notion of *Dis Manibus* was foreign, and made its way into the Imperial epitaphs in the same way as did the formula *sit tibi terra levis,* as a good idea, a pleasant cliché, without fixed doctrinal meaning and without a stereotyped formulation. In this, as in other respects, the Dura epigram is essentially Greek in spirit, not Roman, although there is much fusion in the third century of the Empire.

To the Greeks, on the other hand, though they might refer to the acceptance of the dead by Pluto and especially by Persephone, it was a familiar notion from the time of Homer down to think of individual souls welcoming, some time after their own demise, the individual souls of others. This conception is not common in the epitaphs, but occurs nevertheless.

[11] A fate to which βιοθάνατοι and ἀωροθάνατοι were especially liable, whether or not ἄταφοι (E. Rohde, *Psyche,* 8th ed., transl. W. B. Hillis, 1925, p. 533; Cumont, *After Life,* pp. 128–147; *L'Egypte des Astrologues,* 1937, pp. 199 f.; Nock, *Sallustius,* p. xcii). Soldiers were only with difficulty removed from this group (Cumont, *After Life,* p. 142; cf. however Virgil, *Aen. VI,* l. 660), and if Terentius had died in action (see below), his widow may have had reason to be concerned on this point.

In the Terentius text, it may be assumed that the θεαὶ ψυχαί were the individual spirits of the dead, "the company of the saints," who are to receive Julius Terentius into their number.

The present inscription was found in a private house in the center of Dura, not far from the area of the Roman camp. This is a reasonable place for Julius Terentius,[12] a married Roman officer, the tribune of an auxiliary cohort, to have had his residence, but it is a strange place to have found his epitaph, which, every indication suggests, had simply fallen from the epistyle above. No one would suggest, probably, that Terentius was buried in the house or his ashes deposited there under ordinary conditions, and it may be venturesome to admit the possibility at all. No grave, no body, was found in the house, although it was completely excavated down to bed rock. No niche was found in the court in which a funerary urn might have stood. In diwan H2, the entrance of which was close by the place where the fragments of the stone were lying, were features which might suggest some sort of cult center. The blocked-up doorway on the east presented more or less the appearance of an aedicula, and could have served for one, while the square base before it might have held an urn, an altar, or cult-object of some sort. Possibly the funerary urn had stood there, and the inscription had been set somewhere in the wall of the room. Conceivably the room may have contained a painted representation of Terentius, no trace of which was found. One thinks in this connection of the frescoes with banquet and hunting scenes of a funerary character found in a house near the desert wall of the city south of the Main Gate, and occupied by persons either Palmyrene or strongly under Palmyrene influence. The interpretation of these frescoes is difficult, and certainty has not been reached.[18] Nevertheless it is very likely that they were connected with the cult of the dead in some way, although there also no tomb was found, and, while house burial was a

[12] It is probably unnecessary to devote much space to a discussion of the names of Julius Terentius and his wife, Aurelia Arria. Under the Empire we have often occasion to remember the remark of Plutarch (Vita Marii, 1) on this subject: εἰς μὲν οὖν ταῦτα πολλὰς δίδωσιν ἐπιχειρήσεις ἡ τῆς συνηθείας ἀνωμαλία. No Arrii nor Terentii have occurred hitherto at Dura (note however the *Ter* in *Rep. VI*, p. 488, no. 719), and the tribune and his wife are outsiders, as is natural. Their second gentilicia had been adopted, according to the usual practice, in honor of the imperial family and certainly with its permission, Aurelia from Caracalla (or Heliogabalus, or Alexander), Julius from Maximinus (or Julia Domna).

[18] Published by C. Hopkins, *Rep. VI*, pp. 146–167; cf. Rostovtzeff, *Dura-Europos*, pp. 94 f.

regular Mesopotamian practice to which every excavation bears witness, it was as foreign to Palmyra as to Greece and Rome, and few burials within the city have as yet been found at Dura. On the contrary, every indication points to a regular burial outside the city in the large necropolis west of the city. In this necropolis with its *loculi* and its great tower tombs inscriptions occur only once, two names in a tomb left unfinished at the abandonment of the city. In the entire course of the excavations, which have laid bare roughly one-third of the area of the city, there have been found only four tombstones in addition to the present text, none of them in situ and none giving any indication of its original location. All of them belong to the last period of the city's existence. One is Greek, metrical, fragmentary, found in Street G outside room 39 in Block E4 (*Rep. VI*, p. 34, no. 611). Two are Latin and fragmentary, one re-used in the masonry of Tower 1 (Cumont, *Fouilles*, p. 359, no. 4), the other in the floor of Porch B of the Temple of Artemis (*Rep. VI*, pp. 413 f., no. 805). The fourth tombstone is substantially complete, and was found in the Main Gate. It also is Latin, the epitaph of a former centurion of the *Legio IIII Scythica* (*Rep. I*, p. 49, no. 4).

It is not quite clear what conclusion is to be drawn from these finds. Probably we must conclude, in any case, that while tomb inscriptions may have been used by the early Macedonian settlers, subsequently the practice was given up because of local indifference, and only revived with the arrival of the Roman army. Even then none of the five texts can be shown to refer to a citizen of Dura, and the two which can be identified are of Roman soldiers.

Was there, then, a military cemetery within the walls, from which four, at any rate, of the extant tombstones were plundered and scattered? If so, we have not found it, nor indeed can we well see where it may have been, and while stones may have been scattered after the fall of the city, it is hard to think of them as being carried off and used in buildings during the years of the Roman occupation. In the case of the monument of Terentius, at all events, there can be no question of spoliation. It is possible that the present stone was only a copy of the real tombstone, located elsewhere, or that for reasons unknown the monument was erected apart from the tomb.[14] Possibly the ashes of Terentius, and of course also of other Roman casualties in the fighting during the reigns of Alexander and Gordian III, may have rested in private houses tem-

[14] It is not easy to think of a cenotaph, in view of the verb θάψε. This need not involve inhumation or even deposit of ashes in a tomb, but certainly means that regular

porarily, or in what was expected to be a temporary way, because of conditions which made it impracticable to inter outside of the wall, or because it was planned eventually to remove them elsewhere. It is likely

funerary ceremonies took place. While the diwan may have constituted a heroon without a tomb, I cannot understand the epitaph apart from the grave.

In volume XXV of *The Harvard Theological Review* (1942), p. 81, Professor Martin P. Nilsson submits a note on this inscription, in which he tries to obviate this difficulty by two assumptions, one that the inscription is unfinished, and the other that it was never set into the epistyle. His argument for the first point is, that the red paint of the conclusion of the text was intended as a guide to the stone-cutter only; that all the letters had originally been so delineated, and that the cutter had proceeded thus far and then abandoned his work, for reasons unknown. I have tried to verify this on the original, with indeterminate results. The alabaster is heavily veined in rose and reddish brown, and traces suggesting paint are frequent, due entirely to this except in the final three letters of δέξασθαι. There, however, do occur traces unquestionably of paint, and it is possible to hold, though not to prove, that this was done throughout. Even if true, I do not see that this proves that the inscription was left unfinished, for in addition to the fact that the procedure is otherwise unknown to me at Dura, and is certainly uncommon elsewhere, rubrication is the order of the day, and a perfect parallel at Dura exists in a contemporary altar, a dedication to Jarhibol by the tribune Scrobonius Mucianus from Tower 1, the chapel tower of the Temple of Bel (*Rep. II*, p. 90, no. H3). The last line and some other letters are painted in red only, whereas the remaining text is both inscribed and rubricated. In the case of the present text, there were good reasons why the stone-cutter did not cut further. The lower part of the alabaster is full of cracks and blemishes, and further cutting would have been dangerous.

As to the other theory, that is entirely gratuitous and without foundation. Numerous instances show that the practice of letting stone slabs into plaster walls was normal in the city, and the discovery of a broken stone, with traces of plaster on the back, in the ruins of a fallen epistyle offers archaeological evidence of its original location which cannot lightly be rejected. Where the burial was, cannot be determined. It seems not to have been in the house, unless it was by way of an urn subsequently removed. On the other hand, burials within the city are not as unexampled as was implied in the original publication of this text, although the instances are too few to suggest a regular practice. Dr. N. P. Toll, who prepares a report on the Necropolis which will appear in a later part of this *Report*, gives me the following instances: (1) a double grave, possibly of females, in the House of Lysias in D1, partly under a first century house wall; (2) four burials cut through the plaster floor of a house in X7, 1, probably made after the abandonment of the town; (3) a small necropolis of twelve burials in the northwest corner of the Citadel, made at the time this was no longer considered to be a part of the city; (4) a Babylonian type burial in Tower 10, the pentagonal tower of the south wall, datable in the Second Century B.C.; (5) a rudimentary slipper coffin burial, of Hellenistic date, near the so-called Tower 4 of the north wall; (6) two soldier burials in the ramp along the west wall, one south of Tower 1, the other by Block L7. These are in part burials of necessity, in part burials in unused or remote parts of the city. None argues for the practice of house interment at Dura.

that many of the members of the Dura garrison planned not to remain permanently in the city, although there was in this period a tendency for the troops to take local root,[15] and the units of the garrison had been stationed in the city more than forty-five years at the time of the final Persian siege.[16] All is speculation.

Julius Terentius is a well-known figure at Dura. He it is who is represented sacrificing in the presence of his staff to a Palmyrene trinity of gods[17] on the east wall of the *pronaos* of the Temple of Bel. Below are represented the Tychae of Dura and of Palmyra. His name is written at the left of his head:[18] *Jul(ius) Terentius trib(unus)*.[19] Very possibly the scene is to be connected with one of the cohort's military enterprises, *vota suscepta* before an engagement or *vota soluta* subsequently. This would be an explanation of the presence of the two civic Tychae. The one city was itself threatened in the case of a Persian attack, while the other was endangered in the person of its citizens, the soldiers of the cohort. As it is now known that Terentius failed to return on one occasion, a terminus ante quem is furnished by that campaign or engagement.

It is possible, with reasonable certainty, to establish the approximate date of this event. Among the records of the *Cohors XX Palmyrenorum* found in the Temple of Azzanathkona in 1931–32 were two extensive fragments of the official journal, of the *acta diurna*.[20] The earlier of these (*DP* 3) belongs to the time of Alexander, and the *signum* is given and other instructions issued, as would be expected, by the tribune, Julius Rufianus. In the later (*DP* 9+14), however, which belongs to the year of Gordian's first consulship (A.D. 239), the same office is performed by a legionary centurion, the *praepositus cohortis* Avitus. This was clearly a special situation, due to the temporary absence of a tribune. In view of the fact that there is other evidence to connect Terentius with

[15] Rostovtzeff, *Gesellschaft und Wirtschaft im römischen Kaiserreich* (1931), II, pp. 137–141.

[16] For the units of the garrison cf. Rostovtzeff, *Dura-Europos*, pp. 24–26; *Rep. VII–VIII*, pp. 86 f.

[17] For their identification cf. most recently H. Seyrig, *Syria*, XIII (1932), pp. 190–195; C. Hopkins, *Rep. VII–VIII*, pp. 365–367.

[18] Cumont, *Fouilles*, pp. 89–114, Pls. XLIX–LI; Rostovtzeff, *Dura-Europos*, pp. 71–74.

[19] Cumont, *Fouilles*, p. 363, no. 8a.

[20] Cf. Rostovtzeff, "Papyri und Altertumswissenschaft" (*Münchener Beiträge zur Papyrusforschung und antiken Rechtsgeschichte*, XIX, 1934, pp. 367–370); *Rep. V*, pp. 296 f., 299.

the cohort at just this time, there is no objection to supposing that the absence was caused by his death.

This evidence is furnished by the fresco in the Temple of Bel. In offering sacrifice, Terentius is accompanied by a considerable number of persons (at least twenty), the relative importance of whom is indicated by their size in relation to the tribune, and by their relative nearness to him. It is unfortunate that names and designations have been regularly omitted, for uniforms and equipment vary somewhat, and we might otherwise have derived some information on such matters as insignia of rank. There is, however, one exception. The figure standing immediately to the rear of Terentius, and a little to his left, is designated as follows: Θέμης Μοκίμο[υ] ἱερεύς.[21] Concerning the names, Cumont has said all that is necessary. Both are Palmyrene, both occur otherwise at Dura.[22] Cumont drew the correct conclusion that Themes son of Mocimus held an official position in the cohort, and confirmation comes through the second of the two *acta diurna* just mentioned (*DP* 9 + 14). Column II of that fragmentary and difficult text begins with the statement by the *ord(inatus) princeps* of the Order of the Day, to which obedience is sworn (if that is the correct interpretation of the obscure passage) by him and by his staff. Among the latter Mr. J. F. Gilliam noted the name *Themes Mocimi,* and before it the letters *DOS;* that is to say, *sacer]dos.* In line 9 of the same column occurs also *]R Themes Mocimi,* in the same transaction on a later day, preceded however by a lacuna, but on a little scrap from column I, Mr. R. O. Fink discovered the confirmation: *sacer(dos) Them[es.* In both cases the *bucinator* preceding is named Priscus, so there can be no doubt of the identity of the two *sacerdotes.*

Mr. Fink gives us the following comparative statistics for the cohort as between *DP* 3 and *DP* 9 + 14. In the earlier of the *acta diurna* the strength was as follows: *pedites* 914, including 9 *ordinati,* 8 *duplicarii,* and 1 *sesquiplicarius; dromedarii* 34, including 1 *sesquiplicarius; equites* 223, including 5 *decuriones,* 7 *duplicarii,* and 4 *sesquiplicarii.* In the later text the figures are: *pedites* 781, including 6 *ordinati,* 8 *duplicarii,* and 1 *sesquiplicarius; dromedarii* 36+, figure for the *im-*

[21] Cumont, *Fouilles,* p. 363, no. 8b; cf. *ibid.,* p. 113.

[22] Especially Moqimu, which is common. Taime occurs more properly spelled (Θαίμη) on a fragment of painted wall from the Temple of the Gaddé (*Rep. VII–VIII,* p. 283, no. 913b), and with the spelling Θαῖμος in the southwest tower of the Main Gate (*Rep. V,* p. 23, no. 394).

*munes* missing; *equites* 138 (or possibly 238, or 134–234, it being not quite certain whether to read VIII or IIII), including 4 *decuriones*, 6 *duplicarii*, and 2 *sesquiplicarii*. The contrast is marked, especially with the *pedites* and *ordinati*. Battle losses furnish one, though of course only one of several possible explanations of the loss in strength of the unit during the intervening decade.

Little is known of the political and military situation of the Euphrates frontier between the campaign of Alexander Severus against the Persians, which came to its somewhat ambiguous conclusion in A.D. 233, and the beginning of Gordian's campaign ten years later.

In A.D. 238, either still during the reign of Maximinus or in the confusion immediately preceding and following his death, peace was interrupted by offensive operations of the Persians, led by Ardashir or by his son and later successor, Shapor. Nisibis and Carrhae were taken in the North; later Antioch itself was threatened. Our few sources add nothing more, but a Dura graffito shows that the Euphrates line was endangered also. A tangled mass of scratches from the House of Nebuchelus,[23] a leading Dura merchant who had become Aurelius Nebuchelus through the Constitutio Antoniniana twenty-five years before, yielded clearly the enigmatic remark: Ἔτους νφ′ μηνὸς Ξανδικοῦ λ′ κατέβη ἐφ᾽ ὑμῶν Πέρσης. In the middle of April, then, in A.D. 239, the Persian descended upon Dura, and this or another "descent" of the same period may plausibly be connected with the death of Julius Terentius.

### C. Block G5

### 1. House C

### a. Diwan C2

### 940. Dipinto. (Appendix II, pp. 203–265.)

---

[23] *Rep. VII–VIII*, pp. 172 f., no. 876; cf. p. 179.

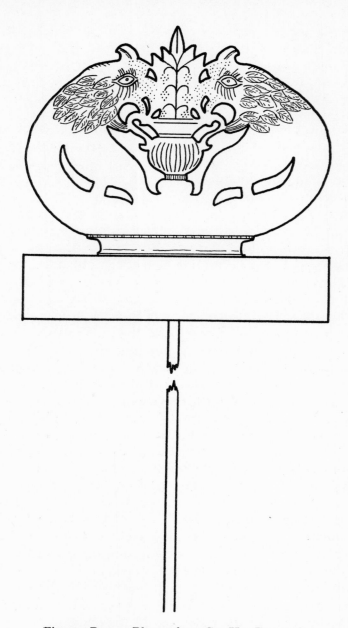

Fig. 91. Bronze Plaque from G3, H4. Restored

# APPENDIX I

## BRONZE PLAQUE FROM G3, H4

THE bronze object found in room H4 is unique in size, shape, and stylistic character. In view of its connection with far-reaching developments of Roman provincial art, it deserves special discussion, though, at the present stage of our knowledge, it may not be possible to answer all the implied questions conclusively.[1]

The object (Pl. XXII, 1, 2) is a thin slab of cast bronze (thickness 2.5–3.5 mm.). Its greatest width is approximately one Roman foot (0.29 m.). The preserved height is 0.206 m. But, inasmuch as the upper center is broken away and as a decorative element might have, and probably did, project upward at this point, the original height was probably somewhat greater. A base-like member with two projecting moldings above and below a narrow frieze supports an open-work bronze slab. This base and the upper part are cast in one piece; the profiles turn around to the short sides (the left lower edge is now deformed by corrosion). The upper molding of the base is decorated by a rhythmical pattern of convex and concave curves. The oval open-work slab has cast and sketchily incised details, which only indicate certain features, i.e., those whose imitative character the craftsman still understood. These details are: the articulation and striated decoration of the central vase, the feather-like hair on the griffins' heads, and the stems with dotted grapes which emerge from the vase in the upper center. The uppermost part of the slab is broken away, including the top of the left griffin's head, its ear, and part of the eye, together with the entire upper finial of the central vine. The back of the slab (Pl. XXII, 2) lacks any such detail. Clearly it was not intended to be seen. This is further indicated by the shape of the base, which projects (10 mm.) beyond the surface of the upper slab on the back as well as on the front, but is open at the back as it is below. The point of a triangular cutting in the center of the horizontal projection reaches the plane of the upper slab. Above this cutting and in the center of the rear face of the slab, even in the photograph, one observes traces of a vertical support which, evidently, passed through the cutting

---

[1] I am indebted to Professor Rostovtzeff for entrusting me with the publication of this piece and to him as well as to Professor Brown for valuable information.

in the center of the projecting base. These traces indicate that this support was a metal staff, the upper end of which was soldered on the back of the object. They also reveal the fact that this ending was of a definite form, i.e., a narrow spearhead or an elongated laurel leaf. A wire or string might have provided an additional means of fastening the object to the supporting staff.

The circumstances of the discovery throw no light on the purpose and use of the object. It is evident that it cannot have been merely part of the equipment of this modest house, but that it was stored here or transported to this place. With it on the earthen floor were found many pieces of carbonized wood and bronze nails which, as Professor Brown suggests, may have belonged to the door leading into the room, though some of them might also have been connected with our object. In addition, a wedge-shaped iron utensil was found rusted on our bronze slab. It has a length of 0.17 m. and, on its broad end, a small section with a ring-shaped perforated ending projects at an obtuse angle (0.05 m. high). This object may possibly have been part of the ensemble to which our bronze slab belonged. But it also might have been part of the lock of the door.[2] Under the circumstances, only the object itself and its formal analogies can possibly enable us to define its use.

Therefore, let us consider its general form. It is a broad oval with two curved lateral elements ending in griffins' heads turned toward the center. From the lower center a decorative unit emerges, composed of a crater from which a vine springs between the griffins' heads; the rhythm of the incised stems indicates an upper ending in the form of a palmette (Fig. 91). The basic form of this pattern is well known to us. Although its origin has apparently been forgotten here, it is the richly decorated "Amazon shield," the *pelta* which from the Augustan period on often had lateral endings with griffins' heads turned inward and flanking a central floral finial (Pl. XXIII, 1).

The origin of this form of crescent-shaped "shield" with two lateral and one central projection on the concave side is unknown.[3] There are

[2] See, e.g., British Museum, *Guide to the Antiquities of Roman Britain* (1922), pp. 44 f.

[3] See G. Hock, *Germania*, VI (1922), pp. 25 f.; J. Zingerle, *Österr. Jahresh.*, XXI–XXII (1924), pp. 229 f. The form differs distinctly from the vertical *ecu* with upper convex edge, with which it is confounded by P. Couissin, *Rev. arch.* (1923), 2, pp. 68 f. and *Les armes Romains* (1926), p. 500. Of course, the Greek term πέλτη mostly refers to the latter which is of Thracian origin (Lammert in *RE* s.v. *Pelta* and Ebert, *Reallexicon der Vorgeschichte*, XI, p. 257). In the following discussion, I shall use

reasons to believe that it was originally rooted in ancient Near Eastern
tradition, as we shall see, but rather as a symbol than as a piece of actual
armor.[4] It occurs from the early fourth century B.C. on in South Italian
and Etruscan representations of Amazons and other oriental warriors,
particularly Persians.[5] Later we find it suddenly in the same period in
three distant regions of the ancient world: in the third and second centuries B.C. as an actual shield used by unidentifiable, but very likely
mythological, warriors, and in decorative funeral symbolism on Etruscan urns;[6] in a heraldic motive of two such forms in the bronze decoration of a La-Tène shield in Great Britain;[7] and around the mid-second
century B.C., among the barbarian spoils in the armor frieze on the
Propylon of the Bouleuterion at Miletus.[8] This strange phenomenon of
regional distribution of the earliest occurrences could best be explained
by assuming that, by this time, the Celtic tribes from Asia Minor to
Great Britain had adopted the *pelta* as a symbol. Thus it could be regarded as a motive characteristic of barbarian armor, though actually
such shields were never worn by Gaulish warriors.[9] This theory would
also account for the immense popularity of the *pelta* motive in provincial

the term in the more limited sense employed for the late Greek and Roman Amazon
shield.

[4] See below, pp. 198 f.

[5] See, in general, M. Greger, *Schildformen und Schildschmuck bei den Griechen*,
Diss. Erlangen (1908), pp. 28 f. Examples, early fourth century B.C.: P. V. C. Baur,
*Cat. of the R. Darlington Stoddard Collection of Greek and Italian Vases in Yale
University* (1922), pp. 189 f., no. 323, Pl. 16; Furtwängler-Reichhold, *Griechische
Vasenmalerei*, III, p. 345, Fig. 164. Later fourth century: painted sarcophagus in
Florence, Giglioli, *L'Arte Etrusca* (1935), Pl. 238, with bibl.; *Mon. dell'Ist.*, II, Pl.
30; *ibid.*, X, Pl. 28; Persae vase, *ibid.*, IX, Pl. 52; *Annali* (1873), Pls. B–C; Furt-
wängler-Reichhold, *op. cit.*, II, pp. 143 f., Figs. 46, 47; compare, also, *ibid.*, p. 161,
Fig. 53 and Persians, *ibid.*, pp. 150 f., Figs. 49, 51.

[6] Brunn-Körte, *I rilievi delle urne Etrusche*, III, p. 212, Fig. 53; p. 230, Fig. 57;
Pls. 110; 112; 127, 9; 146; 148; Hock, *op. cit.*, p. 26, n. 7.

[7] W. J. Hemp, *Archaeologia Cambrensis*, LXXXIII (1928), Pt. 2, pp. 253 f.; Ken-
drick, *Archaeology in England and Wales*, 1914–1931 (1932), p. 186, Fig. 72.

[8] *Milet*, II, Pl. 15; Couissin, l.c.; Hock, l.c.; Löwy, *Jahrb. d. kunsthistor. Samm-
lungen Wien*, N.F. (1928), p. 7. One might also include among the early occurrences,
the *pelta* on the entablature of the palace of Lycomedes in the famous Pompeian painting of Achilles in Scyrus, i.e., in the better copy from the house of the Dioscuri (see,
L. Curtius, *Wandmalerei Pompejis*, 1929, pp. 206 f., Fig. 124), which almost certainly reproduces a Hellenistic original of the second century B.C. See below, note 44.

[9] Hock, *op. cit.*; Couissin, *op. cit.*; also P. Bienkowski, *Les Celtes dans les arts
mineurs* (1928), index s.v. *bouclier* (brought to my attention by Professor Rostovtzeff).

Roman art[10] of the Celtic regions as well as for the common use of the *pelta* shield as a piece of barbarian armor in the numerous Roman armor still-life reliefs in which Gaulish or allegedly Gaulish paraphernalia is very common.[11] Beginning with the Augustan period, however, the *pelta* motive occurs, predominantly in the western Roman Empire, in other connections, too: as a symbolic-decorative form in the group of marble *oscilla* with religious relief representations in Italy and Gaul[12] and as a decorative motive in mosaic patterns.[13] As part of such a decorative system of Roman provincial art, the *pelta* motive also occurs in Dura on the painted slabs from the House of the large Atrium.[14]

The overwhelming majority of examples of the decorative use of the *pelta* motive come from Great Britain, Gaul, the Rhineland and the upper Danube. Obviously, the rhythm of curved lines inherent in this form appealed particularly to the taste of the Celto-Roman provinces. The variety with animal heads turned inward and, as a rule, a floral element in the center occurs first and exclusively in the West in the early imperial group of *oscilla* from Italy and Gaul.[15] This type became extremely popular in the Celtic provinces during the second and third centuries A.D. Here, it generally occurs as an ornamental handle of the inscribed tablets on building inscriptions and funeral monuments. This class of *pelta*-shaped handles with in-turned griffins' heads has been discussed by J. Zingerle in a brilliant paper, which deals with a remarkable piece found in Vienna (Pl. XXIII, 2).[16] He has pointed out the particularly Celtic character of these provincial Roman pieces which occur in Gaul and all along the frontier from Great Britain to Austria.

[10] Zingerle, *op. cit.*

[11] Couissin, *op. cit.*; Crous, *Röm. Mitt.*, XLVIII (1933), pp. 91 f.

[12] M. Albert, *Rev. arch.* (1881), 2, pp. 92 f., 129 f., 173 f., 193 f.; Lippold, *Jahrbuch*, XXXVI (1921), pp. 35 f., n. 82.

[13] Not uncommon in Italy, most popular in Gaul, rare in North Africa and the East; see *Inventaire des mosaïques*, passim; Blake, *Memoirs Am. Ac. Rome*, VIII (1930), p. 104, Pls. passim; *ibid.*, XIII (1936), Pls. passim; Winter-Pernice, *Hellenistische Kunst in Pompeji*, VI, p. 135. For an example from the East: *Milet*, I, Pt. 7, Pl. 8.

[14] P. V. C. Baur, *Rep. IV*, pp. 44 f., Pl. VI, 1. Mr. Baur does not discuss its connection with Roman use of the *pelta* motive. Particularly closely related are: *Inventaire des mosaïques*, Gaule, n. 45; Blake, *op. cit.*, VIII, Pl. 43, 2; XIII, Pl. 19, 4. I am not so sure that the Chinese example of the Han dynasty, to which Baur refers, is related to the *pelta* motive in more than a general similarity of some curved lines of the pattern.

[15] See above, note 12.

[16] *Op. cit.*, with bibliography; add, Crous, *op. cit.*, type 55.

And he has also eloquently discussed the interesting transformations of the motive tending toward a disintegration of its solid structure,[17] and a perforation in the sense of open metalwork which, as is well known, was an outstanding feature of La-Tène and succeeding Celtic-Roman art.[18] Zingerle, indeed, has already proved that a number of the *ansae* of these northern provincial tablets are clearly stone imitations of metal originals. In addition to the evidence which he pointed out, a sarcophagus in York (Pl. XXIII, 3)[19] shows this connection particularly clearly. It is quite possible that the use of the *pelta* motive in open metal work originated in England where we already find a similar application of it in shield buckles of the La-Tène period,[20] and that it made its way thence to France, the Rhine, and the Danube along with the British military detachments of the first and second centuries A.D.[21] The adaptation of the *pelta* with in-turned griffins' heads to the metal *tabula ansata* is quite natural, inasmuch as bronze *tabulae ansatae* were common in the Roman Empire and especially in Gaul.

Thus, the basic *pelta* form with in-turned griffins' heads of the bronze object from Dura is rooted in metalwork and ornamentation of the Celtic-Roman art which flourished along the northern frontiers of the empire from the late first to the early third centuries A.D. This art crystallized in manufacturing centers in the hinterland of the various *limites*. We know such a center, for instance, in Baden in Switzerland which produced armor with open metalwork decoration for exportation to the entire frontier from the lower Rhine to Austria.[22] Many objects of this kind are known from all over this region: pieces of armor for both men and horses, personal ornament of various kinds, and appliqués for utensils and furniture. They show a mixture of classical elements with the curved, whirling rhythms of post-La-Tène Celtic art. Objects derived from this open metalwork art are common among the personal ornaments of military use from the small finds in Dura. The

[17] See also J. v. Schlosser, *Mitt. f. österr. Geschichtsforschung,* Erg. Bd. 6, pp. 760 f. = *Präludien* (1927), pp. 180 f.

[18] *Op. cit.,* p. 246; see also, Hock, *op. cit.,* p. 27.

[19] *Eph. epigr.,* III (1877), p. 313, n. 183; G. Home, *Roman York* (1924), p. 147.

[20] See above, n. 7.

[21] F. Drexel (*Germania,* VI, 1922, pp. 31 f.) has demonstrated that the particular form of the *pelta*-handle with in-turned griffins' heads which occurs in some of the Rhineland camps in the second century A.D. was imported from Great Britain by military detachments.

[22] F. Stähelin, *Die Schweiz in römischer Zeit,* 2nd ed. (1931), pp. 414 f., note 5.

background of this craft, at once unclassical and unoriental, is evident in the bronze slab with its swinging, recurrent and, at the same time, clearly accentuated and centered curves, aside from its previously discussed tangible connections with the in-turned griffins' heads *pelta*. But the bronze slab from Dura is definitely not a product of that well established and refined artistic style. It is somewhat crude and heavy in contrast to the easy play of its Celtic-Roman models. Fortunately, by a happy coincidence, we are able to point out the road along which this superprovincial reflection of a provincial style took place.

We have mentioned above the fact that the craftsman who made this object evidently did not understand the exact meaning of all its elements: he limited his incised details to the griffins' heads, the vase, and the vine emerging from it. But he definitely did not understand the original character of the two antithetic elements which fill the space beneath the griffins' heads between the outer curves and the central vase. The silhouette of these elements nevertheless clearly indicates what they are: two birds which flank the central vase with their backs and tails toward it. In the original version, their heads were certainly turned backward toward the center, in a well-known variety of an old decorative motive.[23] Here, however, the heads of the birds have disappeared, swallowed up by the griffins' heads, and only their bodies, tails, and reduced stumps of their feet remain as a crude ornamental silhouette merged with the linear patterns of the outer frame. Ultimately, thus, the pattern is based on a model in which the *pelta* with in-turned griffins' heads was combined with a substitute for the usual central scroll or floral projection (Pl. XXIII, 1), the substitute being the well-known decorative motive of the vase flanked by two birds. The long and eventful history[24] of this motive deserves special discussion which cannot be given here: ultimately, it was of oriental origin. It spread through the Roman Empire, particularly in the west, whence it migrated back to its

[23] Mr. Toll of the Art Gallery of Yale University has suggested that the basic form of the Dura bronze may be related to the type of "parrots" flanking a vase which is not uncommon on later textiles from Egypt. I can, however, see no specific analogy to any of the textile examples known to me, while the general shape of the object as well as the animals' heads occur in numerous instances in the class of objects quoted above. The late textile motives, of course, are ultimately derived from the same heraldic group of vase and birds which occurs, very early, in Mesopotamia.

[24] The motive of the birds and the vase also occurs in Dura in another context and on a different background in the frieze of Orthonobazos: Cumont, *Fouilles,* p. 68, Pl. LXXXVI, 1 and pp. 226 ff.

land of origin, in this case, in a crude and misunderstood, abstract, linear transformation,—a strange, but by no means insignificant process of historical reversal.

The motive of the antithetic animals flanking a vase was very popular, too, in the Celtic-Roman west, where it was used in the first and second centuries A.D. not only for the crowning groups of funeral monuments[25] but also in the open metalwork appliqués of architectural friezes (Pl. XXIII, 4).[26] Generally, the animals are griffins and this fact may have led even more easily to the combination of the motive of animals flanking a vase with the griffins' heads *pelta* which was so popular in that region. On the other hand, antithetic birds occur on the arch of Orange[27] in shield decoration imitating Celtic metalwork and, also in the same circle, as decoration of *ansae* of inscribed tablets.[28] Fortunately, we possess a monument which demonstrates this fusion of two heterogeneous motives in the eastern part of that Celto-Roman realm, on the Danube. This is a bronze appliqué (Pl. XXIV, 1)[29] for a piece of furniture, a typical product of the Celto-Roman metalwork industry. In its upper section, it shows the *pelta* with griffins' heads endings included in and obscured by the curving scroll work of post-La-Tène ornamentation but, nevertheless, clearly distinguishable. These endings, with their feather-like incisions, are intimately related to the griffins' heads of the Dura slab. But, in addition to this strikingly close formal relationship, the appliqué from Lauriacum combines the motive of the two birds flanking a crater with the in-turned griffins' heads *pelta*. In this case, however—the object may be two to three generations earlier than the Dura slab—the connection is still less intimate. The vase flanked by birds is simply added to the top of the *pelta* though it is brilliantly related to the general pattern by that exquisite linear rhythm peculiar to these artefacts. The next step which apparently was made by a direct forerunner of the Dura slab was to supplant the central floral motive of the *pelta*, still present in the appliqué, by the vase with flanking birds, so that the central floral finial of the *pelta* was now interpreted—as it

[25] *Germania Romana,* 2nd ed., 3, Pls. 21, 4 and 25, 1; Stähelin, *op. cit.,* p. 431, Fig. 110.

[26] *Ibid.,* p. 433, Fig. 112.

[27] Esperandieu, *Recueil des bas-reliefs de la Gaule Romaine,* I, p. 199, left.

[28] *Ibid.,* XI, p. 193, n. 312 (from Obernburg, the site of an outstanding example of the *tabula ansata* with *pelta*-handle and in-turned griffins' heads; Hoch, *op. cit.*).

[29] A. Schober, *Die Römerzeit in Oesterreich* (1935), pp. 95 f. (with incorrect description), Fig. 69. Dated about 200 A.D.

still is on our piece (Fig. 91)—as flowers emerging from the crater. This ingenious combination is the necessary link between the pattern of the appliqué from Lauriacum and that of the Dura bronze.

Professor Rostovtzeff has called my attention to a bronze handle from Colonia Traiana (Xanten) which he allows me to reproduce here (Pl. XXIV, 2).[80] It offers, indeed, a striking analogy to the phenomenon of migration, transformation, and fusion which has just been traced. In this case, the basic, originally Near Eastern, motive of the Lady of the animals forms the background. Already in archaic Greek art, similar motives had been used in combination with a crowning palmette for the decoration of handles (Pl. XXIV, 3).[81] At an early period, forms of this kind passed from Magna Graecia, where they were most popular in bronze vases,[82] via Etruria, to the La-Tène art of Gaul and western Germany.[83] The handle from Xanten, which probably belongs to the second century A.D., shows two birds above the flanking lions. Originally they may have belonged to the goddess; but the griffins' heads which emerge, turned inward, from the necks of the birds were undoubtedly inspired by the familiar *pelta* motive: in fact, this combination with swans' heads relates this piece intimately to the *ansa* from Vienna (Pl. XXIII, 2) which is so typical of this kind of Celto-Roman fusion.

Where the similarly intimate combination of two originally heterogeneous decorative motives which is in the background of our monument was made, we cannot say. It served as the model of the Dura slab whose artist no longer understood its context: the birds were denaturalized and swallowed up by a purely abstract linear pattern. This might have

---

[80] Bonn, Provinzial Museum, inv. no. 8673. I am indebted to Professor Rostovtzeff for the right interpretation of the elements of this curious object, too. Similar handles of Gallo-Roman manufacture showing the bust of Cybele between two lions and two busts of Attis on pine cones are known from France: Babelon-Blanchet, *Bronzes de la Bibliothèque Nationale* (1895), p. 585, no. 1456, with bibliography.

[81] Upper part of mirror handle, Athens, Nat. Mus., inv. no. 6577. Phot. Deutsches archaeologisches Institut, N.M. 2750 (published here, Pl. XXIV, 3 with permission granted by the Institute in 1930). From the Acropolis: A. de Ridder, *Catalogue de bronzes trouvés sur l'Acropole* (*Bibl. Ec. franc.*, vol. 64) (1896), p. 259, no. 722, Fig. 234; Stais, *Marbres et bronzes*, I (1910), p. 275. For the type, see also A. De Ridder, *Bronzes antiques du Louvre*, II (1915), Pl. 96, no. 2646, pp. 106 f., with bibliography (bust!), and nos. 2784 f., with bibliography.

[82] K. A. Neugebauer, *Röm. Mitt.*, XXXVIII–IX (1923–24), pp. 341 f.; *idem*, *Jahrb. Arch. Anz.* (1925), pp. 178 f.

[83] P. Jacobsthal and A. Langsdorff, *Die Bronzeschnabelkannen* (1929), passim; see my review in *Deutsche Literaturzeitung* (1931), pp. 1850 f.

happened anywhere on the long military roads to the east. However, this particular combination of heterogeneous animal forms lacks the Celto-Roman sense of rational order and, on the other hand, does not reflect the wild imaginative curves and phantasms of distorted animals characteristic of the "Scythian animal style." Most probably, therefore, this final transformation took place in the Thracian regions of the lower Danube, where the Celto-Roman provincial style was the dominating influence in sculpture as well as in open metalwork.[34]

Thus, the formal motive of the bronze slab from Dura is the result of a long and complicated process. Its basic ornamental forms, the *pelta* and the vase with flanking animals, are Near-Eastern in origin. But, in the Hellenistic world, these motives spread toward the west. In the Roman period, they were developed and fused in the Celto-Roman art of the northern frontier, hence, reimported to the Near East along the military roads of the empire.[35] But this formal migration and transformation of decorative motives is not the only interesting feature of this strange object. What was its function?

In view of its formal relationship to the *pelta*-handles of the Celto-Roman provinces, it would be natural to consider the Dura slab as an *ansa* of a bronze *tabula*. Its size, silhouette, and ornamental background, as well as its material are compatible with such an explanation. In fact, when Professor Rostovtzeff first showed the object to me, I advanced this theory. However, on the basis of close inspection, there are several reasons to reject it. First of all, the compact and closed ornamental pattern offers no opening adapted in shape or size to the function of a handle, as is invariably the case even with the relief representations of such *pelta*-shaped *ansae* (Pl. XXIII, 1 and 3). In the latter case, whether or not the ends are in the shape of griffins' heads, they are usually free hooks and separated from the center so that they can either be grasped or used for attaching a string; otherwise the empty space between the outer curved parts and the central element allow the former to be used as a

---

[34] The *pelta* motive was common in open metalwork of the Danube and Balkan peninsula during the Roman period as a result of provincial expansion of the more refined Celto-Roman style: A. Riegl, *Spätrömische Kunstindustrie*, small ed. (1927), Pl. 15, n. 6; *Strena Buliciana* (1924), vignettes, particularly p. 8. For the spread of this type of metalwork to Thrace see also, e.g., the tomb of a soldier: *Bull. Inst. arch. Bulgare*, IV (1914), p. 282, Fig. 253.

[35] For other Celtic elements in the art of Dura, see Rostovtzeff, *Dura-Europos* (1938), p. 88.

handle. Our monument affords no such possibility. Secondly, if one were to assume that the *tabula* was not actually carried but used as a decorative feature, e.g., of a building inscription—a common use throughout the Empire—the projecting rear base and the lack of holes for fastening the *ansa* to a wall would obviously conflict with such a use. Thirdly, in the case of an *ansa,* the lateral frame of the inscribed tablet at its base should be at least as long as the largest diameter of the handle, while here we actually have a narrow base from which the broad object unfolds in a lateral expansion. Finally, the traces of a vertical supporting staff at the back as well as the position of the vase make it evident that the object was carried in a vertical position on the upper end of a staff-like backbone. All these facts force one to explain the object as an upper finial which was carried vertically on a shaft. This shaft, as has been said before, was topped with a metal finial in the shape of a spearhead, though its lower part may well have been of wood. These observations combined with the above discussed background of the object in the art of the military zone of the northern frontier suggest that it was used as the upper finial of a standard (Fig. 91).

Religious and military standards with metal finials were a common feature of the Roman Empire, but, ultimately, this type was derived from the ancient Near East. Apparently, a direct line of chronological development and geographical spread leads from the old Mesopotamian empires through the Achaemenid and Hellenistic monarchies to the military and religious standards of the Roman Empire, though the evidence for the Persian and Hellenistic realms is still scanty.[36] Many such standards of military or religious function, with metal finials of various

[36] For the history of standards in general, see A. J. Reinach, *Dictionnaire des Ant. Grecques et Romaines,* IV, pp. 1307 f.; Kubitschek, *R.E.* s.v. *signum.* Near East: Reinach, *op. cit.,* pp. 1307 f.; A. W. Jackson, *Journ. Am. Or. Soc.,* XX (1899), pp. 56 f. (Persia); F. Sarre, *Klio,* III (1903), pp. 333 f.; Ch. Renel, *Cultes militaires de Rome, Les Enseignes, Annales de l'université de Lyon,* n.s. II, fasc. 12 (1903), pp. 52 f.; Kubitschek, *op. cit.,* pp. 2327 f.; E. Unger, in Ebert, *Reallexicon der Vorgeschichte,* XII, pp. 377 f.; R. Dussaud, in Pope-Ackerman, *Survey of Persian Art,* I (1938), pp. 261 f., Pls. 40 f. (Luristan); Ph. Ackerman, *ibid.,* III (1939), pp. 2766 f. (brought to my attention by Miss Mary Crane). Hellenistic: Kubitschek, *op. cit.,* pp. 2329 f. Roman: A. v. Domaszewski, *Die Fahnen im römischen Heere (Abh. Arch. ep. Seminar,* Wien, 5) (1885) and *idem, Westdeutsche Zeitschrift,* XIV (1895), pp. 1 f.; Ch. Renel, *op. cit.;* Reinach, *op. cit.;* K. Ritterling, *Bonner Jahrbücher,* CXXV (1917), pp. 9 f.; Kubitschek, *op. cit.,* pp. 2331 f.; W. Zwikker, *Berichte der Römisch-Germanischen Kommission,* XXVII (1937), pp. 17 f.

shapes, were in general use during the Roman Imperial age. Examples of the common type of military standards which were carried back to their land of origin by detachments of the Roman army as well as religious standards which directly perpetuated the old native types despite the occasional presence of influences from Roman military forms are known, too, from representations in Dura.[37] But actual pieces are rare and most of them have been found on the northern frontiers. They are either of iron covered with bronze or precious metal additions or of bronze, and often they show simple or elaborate patterns of open metalwork.[38] A particularly rich finial of open bronze work, from the Balkan peninsula, is now in the Artillery Museum in Paris (Pl. XXIV, 4).[39] In its combination of open work of ornamental and symbolical character with applied statuettes of protective divinities—compatible with military as well as with religious use—it exceeds the Dura standard. But in its top decoration of a crater flanked by two lions, it offers an interesting parallelism to the motive of the vase with flanking animals on our piece, or rather on its model. If, thus, we are able to relate the material, technique, general type, and even one specific motive of our bronze object to standard finials of the Roman imperial age, the problem arises of how and why the *pelta* with in-turned griffins' heads was adapted to this use. From our former analysis, it results that this very likely happened in the Danube region of Pannonia, Moesia, or Thrace. In view of the fact that small "shields," mostly of oval form, were commonly used on the upper ends of Roman military standards,[40] it would be natural for the decorative form of the *pelta* to be introduced in this place too. And in

[37] Cumont, *Fouilles*, pp. 95 f., 110 f., Pls. 50–51; *idem, Rep. I*, pp. 68 f., Pls. 4 f.; Baur, *Rep. III*, pp. 120 f., Pls. 14 and 19, 1. See also A. S. Hoey, *Transact. Am. Phil. Assoc.*, LXX (1939), pp. 459 f.

[38] For these types, see especially the brilliant paper on the badges of the *beneficiarii* by Ritterling (quoted in note 36).

[39] Le Bas-Reinach, *Voyage archéologique*, Pl. 109; A. Demmin, *Die Kriegswaffen*, 4th ed. (1893), p. 281, no. 80 (with wrong provenance—Asia Minor). It surely comes from Greece, but the Athenian provenance is not certain. Interpreted by Demmin as a military, by Ritterling, *op. cit.*, p. 31, as a religious standard. Another openwork bronze finial (which, of course, is not "Coptic" but Roman, from Edfu), also shows a combination of open circles with heraldically arranged animals, in this case dolphins and hares (?) (J. Strzygowski, *Koptische Kunst*, p. 301, n. 9165). The relationship of the two open circles to the badges of the *beneficiarii* in these instances indicates a military rather than a religious use. In Dura, two smaller "eyes" of this kind occur in the finial of the *vexillum* on side A of the Altar of Tyche (*Rep. I*, Pls. 4–5).

[40] v. Domaszewski, *op. cit.*, passim.

fact, we have documentary evidence for this use in one of the reliefs of Trajan's column (Pl. XXV, 1) where a *pelta* appears in exactly this place.[41] Our bronze finial from Dura which certainly is considerably, probably at least a century, later and in turn based on a misunderstood prototype proves that the *pelta*-finial was a common and widespread form. Therefore it is hardly legitimate to explain it simply as a decorative variety of the normal shield.[42]

This consideration leads us back to the problem of the origin and

[41] Froehner, *Colonne Traiane*, Pl. 135; v. Domaszewski, *op. cit.*, p. 62, Fig. 75; K. Lehmann-Hartleben, *Reliefs der Trajanssäule*, 1926, Pl. 49. Here from my original photo.

[42] I am inclined to assume a military rather than a non-military use for the Dura standard. But it is impossible to decide this question definitely inasmuch as the circumstances of the discovery fail to indicate any specific use. Professor Rostovtzeff has raised several objections against the use of the finial as a standard top, particularly of a military standard. These objections are: (1) The weight of the finial which might seem too heavy. However, the various other metal finials known are hardly less weighty, particularly the bronze finial in Paris (Pl. XXIV, 4). The iron finials discussed by Ritterling, *op. cit.*, when complete, must have been quite heavy. The only piece for which we possess an accurate indication of the weight is the finial in Wiesbaden, which weighs 5½ German pounds = 2750 grams (Ritterling, *op. cit.*). The Dura finial weighs 1048.95 g., to which the spearhead behind should be added. In Roman historical reliefs the standard bearers generally seem to carry a very heavy weight vertically and with both hands. For the heavy weight of the signa, see Ritterling, *op. cit.*, p. 35. (2) The "tactical" *signa* should be visible from the back too and therefore the decoration should not be limited to the front, as is the case of the object from Dura. This objection would, of course, refer only to its use as the finial of a military, not a religious standard and it applies also to the standard finial (Pl. XXIV, 4), the military use of which is equally doubtful. From the description of the badges of the *beneficiarii* (Ritterling, *op. cit.*), it seems that their metal sheet decorations were limited to the front. There is no indication that the finial elements as well as the *phalerae*, etc., of Roman standards were ever duplicated at the rear, while it is always evident that shaft and spearhead pass behind the symbolical decoration of both of them. The imaginifer from Weissenau (last, Zwikker, *op. cit.*, Pl. 2, Fig. 2) shows the image limited to the front. The cloth of the *vexilla* invariably hung in front of the shaft, and whatever decoration it had (see, e.g., the bull's head, *Bonner Jahrb.*, CXVII, pp. 279 f. and the common shields on *vexilla* of Trajan's column and of the base of Diocletian, Domaszewski, *Westd. Ztschr.*, l.c. Pl. 5, Fig. 6) hardly extended to the back, where it would have been overlapped by the pole. The eagles and the statuettes on top of Roman military standards always face forward and turn their backs to the detachments which follow them. The problem, of course, involves to what extent "tactical" standards were made for tactical uses. Their religious, symbolical, and apotropaic character which led to their decoration, was originally overwhelming and always continued. Their tactical value which was considerable during some periods may have been reduced to a very limited

meaning of the *pelta*-symbol. Its widespread, though infrequent, use in the Hellenistic age in which it actually occurs as a shield as well as a symbol proves its pre-Hellenistic origin. Indeed, the repertoire of ancient Near Eastern art includes a motive which is closely and uniquely related to the *pelta*-form while, on the other hand, it is connected with the sphere of standards and badges. Sarre has called attention to the decoration on the pole of Assyrian royal chariots and to its connection with the symbolism and use of standards which are occasionally tied to it.[43] In fact, the most elaborate of these pole decorations shows a metallic *pelta*-form posed on the same support of heraldic bulls' heads as is used to support the standard disks (Pl. XXV, 2). The motive survived on the chariots of Persian kings in the Achaemenid period,[44] and Sarre has already connected it with the standard symbols of the Persian chariot mentioned by Curtius Rufus.[45] Strangely enough, the inverted *pelta*, of exactly the old Assyrian and Persian form, appears many centuries later as the upper metal finial of the poles to which the horns of Roman military trumpeters are fastened on the column of Trajan (Pl. XXV, 3). Here it evidently is their badge. Rooted in an ancient Near Eastern

degree in the later Roman Empire, as it has practically disappeared in modern banners. Our knowledge of the extant varieties of Roman military standards is very limited. Chronologically, it is even less extensive for the third century than for the first and second. Materially, it nearly excludes the auxiliary detachments; and some varieties which according to epigraphical evidence existed do not appear in monuments (see Zwikker, *op. cit.*, particularly p. 15 and p. 20, n. 51). I therefore am unable to decide, e.g., whether the *vexillum* crowned by five eagles on the crossbar in a relief of the arch of Beneventum (last, Snijder, *Jahrb.* [1926], p. 119) is an artistic formula, as v. Domaszewski thought, or whether it existed in reality. As to the restoration of the Dura standard, it is obvious from the lower ending of the top that it was fastened on a horizontal crossbar of wood, the upper center of which projected to be inserted into the base. In the drawing, Fig. 91, I have assumed that this crossbar was the upper edge of a tablet of an otherwise known type. But it also could have been a simple bar with *taeniae* at the ends or the wooden bar to which the cloth of a *vexillum* was fastened.

[43] *Op. cit.*, p. 345. See Botta-Flandin, *Monuments de Niniveh*, I, Pls. 56 and 57 (= our Pl. XXV, 2); II, Pl. 158.

[44] Rawlinson, *Five Great Monarchies*, IV, p. 192; Pope, *op. cit.*, I, Pls. 92A and 93A. The use of the *pelta* on the façade of the palace of Lycomedes (above, note 8) may also be related to this royal badge.

[45] III, 3, 16. Sarre, p. 345, also refers to the occurrence of a similar decorative element adorned with a reclining lion on the chariot of Darius in the Alexander mosaic. The statement, which is repeated by Ph. Ackerman, *op. cit.*, p. 2768, and in both cases given without reference to its foundation, seems to be based on a mistake by Sarre or a drawing which misinterpreted the mosaic. At least I am unable to verify it.

tradition, it must have come down through intermediary Hellenistic usage. Thus we may assume that the *pelta*-form was similarly used in the Achaemenid empire. The fact that it was used on top of Persian standards decorated with or supporting the royal eagle (aside from the *vexillum* which, for example, appears on the Alexander mosaic) is evident from a passage in Xenophon which reads: καὶ τὸ βασίλειον σημεῖον ὁρᾶν ἔφασαν αἰετόν τινα χρυσοῦν ἐπὶ πέλτῃ ἐπὶ ξύλου ἀνατεταμένον (Anab. I, 10, 12). This statement is supplemented by a description of a painting by the Elder Philostratus, where the σημεῖον τὸ βασιλικὸν χρυσοῦς ἐπὶ τῆς πέλτης ἀετός is mentioned (*Imagg.* 2, 31) and it has been shown elsewhere that his descriptions are based on real visual experience of actual paintings.[46] The text tradition of Xenophon is uniform.[47] Nevertheless, since Cobet, the editors and commentators have almost unanimously cancelled ἐπὶ ξύλου as a gloss and translated πέλτῃ as "pole" or "shaft," in view of the fact that, in another passage, Xenophon mentions the royal eagle on top of a spear (*Cyropaed.*, VIII, 5, 13). Only occasionally have scholars protested against this high-handed method of eliminating part of a well-preserved and understandable passage; in doing so they introduced for πέλτη a meaning which is nowhere else documented though, on the basis of this one passage, it has been included in the dictionaries without a question mark.[48] The fact remains that πέλτη means everywhere a light shield and nothing else, and that according to Xenophon and Philostratus some royal standards of the Achaemenid period were in the form of a staff or spear terminating in a *pelta*-shield with the eagle applied to it or on top of it. The precise form of this "shield" cannot be determined from these passages. It may as well have been an *ecu* as a real *pelta*. But, in view of the evidence of the *pelta*-shaped symbol which I have submitted before, it most likely had that

[46] *Art Bulletin*, XXIII (1941), pp. 16 f. See Sarre, *op. cit.*, p. 345; Ackerman, *op. cit.*, p. 2768, n. 3 wrongly refers to the Younger Philostratus.

[47] With the exception that the *deteriores* give ἐπὶ πέλτης instead of ἐπὶ πέλτῃ.

[48] Vollbrecht, as far as I can see, was the only editor and commentator who tried to preserve the complete passage, though he read ἐπὶ ζύγου, which would make sense in view of the above discussed decoration of the chariot pole, but is not needed. M. Fickelscherer, *Neue Jahrbücher*, I (1898), pp. 480 f. (which has escaped Sarre and the other modern writers on Persian standards) protested against the interpretation of πέλτη as "pole," but he too regarded ἐπὶ ξύλου as an "antique" gloss and made a desperate effort to recognize a shield-like ensign in the *vexillum* of the Alexander mosaic. A. Reinach, *op. cit.*, n. 8, was more careful.

form. Such a use of a stylized "shield" form with one convex edge and two concave sections on the other side as part of the Royal Achaemenid standard would be compatible with all the available facts: the tradition of ancient writers; the use of the *pelta*-shaped ornament connected with badges on Assyrian and Persian chariots; the survival of the original reversed form as the finial of poles on the column of Trajan; the occurrence of the *pelta* as a standard finial; and finally the widespread decorative use of the *pelta* which hardly ever was an actual piece of armor, in Roman decorative art, its spread from Asia Minor to England and Italy in the Gaulish regions during the Hellenistic age, and its oriental connotation surviving in its use, already in the fourth century B.C., as a weapon of Persians as well as of Amazons.[49]

If this explanation seems acceptable, we may ask a final question: what is the original meaning of the symbol? The decoration on top of the oriental chariot pole (Pl. XXV, 4) has been called "crescent shaped";[50] in this case, connection with astral symbolism is, indeed, indicated both because of its relationship to the sun-disk shape of the accompanying standards and because of the fact that such disks may well appear in this very place too.[51] On the other hand, in the group of *oscilla* with religious representations mostly of bacchic character,[52] the two types of the *pelta* and the circular disk are also coupled, and it may well be that in such symbolic use they too reflect sun and moon. An original lunar symbolism for the *pelta* was suggested by Couissin.[53] In fact, Vergil (*Aen.*, I, 494) speaks of the Amazons as *"lunatis agmina peltis."* The simple crescent symbol is a very common motive on Roman shields. But the *pelta*, too, occurs in the same function.[54] Also there are cases in which the *pelta* itself is decorated with a crescent or with a bust of the moon-goddess.[55] Finally, the simple crescent-shaped moon symbol as a standard finial is an age-old oriental type which persisted down to the

[49] See above, p. 189 and note 5.        [50] Unger, *op. cit.*, p. 379.
[51] Botta-Flandin, *op. cit.*, Pl. 58.
[52] See above, note 12. Compare also the curious crescent symbol from Herculaneum: *Museo Borbonico*, XI, Pl. 43; *Chefs d'oeuvre d'art antiques* (1862), 2.
[53] *Op. cit.*, p. 401. He refers to the Halstatt moon symbols. Such a relationship would explain the popularity of the symbol in the Celtic regions, aside from its formal appreciation, as due to an ideological substratum.
[54] Lehmann-Hartleben, *Reliefs der Trajanssäule*, Pl. 21, XXXVIII, upper center, closely related to the motive of the painted slabs from Dura (above, note 14).
[55] Baur, *Rep. IV*, p. 45; Crous, *op. cit.*, Pl. 2, no. 54.

Roman period in religious use as well as in military standards. Such crescent-shaped standard finials are common in Dura too.[56]

The bronze object from Dura is the strange result of the movement of a cultural cycle. Its function as a standard finial, its basic symbolism, its decorative motives are ultimately based in old Near Eastern tradition. In all these respects, this tradition spread through Greece to the Roman Empire and its northern provinces. Here the old elements of various provenances were fused and finally confused in a semibarbaric art which developed along the *limites* of the empire from Britain to the lower Danube. And in this deranged and confused state, the old type returned once more, reshaped by influences from classical and Celto-Roman art, to its old land of origin. The importance of this unique object is not primarily due to its being a welcome addition to a rare class of monuments. It illustrates, in a unique way, a cyclic process of cultural and artistic development which can rarely be traced in objects of common form and use but which is nevertheless symptomatic.

[56] For the crescent finial see Unger, *op. cit.,* p. 377; Sarre, *op. cit.,* p. 359; Ackerman, *op. cit.;* Cumont, *Rep. I,* pp. 68 f., Pls. 4 f. (on sides D and C; in my opinion, also on A inasmuch as there was ample space for the representation of a crown if this had been intended); Baur, *Rep. III,* pp. 117 f., with rich material. Among reproductions of Roman military *signa,* those on the coins of Nicaea (v. Domaszewski, *op. cit.,* p. 49, n. 3, Fig. 52) show such a symbol and not a crown, and very likely two monuments which are only accessible in old sketchy drawings: *ibid.,* p. 38, Fig. 14, Fig. 26, both of the early imperial age. A relief vase from Iran in the Metropolitan Museum in New York (M. Dimand, *Bull. Metr. Mus.* (1931), pp. 7 f., Fig. 2; Ettinghausen, in Pope-Ackerman, *op. cit.,* I, pp. 678 f., Pl. 194) as Ettinghausen and Ackerman suggest (*ibid.,* p. 2769), shows a standard rather than a stylized tree. The strange lateral rings on the pole relate it to the crowns and *phalerae* at the shafts of Roman *signa.* I am indebted to Dr. Dimand for permission to examine the vase and for kind information. In spite of its crude workmanship, I am inclined to recognize in the crowning element a *pelta* rather than a crescent with a separate disk in the center: the upper central projection and the crescent are made in one piece, while the entire element and the small disks on the pole are separately attached. Unfortunately, this unique object is undated. Ettinghausen calls it "Late Sassanian or Early Islamic"; Dr. Dimand dates it on the basis of its reputed provenance in the tenth or eleventh century A.D. The metallic shape of the three-lobed mouth and the slightly oblique neck look strangely archaic for such late dates.

# APPENDIX II

## DIPINTI FROM G5, C2*

## ABBREVIATIONS

Cantineau, *Inventaire: Inventaire des Inscriptions de Palmyre,* fasc. I–IX, Damascus, 1930–1933.

*CIS: Corpus Inscriptionum Semiticarum,* Vol. II.

Friedländer: Ludwig Friedländer, *Darstellungen aus der Sittengeschichte Roms,* Leipzig, Vols. 1–3, 10th ed., 1922–1923; Vol. 4, 9th–10th ed., 1921.

Goetz: Georg Goetz, *Corpus Glossariorum Latinorum,* Teubner, 1888–1923.

Lane: *An Arabic-English Lexicon,* I, 1–8, London, 1863–1893.

Lidzbarski, *Ephemeris: Ephemeris für semitische Epigraphik.*

Mayser: Edwin Mayser, *Grammatik der griechischen Papyri aus der Ptolemäerzeit,* Leipzig, Vols. I.1–II.3, 1906–1934; Vol. I.2,3, 1936–1938.

*MUSJ: Mélanges de l'Université Saint Joseph.*

*PEFQS: Palestine Exploration Fund, Quarterly Statement.*

*PAAE: Publications of an American Archaeological Expedition to Syria in 1899–1900.*

*PUAE: Publications of the Princeton University Archaeological Expeditions to Syria in 1904–5 and 1909.*

Reich: Hermann Reich, *Der Mimus,* Berlin, 1903.

*RES: Répertoire d'Epigraphie Sémitique.*

Ryckmans: *Les Noms Propres Sud-Sémitiques,* I–III, Louvain, 1934–1935.

Wüstenfeld, *Register: Register zu den genealogischen Tabellen der arabischen Stämme und Familien,* Göttingen, 1853.

Wuthnow: *Die semitischen Menschennamen in griechischen Inschriften und Papyri des vorderen Orients,* Leipzig, 1930.

## INTRODUCTION

THE following records of a group of entertainers and prostitutes are here presented in what seems the most plausible form. Owing to the unique character of the texts, the interpretation can by no means be

* This paper, with some additions, was presented as a Dissertation to the Faculty of the Graduate School of Yale University in candidacy for the Degree of Doctor of Philosophy, 1943.

considered final, but it is hoped that at least the technical work of reading and placing the fragments has been completed. The study of the fragments as now preserved at Yale has been assisted by photographs taken by Dr. Toll at Dura shortly after the discovery of the inscription in 1935–1936, and by tracings and readings made by Professor F. E. Brown at that time. These earliest records cover the major pieces only, but they provide more complete readings than are now available in a number of cases, notably in Fragment V, since some of the pieces were injured in transportation. The new tracings shown in Figs. 92–98 incorporate all the material; in the commentary only the more important divergences are mentioned. In all cases where the new photographs and the tracings disagree, the latter represent the text as extant at Dura.

In New Haven, most of the fitting of the larger fragments was done by Professor Brown and by Professor C. B. Welles who also made the first complete reading; a number of fragments were assembled by Dr. J. F. Gilliam. To all of them, but especially to Professor Welles, I am indebted for suggestions at various times. In addition I have had the benefit of consulting several letters written by Professor A. D. Nock of Harvard to Professor Rostovtzeff which dealt with the inscription. The work has been under the constant supervision of Professor Rostovtzeff, without whose generous assistance it could not have been written. I have also had valuable help from Professor A. M. Harmon. Professor Harald Ingholt, in addition to giving me several bibliographical references, has kindly undertaken the treatment of the Semitic proper names; his comments are inserted in the notes in quotation marks.

The photographs reproduced on Pls. XXVI–XXX were taken by Dr. Toll at Yale in 1942, and the tracings in Figs. 92–98 were made by Miss D. H. Cox and Mr. T. E. Cooper.

## Location of the Inscriptions on the Walls of Room 2 in House C

The inscriptions, Nos. **940** and **941**, were painted on wall plaster found in over 260 scattered fragments on the floor of room 2 of House C in Section G5 (see above, Fig. 46, p. 117) in the season of 1935–1936. It was impossible to tell from which wall they had fallen from the position of the fragments. The room was the diwan of a private house built on the remains of the city's agora and situated on its northern limit. The entrance of the house itself was on the north side. The block of private houses of which it is a part was rebuilt several times, last about 250

A.D.;[1] the inscription undoubtedly belongs to this latest period of construction. The house is of the usual type found at Dura, containing a court and three rooms on the lower floor plus a number of rooms on the upper.[2] The diwan had a large entrance door from the court, of which the front and its moldings must have been on the court side. A smaller door, with its front in room C2, leads into room C3. A low bench, 0.26 m. high, runs around the four walls, interrupted only by the large door. In the north wall, to the left of the large door, is a small niche, and in the western part of the south wall is a large niche, rising 2.03 m. above the bench, which has a cupboard supported by columns.[3]

Of the wall decoration, nothing was found *in situ*. A small painted plaster relief of Aphrodite found in front of the west wall is probably to be restored on that wall.[4] Several small pieces of painted plaster showing vine scrolls, found with the fragments of the inscription, probably come from an ornamental setting for the relief. Others show similar ornaments in close proximity to the black dividers of the inscription (Frs. V, XXIV, and XXVI). The decoration was therefore not confined to the relief of Aphrodite. Pieces of a cavetto-fillet cornice with no traces of paint preserved were also found. Such moldings usually divide the wall into halves horizontally and continue the lintel of the door.[5] In room C2 only the door leading into room C3 probably had the molding of the lintel on the inside. The height of this door is not preserved, but can be calculated to have been *ca.* 1.90 m. above the bench,[6] or *ca.* 2.16 m. above the floor, which is then the assumed height of the cornice. The total height of the room, as calculated from the staircase in the court leading to the roof, was *ca.* 4.20 m.

The restoration in this setting of the texts forming No. **940** presents no difficulty. The largest continuous body of text (Fr. I, cols. 1–4) is a series of tabellae framed by horizontal and vertical dividers. There are four columns of two panels each. Above is preserved part of a strip of red painted plaster bordered by a dark grey line; immediately beneath it is the top black horizontal divider. The same red decoration is preserved on Fr. I, col. 6 and on Frs. IV and V. The maximum height of Fr. I, cols. 1–4 as preserved is 0.805 m. In the present reconstruction

---

[1] See above, pp. 47 f., 59, 116.
[2] See Fig. 46 and the detailed description above, p. 117.
[3] See above, pp. 117 f., Fig. 47a.          [4] See above, pp. 166 f., Pl. XIX.
[5] Cf. for example *Rep. VI,* pp. 273 f. and Pl. XVII, 1.
[6] 2 x 0.88 m. (width of door at bottom) plus 0.15 m. (height of sill).

there are two groups of text: Frs. I–IV and Fr. V. The first and larger of these has at least ten columns of inscribed panels, but there may have been more; thus the shortest possible arrangement requires about 2.08 m. of wall space including the bare plaster preserved on the left and right of the inscribed parts. Fr. V is smaller than the first group (0.63 m. by 0.59 m.) and probably comes from a different part of the walls, since the dimensions of the panels do not agree with Frs. I–IV. On the assumption that in no place did the framework of a column contain more than two panels, the series of texts of Frs. I–IV can easily be restored immediately below the cornice. This arrangement is perfectly satisfactory, for it places the bottom horizontal divider approximately 1.095 m. above the bench, where it could not be injured by people sitting there. This is confirmed by the excellent state of preservation of the lower parts of the inscription. Essentially the same arrangement holds good for Fr. V also. The exact position of the texts on the walls, however, cannot be determined. Since the north wall has a large door and a niche, the west wall a small door and the relief of Aphrodite, it is evident that the inscriptions could be placed only on the east wall and on that part of the south wall east of the large niche. As the east wall measures 4.51 m. in width, and the free part of the south wall 5.32 m., the texts, which do not require more than 3 m., may have been on either wall, but the south wall, opposite the main entrance, would have been more suitable. Since they formed a major part of the decoration of the room, the texts were clearly placed so that they were well protected but could also be easily read. No. **941**, a short painted text on a recoating of plaster, cannot be placed.

## Description of the Fragments

No. **940**. Thirty fragments of plaster, as reconstructed, painted with red and black letters, with black dividers forming rectangular panels. Pls. XXVI–XXX and Figs. 92–98.

Frs. I, **a–q**. A detailed catalogue of the fragments would be useless, but a word must be said about the combination of those fragments which do not join. Fr. I, **a** contains all of I, col. 1, the lower part of col. 2, and the upper portion of col. 3; on the left is uninscribed space. The central divider continues toward the left, but whether or not the space on the left was divided into panels is uncertain. **b** contains the top portion of a column inscribed alternately red and black and cannot be placed anywhere but at the top of col. 2. The left part of **c** continues the text of col. 3 which, like col. 2, is alternately red and black; the right part contains a list written in red, col. 4. To the same column belongs **d** which its trace of the lower margin and the restoration place in lines 11 and 12. **e** is very similar in lettering and thickness to the lower part of col. 4; there is also a depression on the surface which is continued on **c**. **f–o** have been placed so as to form two complete columns, but this arrangement cannot be given as certain. **f** touches **g**, and probably joins it. **f**, **g**, **h**, and **i** seem to belong together, since the letters and the thickness of the pieces are very similar, and their combination results in a plausible reconstruction of the text. **n** seems to belong at the right of **i** because of the similarity of the letters in cols. 5 and 6, lines 12 and 13, and the identical thickness of the pieces. **j**, **k**, and **o** then belong in the lower panels of these two columns, together with the bottom of **i** and **n**. There are alternately two red and two black lines, and the red letters are larger (0.036 m.) than the black (0.03 m.); only in lines 17–18 do the black letters become large on the right. **l** and **m** belong together because of the restoration of the text, which is the same as that of **q**, lines 1–2. The association of **l–m** with the rest is based only on the trace of a black letter at the left of **l** which should belong to col. 5, line 1, and the restoration of [Αὐρη]λί|α in lines 6–7. The only inconvenience of this arrangement is that the bottom of col. 6, A, and the top of col. 6, B, (both on **n**) are *ca.* 0.01 m. wider than the top and bottom of col. 6 on **l–m** and **o**. In the latter case, there is an inaccuracy in the illustrations: **k** and **o**, which do not join, should be *ca.* 0.01 m. farther apart, making the vertical divider between cols. 5 and 6 *ca.* 0.035 m. wide. The placing of the two columns immediately to the right of col. 4 cannot be strictly proven, and is based on the fact that **g** and **h** have red letters on the left. The letters - -]ος on **h** are best placed in col. 4, line 7, although this entails two difficulties: first, in col. 5 there is not enough space for line 8, and it cannot be determined whether the central horizontal divider sloped downward so as to give room for this line;[7] secondly, the top divider of cols. 5 and 6 is about 0.01 m. lower than that of cols. 1–2. It appears, however, that this is a fact, for in col. 3 the top divider, if continued straight from col. 2, gives a space of only about half the height of the red line which should be restored above the extant black line if it is assumed that the sequence

[7] The dividers are all very irregular, and the panels therefore of uneven dimensions: note especially the vertical divider between cols. 5 and 6. Likewise, the left vertical divider of col. 1 slants, and col. 4 is slightly narrower near the top than at the center.

of red and black lines in cols. 2–3 was unbroken. But the combination resulting from fragments **f–o** suggests that the red line did not exist in col. 3. The top divider, therefore, presumably sloped down to the right. The close combination of the fragments has been adopted because of the general feeling that not much of the text is missing, and because it puts all the remains of full-height panels into one unit, which, in turn, makes possible a uniform interpretation of the ἐξῆλθε texts (pp. 249 f.), a reasonable distribution of these texts and the warnings (pp. 234, 251 f.) and an acceptable relative chronology (pp. 253 f.).

Fr. I, **o** preserves the lower left corner of a panel shorter than any of the previous ones (col. 7, B). From this point on the panels became irregular. That the bottom divider continued at least for a short distance is strongly suggested by the Dura photograph; at present the place is much smeared. **p** touches **o** and may join it. **q** has the same height as col. 7, B and therefore followed that panel at an unknown distance. The last panel of the series was evidently Fr. IV, **a–c** with its blank space and graffiti on the right. **a** is associated with **b** because the right vertical margin was injured on both fragments and the width of the panels, as well as the thickness of the plaster is the same. The vertical distance between them is unknown: it is possible to make lines 3 and 9 coincide, but there is reason to believe that the text was longer (p. 237); therefore **b** has been tentatively placed below the central divider of Fr. I. Fr. IV cannot have followed Fr. I immediately for the lower divider of cols. 7 ff. should then be visible on the left of Fr. IV, **b**. For the intervening tabellae we have only Frs. II and III and also Frs. VI–IX which presumably belong together (p. 219). They are perhaps to be inserted at the height of the lower panels in cols. 7 ff. leaving the upper panels uninscribed. But since it is not impossible that a large portion of plaster fell down at a different time and was destroyed, this suggestion is purely hypothetical.

If this reconstruction is correct, it follows that Frs. I–IV form a series begun at one time with six columns of two panels each, which was abandoned when shorter panels were added later.

Fr. V cannot be combined with the first group of dipinti (Frs. I–IV). It preserves part of the same red and grey decoration found in the other group, but a graffito incised upon and below the decorative band made it necessary to paint the top divider of the dipinto *ca.* 0.09 m. below the decoration. The framework of the black dividers differs from that of Frs. I–IV in that some lines are thinner than others, and in that the central vertical divider is not carried through col. 1. The upper left corner of the framework shows that there were no panels to the left of col. 1. The red stroke on the left of Fr. V, **a** is presumably a piece of ornament, since it is not formed like the bottom stroke of a letter. On the right are the remains of an uninscribed column. There seems to have been no bottom divider.[8]

Fr. V, **b** is placed by three observations: 1) a narrow horizontal and a wide vertical divider can meet only in the lower right-hand corner of **a**; 2) **b** is very thin on the right and thickens toward the left; this is exactly paralleled by the corresponding portions of **a**; 3) the spacing and height of the letters in lines 8–9, cols. 2–3 is the same. From general considerations it is unlikely that **b** should be put a whole column farther down, which would mean that a great deal of text has been lost in col. 1 (p. 243).

### Paleographical Note

A study of the letter forms has convinced me that all the texts of No. **940** were by one hand. No. **941**, of course, is by a different hand. It is particularly the sequence of strokes in one and the same letter which is uniform throughout, wherever it can be distinguished. The graffito in Fr. V must also be considered to be by that hand, since it repeats rather unnecessarily the finials at the bottom of uprights in the dipinti. The incised ω, φ, υ, ε (in three strokes), as well as the other letters, show the same technique as the painted letters. The differences in writing can all be explained by different brushes used by the painter. The following groups can be distinguished:

Fr. I, cols. 1–3, line 9.

Fr. I, col. 3, lines 10–11, and col. 4, more hastily written and resembling Fr. I, col. 8 (?) and Fr. V.

Fr. I, col. 5, A and cols. 5–6, B, the latter being especially well written, with wavy lines for the horizontal strokes. Col. 6, A, lines 1–3, are more irregular.

It seems certain, therefore, that only one man was employed by the

---

[8] The top divider of **a** is not correctly shown in the photograph: when the pieces were put in plaster, the top margin of that divider was thought to be straight. It is clear, however, that the original top line in its right portion lies below the present one, and that the line was heightened when the painter saw that he had painted a gentle curve. The piece of Fr. V, **a** farthest to the right has therefore been turned counterclockwise in the tracing, giving space for **b** below.

entertainers as the scribe of No. **940**. But the impression gained is that Fr. I, cols. 1–4; Fr. I, col. 5, A and cols. 5–6, B; Fr. I, col. 6, A, lines 1–3; Fr. I, col. 8 (?); Fr. III; Fr. IV; and Fr. V were not written at the same time. For the different parts of Fr. I, cols. 1–6, this may mean only a short difference in time since these columns seem to have been designed as a unit. In any case, there can be little doubt that the whole group of texts from the paleographical point of view forms a unit and that only a short period of time should be assumed for them.

### MEASUREMENTS OF FRS. I–V

Fr. I,[9] col. 1, A: Height: 0.35 m., width, at top: 0.14 m.

Col. 1, B: Ht. (as restored): 0.33 m. W., at bottom: 0.128 m. Width of left divider: 0.023–0.031 m.; of right divider: 0.025 m.; of central divider: 0.03 m. All dividers black. Ht. of letters (red): *ca.* 0.03 m.

Col. 2, A: Ht.: 0.355 m. W.: 0.185 m.

Col. 2, B: Ht.: 0.33 m. W.: 0.19 m. Ht. of letters of A and B (red and black): 0.02–0.025 m.

Col. 3, A: Ht. (as restored): 0.365 m. W.: 0.147 m. Ht. of letters (black and red; last two lines red): 0.022–0.03 m.

Col. 4, A: Ht. (as restored): 0.363 m. W. (line 5): 0.118 m. Ht. of letters (red): *ca.* 0.026 m.

Col. 5, A: Ht. (as restored): 0.36 m. W. (as restored): 0.17 m. Ht. of letters (black; line 12 red): line 1: 0.029 m.; lines 2–4: 0.024 m.; lines 6–7: 0.021 m.; lines 9–11: 0.024 m.; line 12: 0.034 m.

Col. 5, B: Ht. (as restored): 0.342 m. W., at bottom: 0.162 m.

Col. 6, A: Ht. (as restored): 0.363 m. W., at top: 0.175 m.; at bottom: 0.181 m. Ht. of letters (red): lines 1–3: *ca.* 0.04 m.; lines 10–11: 0.026 m.; line 12: 0.034 m.

Col. 6, B: Ht. (as restored): 0.335 m. W., at top: *ca.* 0.17 m.; at bottom: 0.162 m.

Cols. 5, B–6, B: Ht. of letters (2 lines black, 2 red, etc.): lines 13–14: 0.03 m.; lines 15–16: *ca.* 0.036 m.; lines 17–18, col. 5: *ca.* 0.031 m.; col. 6: *ca.* 0.04 m.; lines 19–20: 0.036 m.

[9] Thickness of **a**, at left: 0.025 m.; at right, top: 0.015 m., bottom: 0.007 m. **b**: 0.02 m. **c**, at left, bottom: 0.015 m.; at right: 0.01 m. **d**: 0.015 m. **e**: 0.006 m. **f**: 0.02 m. **g**, top: 0.018 m.; bottom: 0.01 m. **h**: 0.014 m. **i**: 0.012 m. **j**: 0.006 m. **k**: 0.008 m. **l**: 0.025 m. **m**, top: 0.025 m.; bottom: 0.012–0.022 m. **n**, top: 0.013 m.; bottom: 0.005 m. **o**, top: 0.01 m.; bottom: 0.015 m. **p**: 0.01–0.016 m. **q**: 0.011 m. All figures approximate, since the backs are quite irregular.

Col. 7, B: Ht. (as restored): 0.16 m. Ht. of letters (red): 0.029 m.

Col. 7, C: Ht.: 0.142 m.

Col. 8(?), B: Ht.: 0.166 m. W. (as restored): 0.202 m. Ht. of letters (red): 0.03–0.035 m.

Fr. II:[10] Ht. (as preserved): 0.119 m. W. (as preserved): 0.115 m. Ht. of letters (red): line 1: 0.035 m.; line 2: 0.04 m.; line 3: 0.019 m.

Fr. III:[11] Ht. (as preserved): 0.07 m. W. (as restored): 0.166 m. Ht. of letters (black): 0.02–0.025 m.

Fr. IV,[12] A: Ht. (as restored): 0.393 m. W. (as restored): 0.179 m.

Fr. IV, B: Ht.: 0.23 m. W.: 0.175 m. Ht. of letters (red): lines 1–2: 0.036 m.; lines 10–11: 0.029 m.; lines 12 ff.: *ca.* 0.039 m.

Fr. V, Graffito: Ht. of letters: 0.021 m.

Dipinto:[13] Width of dividers (black): top, *ca.* 0.02 m.; central: 0.017 m.; left vertical: 0.027 m.; right vertical: *ca.* 0.03 m.; others: 0.015 m.

Col. 1: Ht. (as preserved): 0.425 m. W., at top: 0.127 m.; at bottom: 0.114 m. Ht. of letters (red): *ca.* 0.025 m.

Col. 2, A: Ht.: 0.305 m. W.: 0.152 m. Ht. of letters, lines 1–4 (red): *ca.* 0.037 m.; lines 5–6 (black): 0.027 m.; line 7 (red): 0.036 m.

Col. 2, B: W.: 0.148 m. Ht. of letters (red): line 8: 0.037 m.; line 9: *ca.* 0.03 m.

Col. 3, A: W., at top: 0.156 m. Ht. and color of letters as in Col. 2, A.

Col. 3, B: Ht. (as preserved): 0.162 m. W. (as restored): 0.165 m. Ht. of letters (red): line 8: *ca.* 0.04 m.; lines 9–10: 0.03 m.

---

[10] Thickness: 0.007 m.      [11] Thickness: 0.004 m.

[12] Thickness, **a**: 0.025 m.; **b**: 0.025 m.; **c**: 0.016 m.

[13] Thickness of **a**, at top: *ca.* 0.025 m.; at bottom: *ca.* 0.01 m. **b**: 0.007–0.015 m.

# TEXT
## Figs. 92–97

Fr. I, Col. 1, A:    ˏΟτε ἐξῆλ[θο]ν

ἀπὸ Ζεύ[γμα(τος),]

Περιτίου ιγ΄.

Δύστρ[ο]c

5 Ξαγδικόc

Ἀρτε[μ]ίσιος

Δέσιος

Πάνημος

Λῶος

10 Γορπιᾶος

B:    Ὑπερβερετᾶος

Δῖος

Ἀπελλᾶος

Ἐδυνᾶος

*vacat*

Col. 2, A:    [Ὀλ]υμπιὰc μωρά

[. .]νκυβις ἱλαρά

[1.2]μις μωροκυστα

[. . .]ΙΛΙΓΓΙΚΛΙΓ[.]Ι--Α

5 Σαλμα[θη?. ᶜᵃ.⁶..]α

Κλεοπάτ[ρα..] ΡΑΛΑΒΑ

[. ⁴·⁵. ϹΟΔ[²·³]] *vacat*

Θικιμη βλαρά

Ἀφροδιςία μωρά

10 Σαλμαθη κό[ππ]α

Ῥε[1.2]υθη σπάθη

Βλ[. ᶜᵃ.⁴.]c καλή

B:     ....[.<sup>ca.6</sup>..] κομϲή

Δόμνα μ[ω]ρά

15 τῶν ἡμετέρων

Θικιμη μικκὴ καϙεν

Θεννιϲ ἡ παλεοπόρ(νη)

Ἀ[λ?]βῖνα *vacat*

[.<sup>ca.5</sup>.]ουϲ γρέοψιϲ

20 [.] ⟍ΙΙ αβαιθα καλή

['Α]γνα Βαδϲιϲαια

[1-2] ιϲιῖθαϲ *vacat*

Σαλιφθαϲ γρ[έοψιϲ?]

Καμαθη εὔϙ[ουϲ?]

Col. 3, A:     [.<sup>ca.6</sup>..]ΙμεαΙ[.<sup>ca.4</sup>.]

ΙΝΟΜΑϹ βλ[αρά]

Αβεδϲιμ[εια]

Κάϲτα μεγά[λη]

5 Βαδϲημε[ια]

καλὴ Ζευγμα(τῖτιϲ)

Βα[δϲη(μεια)] ἡμετέ(ρα)

Ι ανθελο[υ]ϲ

[.]αρβαιθη κηλητρ(ία)

10 Αβϲαλμαϲ καλή

Κυρίλλα κάππα

B:     *vacat*

Col. 4, A:     [--------]ΙΙ ει

[------------]

[------------]

[-------]Ι ΟΙΟϹ

5 Ομαναϲ ϲκ(ηνικόϲ)

Σαμακους [..]

ΙΑΓΑΠΕΛΘΟϹ

Ἀσβόλις  *vacat*

Γαιι[ - - - - ]

10 Μαρ[ - - - - - - ]

Οὐάλ[η]ϲ ὁ πρε(σβύτεροϲ?)

Ἀντιοχίδ[ηϲ]

B:    Καῖ[οϲ] σκην(ικόϲ)

['Αβάσκ?]αντ(οϲ)

    *vacat*

Cols. 5–6, A:    Ἐξῆλθε Τά[τιοϲ ?]      Μετέβημεν

     A   ⟩ [ - - ]        [ὧδε] Δείου

     Δερίου δευ[τέρ -]      νεομηνί[ᾳ.]

     [ᾳ καὶ Σα]ββᾳ   [τῇ *ca.4*.]

5 [ - - - - - - - - - - - - - - - ][ ∂ ]   ∂   ∂   ∂

     Ἔπεμσα [ἐγὼ Αὐρη]λί-

     α εἰς Ζε[ῦγμα....]

     ..[ - - - - - - - - - - - - ][ - - - - - - - - - - - - - ]

     ['Υπερβε]ρετέο[υ]     [ - - - - - - - - - - - - ]

10 [πρώτ]η καὶ Σαββα     [...]Ι ∪ ∕ [ - - - - - - - ]

     [τῇ δε]υτέρᾳ. *vacat*     [..]ΩΕΟΝΙΙ[..]ΟΙΙΙ[εἰ-]

     [πιστε?]ύει σοὶ οὐδ[είϲ.]   ϲ οἶ[κο]ν εἰσενίκηϲ.

B:    [.*ca.5*.]ΠΕΡΕ[*ca.3* ἰδ]οῦ μὴ πιστε-

     [ύσῃϲ .*ca.6*..]ι σὺ ἔδωκαϲ *vacat?* [.*ca.4*.]

15 [.*5-6*..]ι πιστευσε [...*7-8*...]

     τρα[.*3-4*.] ..ΙΙ[.]Ι [ - - - - - - ]

     μηδε.[ - - - - - - - - - - - - ] α

     ἀνε.[ - - - - - - ] εἰς οἴκόν σου,

     βλέπε, ὅτι οὐδ[ε]ὶϲ τῷ ἑτέρῳ δίδει· ἐ{ξ}-

20 ξήχθηϲ ὑπὸ Οὐικτωρίνου   ∂

Col. 7, A:          missing

   B:      [ - - - - - - - - ]

           [ - - - - - - - - ]

           [ - - - - - - - - ]

           [ .³⁴. ] Ιυ [ - - - ]

        ₅ Αἰδυνἑος [ - - ]

   C:      *vacat*


Col. 8 ?, A:        missing

   B:   [Μ]ετἑβημεν *vacat* ῷδ̣[ε]

        [Δ]είου *vacat* νεομη[νία.]

        [ἔ]χει ὁ σταθμ[οῦχος]

        [π]ροχρείαν *vacat* [ .³⁴. ]

   C:      missing

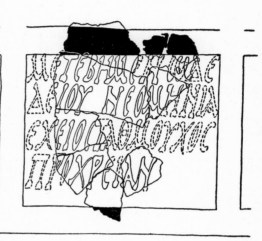

Fig. 93


Fr. II:    - - - - - - - - - - - - - -

        [ - - ] ι Κạ[ο]σιαγ[ - - ]

        [ - - ] ⁄ της Εσμạ[ - - ]

        [ - - ]. πιστευσε[ - - ].

Fig. 94


Fr. III:   - - - - - - - - - - - - - -

        [ - - - - - - - - - - ] ι⁄ιιΟι

        [Δ]ίọυ Ṣκ, Σαββα

        [ε]ἰσαγούσης Ṣ

        [ .ᶜᵃ.⁴. ] ſ ſ ∩ - [..] ` [ - - ]

        - - - - - - - - - - - - - -

**Fr. IV, A:**     Ἐξῆλθε Κασσια-
        *vacat* νὸς κὲ Ῥοῦφ[ος]
        ['Απ]ελλέο[υ..]
        [ - - - - - - - - - - - - ]
    5 [ - - - - - - - - - - - - ]
        [ - - - - - - - - - - - - ]
        [ - - - - - - - - - - - - ]
        [ - - - - - - - - - - - - ]
        [ - - - - - - - - - - - ]ος

**B:**     10 [Εἰσά]γων δύο μῆ-
        γας εἰς οἶκόν σου
        βλέπε μή τι-
        νι πιστεύ-
        σῃς πολύ,
    15 μηδὲ ἑαυτῷ, βλ[έ-]
        π[ε.]

            To right: graffiti

**C:**     *vacat*

Fig. 96

Fr. V, Graffito:

- - - - - - - - - - - - - - - - - - - - - - - - - - - - - - - -

[ - - - - - - - - - - - - - - - - - - ] ЄΡΕΙΟ [ - - - - - - - - ]

[ - - - - - - - - - - - - - - - - - ] ι γὰρ φιλ [ - - - - - - - - ]

[ - - - - - ] ΟΝΟ [ - - - - - - - - - - - ἀ]νδρῶν [ - - - - - - - - - - ]

[ - - ] νιν δὲ ἐπ[ . . . . *ca. 9* . . . . ] . [ . ]ωδια χρήματα [ - - - - - - - ]

5 [καὶ] ξίφος ὠκύ *vacat* [ . *ca. 5* . ] *vacat*

Dipinto, Col. 1: Ὅσοι δουλο-

παράσειτοι,

ἀφ' ὅτε ἀνέ-

[*vacat*] *vacat* βη τὰ πε-

5 δία εἰς Ζεῦγμ[α,]

ἢ τὸ ὕστ[ερον·]

Ἀσβόλις ὁ τρα(γῳδός).

Ῥωμανὸς ᾧ

Θεοδώρα ὑποτρ(αγῳδεῖ.)

10 Ἄχαβος

[Φι]λόπα[ππ]ος

[Κ]ασσιανός

[ . ] ΓΥΝΗΛΙΦΟ

Ὕμνος [ - - ]

15 [ . . ] Κ[ - - - ]

- - - - - - - - - -

Cols. 2–3, A: Καταφαγᾶς       Κοττιστής

Χαρίσιος ὃς       [ . . . . ] ιος *vacat*

ἀγαθὸς [μου-]       [ - - - - ]

[σι?]κός. [*vacat?*]       [ - - - - ]

5 ΟΧ . Є [ - - - ] . . [ - - - - - - - - - - ]

ἔχον [ - - ] . ΟΙ / [ . ] . [ . ] . / [ - - ]

φιλῶ[ν τ]ρόπους γελ[οίου-]

B:  ϲ κὲ μίμο[υϲ,] ἰδὲ μὴ

ἐγε[. .ᶜᵃ.⁷˙⁸. .] ποιῆϲθ⟨ε⟩· ὀπτίων

10 [ὁ δεῖνα ? πα]ρὰ Σατυρίλλῳ.

*vacat*

There remains a number of fragments which could not be placed ( Pl. XXIX and Fig. 98).

Fr. VI : 0.092 m. across. Th.: 0.004 m. Black letters; Ht.: 0.031 m. Broken on all sides.

MON
ΟΙΕΧΙ
ΟϹ

Fr. VII : Ht.: 0.055 m. W.: 0.042 m. Th.: 0.01 m. Black letters; Ht.: *ca.* 0.023 m. Broken on all sides, but the purple decoration at the right shows that the letters are from the end of two lines.

ΕΙ
/Γ

Fr. VIII : 0.066 m. across. Th.: 0.002 m. Same description as Fr. VII.

ΙΕ *vacat*
Ι *vacat*

Fig. 97. No. 940. Fragment V

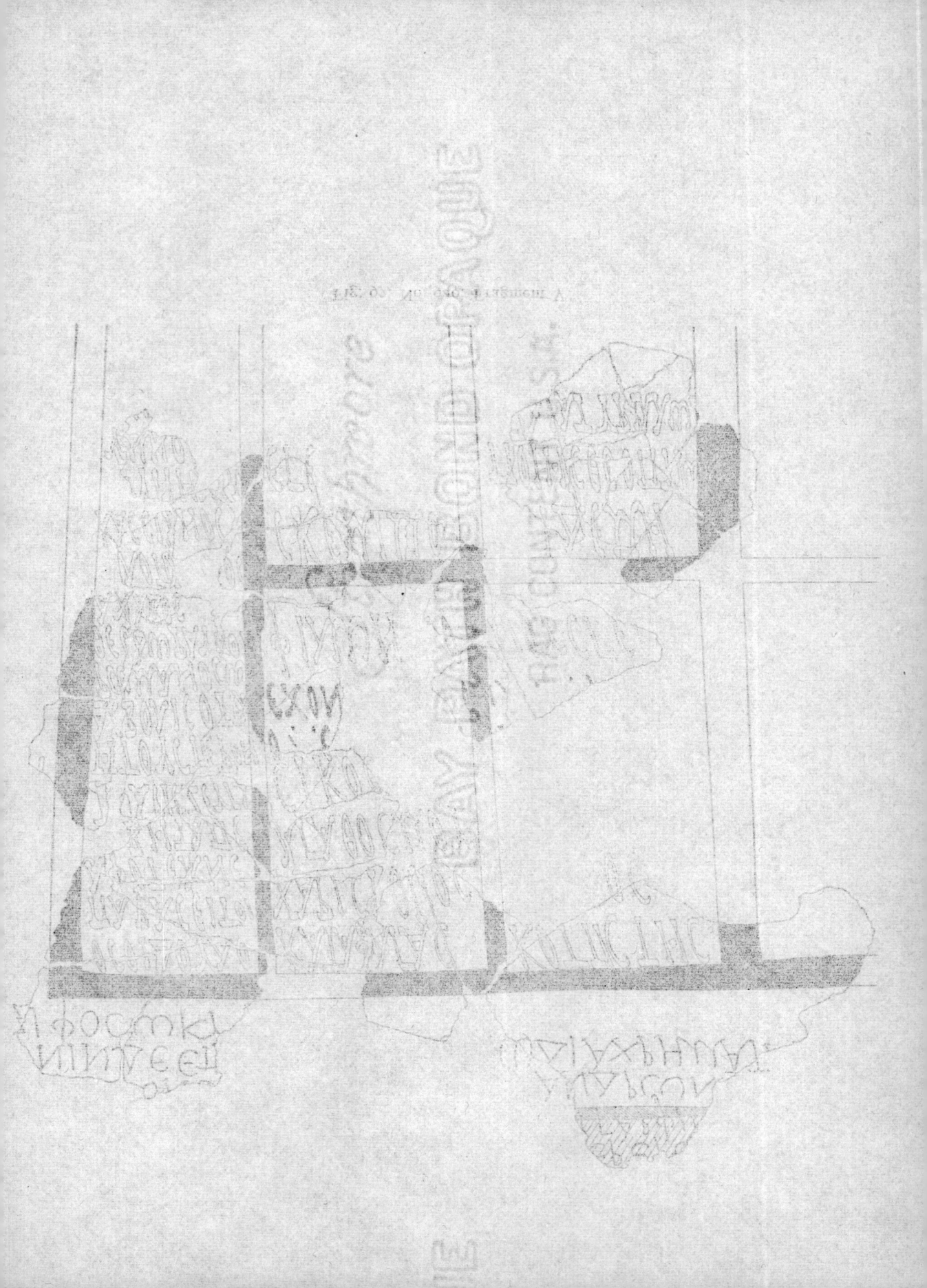

Fr. IX: Ht. 0.04 m. W.: 0.057 m. Th.: 0.003–0.004 m. Black letters; Ht.: *ca.* 0.03 m. Broken on all sides.

Frs. VI–IX seem to be the remains of one tabella; see p. 208.

Fr. X: Ht.: 0.047 m. W.: 0.056 m. Th.: 0.008 m. Black letters; Ht.: 0.034 m. Broken on all sides.

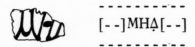

Judging from the letter forms and thickness this fragment certainly belongs with Fr. I, cols. 5–6, B; see p. 234.

Fr. XI: Ht.: 0.049 m. W.: 0.055 m. Th.: 0.01 m. Black vertical divider in center, horizontal divider at the top. *vacat* at left; at right in red letters (Ht.: 0.023 m.):

Fr. XII: 0.037 m. across. Th.: 0.01 m. Trace of black divider at left (?). Broken on all sides. Letters red; Ht.: *ca.* 0.03 m.

Fr. XIII: Ht.: 0.044 m. W.: 0.051 m. Th. 0.01 m. Broken on all sides. Letters red; Ht.: *ca.* 0.035 m.

Fr. XIV: 0.042 m. across. Th.: 0.012 m. Broken on all sides. Letters black; Ht.: 0.022 m.

ΙΕΓ

Fr. XV: 0.037 m. across. Th.: *ca.* 0.011 m. Black divider at left. Red letters; Ht.: *ca.* 0.022 m.

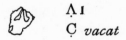

ϹΟ̣[- -]

Fr. XVI: 0.03 m. across. Th.: 0.007 m. Broken on all sides. Red letters.

Ṇ̣Ạ̣
Ϲ

Fr. XVII: 0.036 m. across. Th.: 0.007 m. Broken on all sides. Red letters.

Λ̣Ι
Ϲ̣ *vacat*

Fr. XVIII:[14] Ht.: 0.017 m. W.: 0.029 m. Th.: 0.008 m. Broken on all sides. Red letters; Ht.: *ca.* 0.023 m.

ΛΙ̣Θ/

[14] Twelve additional fragments are too small to be described. Frs. XIX–XXIII show traces of red letters, Frs. XXIV–XXIX have dividers, partly with ornament. Fr. XXX, with traces of letters, is visible on the Dura photograph, but could not be found. See Fig. 98.

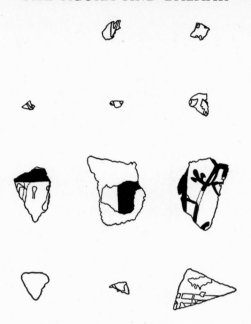

Fig. 98. Inscription No. 940. Minor Fragments

No. **941. a–e.** Painted in light red on a second coating of white plaster, with a red line above and below, apparently forming a tabella.[15] Fragments **b** and **c** are placed with reference to the brush marks; the position of **d** is quite uncertain, that of **e** is unknown. Ht. of inscribed space: 0.08 m. Ht. of letters: 0.02–0.03 m. Pl. XXIX.

[Μνησθῇ (?) - ]⌒ ˋ [- -] Αὐρηλία[- -]

[ - - - - - - - - - ] αζειαβ [- -] ⌒ [- -]

[ - - - - - - - - - ] υτης [- - - - - -]

*vacat*

## Notes

Fr. I, col. 1, lines 1–3: This entry must be considered complete, since nothing was inscribed in the column to the left, and nothing could have been inscribed above. The form of the date is peculiar; the month should have preceded the ὅτε construction. The change may have been

---

[15] Cf. e.g., Cumont, *Fouilles*, p. 390, no. 28 (graffito).

made with a view to the following list of months. The traces of red letters in the right portion of lines 1–2 do not preclude the restorations
ἐξήλ[θομε]ν and Ζεύ[γματος], but the spacing is better with the text as
adopted. This must be the heading of the two lists, of women and of
men respectively, in cols. 2–3. The list of months (lines 4–14), evidently written by the same hand at the same time, is very puzzling. The
use of the nominative case shows that the months were not intended as
dates to be completed; a possible significance of the list will be discussed
on pp. 246 f.

Fr. I, cols. 2–3 contain a list of 33 women, 26 of whom originally had
epithets accompanying the name, while two others have other special
designations. The alternation of red and black lines is regular for col.
2, A–B, which have 12 lines each; col. 3, A, apparently had only 11
lines (see pp. 207 f.), beginning with black. The last two lines are in
red and thicker lettering, resembling the letters of Fr. I, col. 4, but it is
doubtful whether they were written later.

Fr. I, col. 2, line 1: μωρά, here and below in lines 9 and 14 is no doubt
the common Koine word of vulgar abuse, best known from Matth. V. 22,
where the context requires a very mild term.[16] That μωρά here is not the
equivalent of *stupida* as a technical term of the mime will be seen from
the other adjectives (below, pp. 255–257).

Fr. I, col. 2, line 2: [..]νκυβις. This name seems to be unknown. ἱλαρά
"merry" rather than "gracious." This quality is often mentioned in
connection with banquets,[17] and especially in connection with entertainers acting at banquets.[18] It is not impossible that the epithet implies
that the woman was a singer of ἱλαρὰ ᾄσματα,[19] but no certain clue either
to her character or her profession can be derived from the word.

Fr. I, col. 2, line 3: The M of [.]μις is uncertain. μωροκυστα is un-
known and the ending is not Greek but may be Aramaic (S. Krauss,
*Griechische und lateinische Lehnwörter im Talmud*, 1898, I, pp. 83 f.).
Compounds with μωρός are frequent in late Greek,[20] but the element

[16] E. A. Barber in J. U. Powell, *New Chapters in the History of Greek Literature*,
Vol. I, 1921, p. 122, note 1.

[17] E.g., Theophrastus, *Charact.* XVII. 9.

[18] Petronius, ch. 23, 1: *adjuvit hilaritatem commissantis cymbalistria*.

[19] Athenaeus, XV, 697 D. Cf. the doubtful restoration κιναίδωι ἱλ[αρῶι?] in *P. Co-
lumbia* 94,[r] line 2 (Westermann-Keyes-Liebesny, *Zenon Papyri*, II, 1940, p. 111; C. B.
Welles, *Classical Philology*, XXXVII, 1942, p. 436).

[20] For Byzantine nicknames with μωρο- see S. M. Psaltes, *Grammatik der Byzantinischen Chroniken*, Göttingen, 1913, p. 345.

-κυστα is not clear although perhaps to be connected with κύστις, "bladder" in an obscene sense.[21] The woman may have used bladders in theatrical skits, see below, p. 256. Another possibility is κύσθος, "pudendum muliebre," since *theta* frequently appears as *tau* in vulgar Koine especially in Asia Minor.[22]

Fr. I, col. 2, line 5: Σαλμα[θη?] : see below, on line 10.

Fr. I, col. 2, line 6: ΡΑΛΑΒΑ is unintelligible, but Ρ̣ may be read Τ̣, Π̣, Ψ̣, Υ̣(?), Γ and Α̣ may be Λ or Δ̣. Perhaps [μω]ρ̣ὰ λάβδ̣(α)? Letters are used as epithets below, line 10 and col. 3, line 11, and the erotic implications of λάβδα are alluded to several times in ancient literature.[23]

Fr. I, col. 2, line 8: Θικιμη: "This name I take as rendering the Arabic Tuqîm, already found under the form Θοκιμη in an inscription from southern Syria. The first vowel, ι instead of ο might be taken as evidence of carelessness in rendering a Semitic word in Greek; on the other hand, an original u near an î easily becomes i, as for instance in the name Ἰκειμος."[24]

βλαρά: this word is not listed in the dictionaries, since it is only known from the Graeco-Latin glossaries: βλαρός *insulsus*, βλαρόν *inconditum*, βλαροῦμαι *insulsor*, Goetz, II, 257, 57–59; *blarus vanus*, III, 490, 74. Compare also the proper names Blarus (*Not. Scavi*, 1895, p. 452) and Βλάριος (C. M. Kaufmann, *Handbuch der altchristlichen Epigraphik*, 1917, p. 391). βλαρία as the popular name for a mental condition is quoted from a Byzantine medical source by Du Cange, *Glossarium*, appendix. βλαρός, then, much like μωρός means "inept."

Fr. I, col. 2, line 10: Σαλμαθη. "This name corresponds no doubt to the Semitic Shalmat, often found in Palmyra, once in Djebel Sha'ar, and once in Nabataean."

κ̣ο̣[ππ]α: the traces of letters between ο and α are not decisive. The restoration depends on Fr. I, col. 3, line 11, *q.v.*

Fr. I, col. 2, line 11: ʽΡε[..]υθη: Semitic?

---

[21] Juvenal, 1, 39: *vetulae vesica beatae.*

[22] K. Dieterich, *Untersuchungen zur Geschichte der griechischen Sprache*, Leipzig, 1898, pp. 84 ff. and 100 ff.; *Rep. VI*, p. 249, no. 742 (μνηστῇ) ; above, p. 177.

[23] Aristophanes *Ecclesiazusae*, 920; Ausonius, *Epigrams*, L.C.L. p. 204, LXXXVII; *Anth. Pal.* XII, 187, 6 (Straton). Probably also in Varro, *Sat. Menipp., Bimarcus*, fr. IV Buecheler (XVII, Riese).

[24] Littmann, *PUAE*, IV, Leyden, 1914, p. XXVIII. These comments of Professor Ingholt are somewhat abbreviated, by his permission. The whole question of the Semitic names at Dura must be taken up later and dealt with as a unit [Ed.].

σπάθη: "sword," evidently metaphorical. A comparison of some sort with a sword may be implied, but after Aristophanes, *Clouds*, 55 (ὦ γύναι, λίαν σπαθᾷς) the idea may rather be that of "squandering," a meaning common in comedy and late Christian authors. If the word is abbreviated, like some others in this text, one might compare Photius, *Lex.* p. 529: σπάθημα φρενῶν · τὸν ἄγαν φρόνιμον.

Fr. I, col. 2, line 12: καλή: the καλός acclamation which is so well known from Attic vases appears to continue through Hellenistic and Roman times in various uses. It is common for men in an erotic sense;[25] it is also addressed to women.[26]

Fr. I, col. 2, line 13: - -] κομσή, i.e. κομψή, or a compound on the analogy of Πασικόμψη, the name of a hetaera in Plautus, *Mercator*. The last letter is Ḥ rather than Ạ. The only difficulty here is whether κομψή should be taken as *composita, decorata* (Goetz, V, 446, 60) or in the meaning indicated by Pollux VI, 123, where κομψός, πανοῦργος, γόης, ἀπατεών are listed as terms appropriate εἰς κόλακα. Since Κόμψη occurs very frequently as a woman's name, the former may be the case: κομψότης seems to be characteristic of women rather than men. For the loss of π between μ and σ, compare ἔπεμσα in Fr. I, col. 5, line 6. This is merely a matter of spelling and of no phonetic significance.[27]

Fr. I, col. 2, line 14: Domna is no doubt derived from Julia Domna, and therefore Semitic. μ[ω]ρά: the reading is certain. See Fr. I, col. 2, line 1.

Fr. I, col. 2, line 15: the list is divided into two parts by this heading, on which see below, Fr. I, col. 3, line 6, and pp. 249 f.

Fr. I, col. 2, line 16: Θικιμη: above, line 8.

ΜΙΚΚΗΚΑΠΕΝ presents difficulties, and it is possible that either the whole line, or at least ΚΑΠΕΝ, is Semitic, though no certain solution was found by several Semitists consulted. Π is the only uncertain letter, and it can be read ΙΤ since the place where the top of I and the horizontal stroke of Τ would meet is damaged. Possibly καὶ τέν(θις), an un-

---

[25] E.g., an inscription from Pompeii, *C.I.L.*, IV, 1256: *Sabine calos Hermeros te amat*. Numerous other examples in Index IV of *C.I.L.*, IV and in Index XVI of *C.I.L.*, IV, *Suppl. s.v. calos*. See the two inscriptions from a brothel quoted below, p. 256, n. 156.

[26] Σίμη καλὴ δοκεῖ ἐμοὶ Δ. (or Λ.?) Νικατείδ[ει?] from a columbarium in Eleutheropolis in Palestine, Ch. Clermont-Ganneau, *Recueil d'Archéologie Orientale*, IV, 1901, pp. 237 ff.

[27] E. Mayser, *Grammatik der griechischen Papyri aus der Ptolemäerzeit* I, 1, p. 166 (on πέμτη). Mayser has no unquestionable example of μψ>μσ: *ibid.*, p. 211 and p. 167, note 6. ἔπεμσα, in Roman times, occurs in *P. Oxy.* 528, 24.

known feminine form of τένθης (glutton). μικκός, the hypocoristic form of μικρός, is common in late Greek.[28]

Fr. I, col. 2, line 17: Θεννις: "With this name I should compare the Safaitic Tinn which, according to Ryckmans, goes back to the same root as the Arabic *tinn*, companion, equal."[29]

ἡ παλεοπόρ(νη): As a compound, this word seems to be new, but it may be translated "prostitute from of old" and compared with παλαιόδουλος (Philo Jud. VI. [Ed. Cohn and Reiter] p. 3, l. 16; p. 42, l. 3) "slave from of old," παλαι(ο)στρατιώτης, παλαιόκαστρον, etc. The Old Testament term בלהנאפים (Ez. 23, 43), probably to be rendered "waxen old in adultery,"[30] conveys a similar idea. A Rabbinical commentary even translates this term by פיליאפורני, the transcription in Hebrew letters of παλαιὰ πόρνη, further explaining these words as "a wasted harlot."[31]

Fr. I, col. 2, line 18: Ἀ[λ?]βῖνα: the restoration is very uncertain, since Λ or Δ can be read for Ἀ and Ρ for Ḅ.

Fr. I, col. 2, line 19: γρέοψις, i.e., γραίοψις is likewise new, but formed after the pattern of μάκροψις, ξήροψις, πλάτοψις, στρογγύλοψις, words occurring in Malalas and Tsetses.[32] The reference in all cases seems to be to a person's face. Pre-byzantine is only κάκοψις in *P. Lips*. I, 9 and *P. Grenf*. II, 28, 4, both of the second century B.C., where the word is applied to women and possibly refers to eyesight. Vettius Valens, 14, 23 has κακόψιδες, *sc.* γυναῖκες. The first part of our compound occurs also in γραιωπίας glossed by Hesychius γραίας ἐμφερής. "Having the face of an old woman" is probably the correct translation here.

Fr. I, col. 2, line 20: καλή, see above, line 12.

Fr. I, col. 2, line 21: [.]γναβαδσισαια: "I venture to restore [Ἄ]ννα Βαδσισαια, that is 'Anna, daughter (or client) of Sisaia.' The name Ἄννα is known in Dura,[33] and we meet it in Palmyra, either under the form אנא[34] or חנא.[35] This Anna is the first of the women with Semitic names to receive what looks like an additional epithet. The reason is to seek

---

[28] Preisigke, *Wörterbuch*, *s.v.*     [29] Ryckmans, I, p. 214; cf. also Lane, *s.v.*

[30] G. A. Cooke, *The Book of Ezekiel*, New York, 1937, I, p. 263: "old by reason of adultery."

[31] מבליאגירא. The exegesis is given in the *Midrash Rabba, Leviticus*, §33.6, in the commentary to Leviticus 25[14]. The rendering is there ascribed to Aquila, whose real reading, however, is: τοῦ κατατρῖψαι μοιχείας.

[32] See Stephanus, *Thesaurus, ss.vv.* and Psaltes, *Grammatik der Byz. Chron.*, p. 361.

[33] *Rep. IV*, no. 284, p. 148. Cf. likewise Wuthnow, *s.v.*

[34] *Berytus*, V, 1938, p. 135, note 6.

[35] Cantineau, *Inventaire*, VIII, no. 134; *RES*, 2180; cf. the Arabic feminine name Hanna (Wüstenfeld, *Register*, p. 204).

either in the fact that Anna was a very common name, or, if we choose the derivation from אנא, because this latter name could be used both as a masculine and as a feminine name.[36] As to the epithet, Bad Sisaia, it probably is to be translated "daughter of Sisaia,"[37] an epithet which would establish without doubt the identity of the bearer. As to the name Sisaia, it looks feminine, so that we seem to have one of the rare cases where a matronymic is given instead of the usual patronymic,[38] probably from the maxim *pater incertus, mater certa*.[39] A name Σισεος occurs in Dura,[40] possibly, like Sisaia, ultimately derived from the root sîsâ, 'flower' or that from which comes the Palmyrene feminine name Shîshtâ, cf. the Syriac *shishta* 'alabaster, white marble.' "

Fr. I, col. 2, line 22: [..]ιοιϊθας: doubtless an unknown Semitic name.

Fr. I, col. 2, line 23: Σαλιφθας: "Undoubtedly of the same root as the name Σαλιφα, found once in a graffito from Dura.[41] As to the meaning, many possibilities present themselves. The most probable to me is to compare the Arabic *salifat* 'a woman's husband's sister' or her 'brother's wife.' "

γρ[εοψις]: fills the space exactly, but there is a dark spot near the break where the third letter should be, high above the line. If this is paint, there would be a choice of the letters ι, κ, φ, ψ.

Fr. I, col. 2, line 24: Καμαθη: "Probably this word comes originally from the same root *qam* as Θικιμη (above, line 8). I take it to be equivalent to Ακαμαθη, a proper name known from Palmyra,[42] where the Palmyrene counterpart is quite common.[43] It is true that an initial א with a short vowel is dropped only very rarely, but similar examples are known in proper names from Syria."[44]

---

[36] Cf. *Berytus*, II, 1935, p. 92. The Palmyrene אנא seems so far to have been found only as a feminine name, but הנא is also a man's name, cf. *RES*, 973. Cf. also Annas, the father-in-law of Caiaphas the high priest of Jerusalem during the year of the crucifixion, John 18.13, and the prophetess Anna, Luke 2.36.

[37] Cf. below the name Bad Semea (Fr. I, col. 3, line 5).

[38] Cf. *Berytus*, III, 1936, p. 96, inscriptions A and B: Maqqai, son of Omabi. As Professor Littmann suggested in a letter to me, Omabi might here rather be the mother's name than a surname.

[39] Cf. H. Seyrig, *Berytus*, I, 1934, p. 5.

[40] *Rep. V*, p. 241, no. 595.        [41] *Rep. V*, p. 125, no. 438.

[42] *Berytus*, III, 1936, pp. 99 f. (Palmyrene equivalent in the same inscription). Greek form alone in Mouterde, *MUSJ*, XVI, 1932, pp. 93 f.

[43] Cantineau, *Inventaire*, IV, no. 271; *CIS* 4190, 4200; *RES* 147, etc.

[44] Μαθγα, *PUAE*, III, no. 512, p. 221; Μαθβαβεα, *PAAE*, III, no. 263, pp. 222 and 206; Μαθσημεα, Seyrig, *Syria*, XX, 1939, p. 305.

εὐπ[ους?], suggested by Professor Nock, fits well in view of the occurrence of adjectives in -πους in late Greek,[45] but since there is space for *ca.* 6–7 letters, the possibilities are many. εὐπ[υγος] would fit equally well. In any case, this is one of the few laudatory epithets.

Fr. I, col. 3, line 1: --]Ιμεα Ι[--: presumably the end of a proper name and the beginning of an epithet.

Fr. I, col. 3, line 2: ΙΝΩΜΑΣ: This name has defied reading. Ν is given in accordance with a faint trace of the central stroke, also seen by Professor Brown in Dura, but the letter may be Η, or merely two uprights.

Fr. I, col. 3, line 3: 'Αβεδαιμ[- - -]: "This name is probably to be read Αβεδαιμ[εια] which means 'the servant of (the goddess) Simea.' In Dura two masculine names have been found, similarly constructed, namely 'Αβιδσημιατος,[46] and 'Αβιδσημις.[47] In a feminine name we should have expected the regular feminine of *'abd,* which is *'amat,* a form we actually meet in two names composed with Simea, 'Αμασσημια[48] and Μαθσημεα,[49] one from Haurân, the other from northern Syria. *'Abd* in our name is most likely used 'e parte potiori,' just as in Arabic *'abd* can be applied both to a male and a female."

Fr. I, col. 3, line 4: Καστα: "This name probably is to be derived from the root *qašaṭa,* 'acting justly, equitably,' found in Jewish Aramaic, Nabataean and in Palmyrene.[50] As a proper name Qâsit is known in Arabic, the comparatively frequent Χασετος found in a number of inscriptions from Syria no doubt being the same name, even if the strict grammatical form would have been Κασετος." Καστα is of course also the equivalent of Latin *Casta* and therefore this may be one of the cases where a Latin name was chosen because of its similarity to a Semitic one. Another case is Κασσιανός below, Fr. IV, lines 1–2.[51]

Fr. I, col. 3, lines 5–6: Βαδσημε[: "This name, too, probably contains

[45] Psaltes, *Grammatik der Byz. Chron.,* pp. 347, 361, 367. Cf. βαρύπους, the nickname of a certain Philip of Antioch according to Malalas, 225, 10; καρκινόπους (poet.) *IG*² II/III, 4514, l. 24, meaning "lame"; χηνόπους, *I.G.,* XII, 3, 388 (Thera); and 'Αγαθόπους as a name of runners, L. Robert, *Études Anatoliennes,* Paris, 1937, pp. 143 f.

[46] Cumont, *Fouilles,* p. 382, no. 20; cf. p. 389, no. 27, line 13.

[47] *Ibid.,* p. 383, no. 21.

[48] Lidzbarski, *Ephemeris,* I, p. 218, no. 21; *PEFQS,* 1915, p. 144 n. 2.

[49] Seyrig, *Syria,* XX, 1939, p. 305 (caza of Carchemish).

[50] Cf. *Berytus,* II, 1935, p. 110, no. II, l. 1.

[51] See Wuthnow, p. 2; *Berytus,* II, 1935, p. 98, note 245, and p. 106, note 309.

the name of the goddess Semea, the whole name being Βαδοημε[ία], 'daughter of Semea.' Cf. on Βαδσισαια, Fr. I, col. 2, line 21 above."

The correct position of fragments **a** and **c** at this point will be seen in the tracing; the position in the photograph is not quite right. With Professor Ingholt's restoration of the name in line 5, there is no space in the break for an epithet; the preserved portion on the right is blank. καλή in line 6 is therefore not a proper name (see above, Fr. I, col. 2, line 12), and ΖΕΥΓΜΑ must belong to the same entry. This last is preserved on a piece which makes a slight but certain join on the right. The top of the *zeta* is preserved on **a**, the vertical stroke on **c**. Lines 5–7 are written in very large sloping letters except for ḤΜΕΤΕ. The appearance of the name of the city of Zeugma in this place is surprising, but can best be understood as an abbreviation indicating the place of origin of Βαδοημεία. As such, it must be connected with the heading τῶν ἡμετέρων in Fr. I, col. 2, line 15, which seems to divide the group of women into those from Zeugma and "ours." (See below, pp. 249 f.) It seems reasonable, therefore, to restore ἡμετέ(ρα) in line 7, rather than a nickname (μετε(ώρα)), and to assume that the name of the beautiful Badsemeia had been accidentally omitted in the list preceding τῶν ἡμετέρων. On this hypothesis, the same name has been restored in line 7, assuming that a dark spot high above that line is part of an abbreviation mark similar to the sign used in Fr. III. Βαδοημεια καλή Ζευγμα(τῖτις), then, means not that the woman was a native of that place, but that she belonged to a group contrasted with that of ἡμέτεραι.

Fr. I, col. 3, lines 8 and 9: ΙΑΝΘΕΛΟ[Υ]Σ and [ ]ΑΡΒΑΙΘΗ are Semitic but cannot be restored.

κηλητρ(ία): under this form, the word is not attested. Nevertheless, it would be the regular feminine form of κηλήτης,[52] *herniosus,* a term common in the literature of the mime and Atellana.[53] It may be that this woman was possessed of, or suggested, this affliction. It is also possible

[52] Hesychius gives the gloss κηλήτειρα · ἡσυχάστρια, but this is comment on εὐκηλήτειρα in Hesiod, *Works and Days,* 464 (cf. the glosses in Suidas, Hesychius, and the Etym. Magn. 59.35), and hence a grammarian's invention (cf. Lobeck, *Pathol. Elem.,* p. 54, note 11) or a corruption.

[53] Reich, p. 65, n. 1; A. Dieterich, *Pulcinella,* pp. 37 ff. It was a term of general abuse as well, cf. *Anth. Pal.* VI, 166; XI, 342, 393, 404; Martial XII, 83; Cass. Dio, LXXIII, 2, 2 (cf. *S.H.A.* Commodus, 13, 1); Synesius, *Ep.,* p. 160 A. The point of the jokes in *Philogelos,* ed. Eberhard, nos. 113, 116 (=252), 117–119, 259, is similar to that of Catullus 11, 20, and would not be applicable to a woman.

that she was a hunchback, for κήλη has that meaning.[54] These misformed figures were notoriously popular as entertainers.[55]

Fr. I, col. 3, line 10: 'Αβσαλμας: "The first element of the name is probably a contraction of 'Αβιδ-, 'servant of,' an abbreviation well known from Palmyrene and Syriac. One of the Palmyrene examples even offers the exact equivalent to 'Αβσαλμας, namely עבשלמא;[56] the un-contracted form 'Abd-shalmâ also occurs. As in 'Αβεδσιμεια[57] we should have expected Amat- instead of 'Abd. The god Shalma or Shalman is found both in Djebel Sha 'ar[58] and in Palmyra."[59]

Fr. I, col. 3, line 11: κάππα is in all probability the letter of the alphabet used as a nickname. For this practice we have some evidence in Photius' excerpts from Ptolemaeus Chennus, Καινὴ Ἱστορία, V, 25 ff.,[60] where eight letters are given as the nicknames of a variety of personages. In spite of Ptolemaeus' general unreliability, this list can be accepted for the most part, and we can add to it Eratosthenes, βῆτα,[61] and Dionysius ψῖ (an athlete).[62] For κάππα in particular, parallel evidence can be adduced from the cognomen *Cappa* found in two Latin inscrip-

---

[54] Cf. also Goetz, III, 252, 59: κυρτός, κυλήτης, *gibberosus, curvus*.

[55] Especially Aesop, cf. Lucian, *Vera Hist.*, 2.18. Cf. further Horace, *Ep.*, II, 1, 173; Pliny, *Nat. Hist.*, xxxiv, 3. §11 (*CIL* I², 1004); Martial XIV, 182; *Anth. Pal.*, XI, 120; *S.H.A.*, Commodus, 11.2; A. J. B. Wace, *Annual of the British School in Athens*, X (1903/4), pp. 105 f.; G. M. A. Richter, *AJA*, XVII (1913), pp. 149 ff.; M. Bieber, *History of the Greek and Roman Theater* (1939), p. 419, n. 40; 422, fig. 559; Doro Levi, *Antioch on the Orontes*, III (1941), p. 229; Hetty Goldman, *AJA*, XLVII (1943), p. 25 and fig. 7. Cf. Reich, pp. 65 and 682, Dieterich, *op. cit.*, pp. 37 and 220, note 1, and R. Delbrück, *Die Consulardiptychen* (1929), p. 132, N 21; *Thesaur. Ling. Lat.*, s.v. *gibber*. The adjective κυρτός is used as a personal designation (*SB* 4425, 7, 6; *Fayum Towns*, 121, 15) and Γίββηρος as a slave name (*Inscr. Délos*, 1763, 1769). A similar explanation may lie back of the name Διτύλας in Aristoph., *Frogs*, 608 (L. Radermacher, Wiener Akademie, *Sitzungsberichte*, vol. 198, Abhandlung 4, 1921, p. 230).

[56] *CIS* 4198 B, l. 2; there a masculine name.

[57] Above, Fr. I, col. 3, line 3.          [58] Unpublished inscription.

[59] Cf. *Berytus*, V, 1938, p. 121, note 3.

[60] Cod. 190. See A. Chatzis, *Der Philosoph und Grammatiker Ptolemaios Chennos* (*Studien zur Geschichte und Kultur des Altertums*, VII, 2, Paderborn, 1914), pp. 37 f.

[61] Suidas, *s.v.* Ἐρατοσθένης = Hesychius Miles., *De vir. ill.*, no. 27 Flach; cf. F. Susemihl, *Geschichte der griechischen Literatur*, I, Leipzig, 1891, p. 413, n. 27.

[62] Plutarch, *De proverbiis Alexandrin.*, no. 29; O. Crusius, *J. Kl. Phil.*, CXXXV, 1887, pp. 256 f. Cf. also a story told of Herodes Atticus, Philostratus, *Vita Soph.*, II, i, 22–23 (p. 164 W.). On the significance of letters used as nicknames, see K. Lehrs, *Quaestiones Epicae*, 1837, pp. 18 ff., and esp. Martial V, 26 and II, 57.

tions.[63] As for the meaning of the nickname, one may refer to Suidas, *s.v.* κάππα διπλοῦν · ἀντὶ τοῦ κακά. τρία κάππα κάκιστα · Καππαδοκία, Κρήτη, καὶ Κιλικία. As a contemptuous expression, κάππα fits in well with the majority of the epithets.[64]

Fr. I, col. 4, A–B, contains a list of men's names written in red, as are lines 10–11 in col. 3, and with letters of the same average height as those of col. 2, A–B. Twelve lines are therefore to be restored in col. 4, A, giving 14 names in all, or 13, if line 1 contained a heading, as might be thought from the letters ει in that line.[65] It seems much more likely, however, that this list belongs with that of women under the heading in col. 1.

Fr. I, col. 4, line 5: Ο̣μ̣ανας: ΟΜ are uncertain, especially because of the red stroke between Μ̣ and Α; it probably is part of the Μ̣. "This masculine name one might consider derived from the root אמן, 'be faithful, trustworthy,' comparing the Safaitic Amin (or Umayin)[66] and the Nabataean Amînu (or Umaynû)."[67]

σκ(ηνικός) occurs again in line 13 in the form σκην(ικός). σκηνικός means "actor" in Plutarch, *Otho,* ch. 6, but it is significant that the reference is evidently to low-class actors. A similar connection with popular plays is implied in some Graeco-Latin glosses.[68] In this sense, *scenicus* occurs in a number of Latin inscriptions in which soldiers appear as actors of mimes,[69] and in Dura itself, in the Mithraeum two Latin inscriptions dealing with the same soldier have *scenicus* and a Greek graffito has σκηνικός.[70] Since there is reason to believe that our group had close connections with the Roman camp at Dura, it is likely that the same interpretation should apply to all these inscriptions and

[63] Dessau 5239 (=*CIL,* XI, 4424) from Ameria; *CIL,* VIII, 23697, from Uzappa in Africa. Cf. F. Buecheler, *Rhein. Museum* XXXVII, 1882, pp. 332 ff.

[64] Possibly the surname was given because of the fact that the woman's name began with a *kappa;* cf. Julian, *Misopogon,* 357A.

[65] As to the uncertainty of placing this fragment, see above, pp. 207 f.

[66] Ryckmans, I, p. 45.                    [67] Cantineau, *Le Nabatéen,* II, *s.v.*

[68] *scenicus mimicus,* Goetz, II, 592, 36; Atellani σκηνικοὶ ἀρχαιολόγοι βιολόγοι etc., II, 22, 40 (on this gloss see L. Robert, *Rev. Ét. Gr.,* XLIX, 1936, p. 237; W. Heraeus, *Rhein. Museum,* LXXIX, 1930, pp. 395 ff.; and L. Robert, *Hellenika,* Limoges, 1940, p. 135, note 1); σατυριστὴς ὁ σκινηκός (!) *ludio,* II, 430, 2; cf. II, 124, 47. Cf. Reich, p. 225, note 2 (p. 227).

[69] Dessau, 2178 and 2179.

[70] One of the texts is published in *Rep. VII–VIII,* p. 121, where all the pertinent material is quoted. Professor Rostovtzeff now suggests the reading *scenicus* for a fragmentary inscription from the praetorium, *Rep. V,* p. 233, no. 585.

that the *scenici* of the Mithraeum were actors. The exact meaning, however, remains obscure. The men listed in Fr. V were entertainers, but those listed here may have been attendants of the stage, or else only certain members of the group were actors. However, it may be recalled that several of the sailors from Misenum (Dessau, 2178 and 2179) are called *scaenici Graeci* as members of a company of mimes, and thus were undoubtedly a special type of performer. This may also be the case in our inscription.

Fr. I, col. 4, line 6: Σαμακους: "The most probable derivation is from the Arabic root *samaqa* 'was or became tall,' which is used particularly of palm trees."[71]

Fr. I, col. 4, line 7: ỊẠΓΑΠΕΛΘΟϹ: This name remains unexplained. It must be noted that ỊẠ are quite uncertain and that the ending ΟϹ is found on Fr. I, **h**, which is not placed with certainty.

Fr. I, col. 4, line 8: ’Ασβọ́λις, i.e. ’Ασβόλιος, a Greek nickname meaning "sooty one," known as a proper name,[72] as ἐπίκλησις,[73] and as a gladiator's name.[74] Since it is by origin a nickname,[75] it is particularly well suited to a parasite; in all probability the same person appears in Fr. V, col. 1, line 7. To blacken the face of the γελωτοποιός with soot (ἄσβολος) seems to have been a standard joke at banquets.[76]

Fr. I, col. 4, line 11: Οὐάλ[η]ϲ, a very uncertain reading, would be Latin Valens.[77] The last letters of ΟΠṚẸ were still preserved in Dura. A dark spot visible on the Dura photograph after Ε and hence shown in the tracing (Fig. 92) is probably a depression, not a letter.

Fr. I, col. 4, line 12: The last letter preserved can only be Α, Λ, or Δ. Hence the rare ’Αντιοχίὃ[ης], or, with less likelihood, ’Αντιοχιạ[νός] must be restored.

Fr. I, col. 4, line 13: Καị[οϲ]: A very short name is required. This

[71] Lane, *s.v.* Compare the expression used in Cant. 7, 7, "Thy stature is like to a palm tree."

[72] *PUAE*, III, A, no. 628.

[73] A. Audollent, *Defix. Tabellae*, 1904, no. 27, l. 12.

[74] Ammianus Marcellinus, XXVIII, 1, 8 and L. Robert, *Les Gladiateurs dans l'Orient grec,* Paris, 1940, no. 191 a (cf. ibid., p. 298, note 5).

[75] M. Lambertz, "Zur Ausbreitung des Supernomen oder Signum im römischen Reiche," *Glotta*, V, 1913–1914, p. 134.

[76] Lucian, Τὰ πρὸς Κρόνον, 22; Alciphron, III, 12, 2; cf. also John Chrysostom, *Hom. in Matthew*, 35, 3 (Migne, vol. 57, p. 409).

[77] See *Rep. VI*, p. 187.

spelling of Γαῖος is not infrequent in papyri,[78] and is found also in a late Christian inscription from Syria.[79] σκην(ικός) : see above, line 5.

Fr. I, col. 5, A, lines 1–11, as conjecturally reconstructed, contain a series of entries under the heading: Ἐξῆλθε - -, followed by a similar list under the heading: Ἔπεμσα - -. In the latter, Sabba is the same name as that occurring in line 4, so that it would seem that the two lists deal with the same persons. In fact, it is the double occurrence of this name which makes desirable the insertion of a second heading such as is preserved on Fr. I, **h**. Although the text cannot be restored completely, it seems that three persons were listed in lines 1–5 as having arrived in Dura. The order was presumably chronological, for in lines 8 (or 7)–11, the same people are listed in the chronological order of their departure for Zeugma. Essentially, the tabella is of the same kind as Fr. I, cols. 1–4, an additional reason for preferring the present arrangement of the columns.

Fr. I, col. 5, lines 1–2. The first line is larger than the following, and lines 2 and 3 are curiously indented. The reason for this, and the two letters of line 2 are not clear to me. It is preferable to restore a proper name in line 1, rather than τὰ [πεδί]|α,[80] because a name is needed for the first date, and because the separation of the A in line 2 from the rest would otherwise be unaccounted for. Possibly, however, a woman's name should be restored instead of Τά[τιος?], for Sabba is a woman (see below). Yet Sabba seems to have led a group of entertainers or of women (see the discussion of Fr. III), and in such leading positions men are mentioned in Fr. I, cols. 5–6, line 20 (Οὐικτωρῖνος) and Fr. V, col. 1, line 8 (Ῥωμανός). I therefore prefer a man's name. If it were not for the trace of a second letter in line 2, the A in that line could be read as a numeral: Τά[τιος?] α΄. Possibly we have an abbreviation: ἀ(πὸ) Ζ(εύγματος)?

Fr. I, col. 5, lines 3–4: δευ[τέρ|ᾳ] : The width of this tabella depends upon the restoration of this word and of [καὶ] before [Σα]ββᾳ which seems necessary on the analogy of line 10. Keeping the width of col. 5 at the bottom, there is space only for two letters after δευτέρᾳ; this, as well as the restorations in all the other lines, especially in line 6, required a slight widening of column 5, A (0.008 m.). The irregularity

---

[78] Preisigke, *Namenbuch, ss.vv.* Καῖος and Καῖα.

[79] *PUAE*, III, no. 937. Cf. also Pape, *Wörterbuch d. gr. Eigennamen, s.v.* Καῖος where, however, the reference to *C.I.G.*, III, 4036 (=*IGRR*, III, 187) is mistaken.

[80] Compare Fr. V, col. 1, lines 4–5.

of almost all the other tabellae permits this procedure. Syllabic divisions had to be abandoned if [καί] was to be kept in preference to [κέ].[81]

Fr. I, col. 5, line 4: Σα]ββα: The Dura photograph, as well as Professor Brown's tracing, leaves no doubt about the first B, which is now partly broken. Σαββα occurs again in line 10 and in Fr. III, line 2. Attempts to interpret it in all three places as a date, by reading either Σάββα(τον) "week" or "seventh day of the week" or else as σαββα, Semitic for "seven," have led to no result. Fr. III, lines 2–3: Σαββα [ε]ἰϲαγούϲηϲ can only refer to a woman. On this name Professor Ingholt has given the following information. "A number of different possibilities present themselves. Greek inscriptions and papyri have similar names but they may go back to different Semitic roots. In the Palmyrene feminine name תשבב, Toshabeb[82] we seem to have a name of the same semantic origin, presumably derived from the same root as the Safaitic name Shabab[83] and the old Arabic Shabîb,[84] both meaning 'young man.' Our name Σαββα would thus be an abbreviated feminine name of the same root, meaning 'young woman.' "

Fr. I, col. 5, line 6: Ἔπεμϲα: on the spelling, see above, p. 224 and n. 27. It is not difficult to choose between ἔπεμϲα and ἐπέμϲα[μεν] since the first person plural in Fr. I, col. 6, line 1 and Fr. I, col. 8 (?), line 1 refers to the group of entertainers as a whole, which cannot be the case here. The first person singular has been restored after several graffiti from the House of Nebuchelus at Dura, e.g. ἔπεμψα εἰϲ Ἀπάδανα ἐγὼ Νεβουχῆλοϲ as the heading of a list of miscellaneous goods shipped to Apadana.[85]

[Αὐρη]λί|α is restored from No. 941, a μνηϲθῇ inscription put up by her and some other people. As a Roman citizen she may have been the owner of the establishment (below, p. 254). Her Semitic name is lost, but there is hardly enough space for assuming that it stood in line 6 instead of ἐγώ. The addition of ἐγώ contrasts with classical usage, but is a feature of the Koine.[86] Aurelius Nebuchelus was commonly called by his Semitic name, but Aurelia seems to have used her Roman name.

Fr. I, col. 5, line 8: This line seems necessary in order to make space for the third name; of course line 5 may have been vacant. The difficulty

---

[81] Cf. the awkward division in Fr. V, cols. 2–3, lines 7–8.

[82] *Berytus*, II, 1935, p. 115.                [83] Ryckmans, I, p. 204.

[84] Wüstenfeld, *Register*, p. 414.

[85] *Rep. IV*, p. 98, no. 227; cf. *ibid.*, p. 119, no. 240, line 7.

[86] This can be gathered from the examples collected by Mayser, II, 1, pp. 62 f.

of spacing in this place has been mentioned above, p. 207. Lines 8 and 9 cannot be made to coincide because of the top margin of col. 6.

Fr. I, col. 6, lines 1–3: This complete entry, restored with certainty from Fr. I, col. 8 (?), lines 1–2, which are identical, announces the occupation of the house by the whole group on Dius 1. The precise meaning of μεταβαίνω, "to change one's residence," is probably implied here, and the group seems to have lived previously in other places in Dura (see p. 254). In the present arrangement, this notice occupies a prominent place in the upper right corner of the series of large tabellae.

The lower parts of cols. 5 and 6 are filled with a series of notices, apparently dealing with the life of the group, but very difficult to understand. In this place they look like space fillers, as does the similar notice in the last line of Fr. II, but in Fr. IV they occupy a tabella especially designed for them. They seem to be warnings of some sort placed at the end of the regular lists and entries. Similar sentences are added to the main text in Fr. V. The first sentence of this sort is in col. 6, lines 8–12, of which only the end can be read: - -[εἰ]ς οἶ[κο]ν εἰσενίκης, where εἰσενίκης is clearly 2nd singular aorist subjunctive of εἰσήνικα, Ionic and Koine form for εἰσήνεγκα. βλέπε μή should be restored somewhere in the preceding lines. Then the scribe went over to col. 5, line 12, with a short sentence consisting of three words [πιστε?]ύει σοὶ οὐδ[είς], which cannot be combined with the corresponding line in col. 6. It would be natural to assume that line 12 in col. 5 was written after col. 5, A, lines 1–11, had been inscribed. But an ancient black blot covering the letters IO of line 12 probably was made when the black lines above were painted. The text of cols. 5–6 apparently was written from right to left, starting with the large Μετέβημεν notice which was the first text to be inscribed.

In cols. 5–6, B, the scribe went over two panels and chose an ornamental arrangement of black and red. The first two lines (13–14) may be a complete sentence since there seems to be a very worn *vacat* after ἔδωκας. Lines 15–20 possibly belong together. Warnings with πιστεύειν occur in two different forms: lines 13–14: ἰδ]οῦ μὴ πιστε[ύσῃς], which is paralleled by Fr. IV, B; and line 15: πιστευσε[- -, also found in Fr. II, line 3. This latter form is not altogether clear. Lines 18–19 contain the end of a βλέπε μή warning with βλέπε repeated exactly as it is in Fr. IV, lines 15–16; there follows "because nobody gives to the other." With these panels, and in all probability at the end of line 17, belongs Fr. X, giving --]μηδ[έν]α. The sense may be, as Professor Nock suggested: "Do not let anybody into your house without money." More likely the sentence refers to the admission of entertainers by the leader of a group, for this is the sense of εἰσάγειν in Fr. IV, line 11. δίδει in late Greek is a regular form for δίδωσι.[87]

Fr. I, cols. 5–6, lines 19–20: ἐξἐξήχθης ὑπὸ Οὐικτωρίνου: double spellings of ξ are not infrequent in inscriptions,[88] but here no doubt the phenomenon is to be classified with other cases of the doubling of a consonant at the end of the line and the beginning of the next. Most common are the cases of μμ, νν, etc., a fact perhaps to be connected with the doubling of nasals and liquids in popular speech.[89] It may be suggested that the mistake here was caused by an uncertainty felt about the syllabic division: the phonetic division, which is that prescribed by the grammarians, required ἐ|ξήχθης, while ἐξ|ήχθης is the etymological spelling which is also widely used in epigraphical texts. It may also be recalled that as early as Ptolemaic times ἐξ- is found written and pronounced 'ξ, as it is in modern Greek.[90]

The sentence gives the reason for the preceding warning, whatever it was. For us its main significance lies in the fact that it clearly shows that the sentences here are addressed to members of the group (see p. 251). ἐξήχθης presumably refers to travel from Zeugma, but one cannot be certain. Victorinus, a man with a Latin name, occupied a prominent position in the group.

Fr. I, col. 7, B: the end of a short tabella perhaps similar to the following. Αἰδυνέος is also the last month mentioned in Fr. I, col. 1. The traces in line 4 do not favor the assumption that this was another list of months, but they are much worn and not decisive. The reading Αἰδυνέος itself is based on an uncertain joint.

Fr. I, col. 8 (?), B: a short notice concerning an advance payment, no doubt on the rent, to the landlord. The notice concerning the date of

---

[87] Mayser, I, 2, pp. 123 f. Dieterich, *Untersuchungen zur Geschichte der griechischen Sprache,* p. 221 (cited above, n. 22).

[88] E. Hermann, *Silbenbildung im Griechischen,* Göttingen, 1923, pp. 112 f.

[89] W. Schulze, *Zeitschrift für vergleichende Sprachforschung,* XXXIII, 1895, p. 397; cf. C. B. Welles, *Royal Correspondence in the Hellenistic Period,* New Haven, 1934, p. LIV, note 10; F. Solmsen, *Untersuchungen zur griechischen Laut- und Verslehre,* Strassburg, 1901, p. 164.

[90] Mayser, I, 1, p. 144. Cf. Dieterich, *op. cit.,* p. 30. On syllabic division in general see the lists compiled by E. Hermann, *op. cit.,* pp. 132–181 and pp. 202 f. Cf. pp. 123 ff. for the rules of the grammarians. Further bibliography in E. Schwyzer, *Griechische Grammatik,* I, 1939, p. 236; R. P. Austin, *The Stoichedon Style in Greek Inscriptions,* Oxford, 1938, pp. 43 ff.; C. B. Welles, *loc. cit.*

arrival in the house is repeated from col. 6, lines 1–3, a fact well explained by the present arrangement according to which the space below the first notice had already been filled when this tabella was written. In line 3, ΕΙΟΣΤΑ is quite certain, and the next letter can only be Ο or Θ. The reading σταθμ[οῦχος] is therefore reasonably assured. σταθμοῦχος is in the first place a military term denoting the owner of a house in which soldiers are billeted.[91] Probably in this sense the term has already occurred in Dura.[92] In late texts and inscriptions σταθμοῦχος can also mean simply "landlord."[93] Since there is reason to believe that our group lived in close contact with soldiers (below, pp. 245 and 260 f.), the term may well be military here. The group may have been assigned to quarters by the military authorities at Dura, or they may simply have used a familiar word. That it was not a case of ἐπισταθμία is shown by the fact that they paid rent. I have found no direct parallel for a partial advance payment on the rent of a house, but in *P. Teb.* 372 of 141 A.D., a contract for the lease of a house for six years, the rent for the whole period is paid in advance, and the same is true of the contract *P. Rendel Harris* 82 of 345 A.D., which runs for four years. After [π]ροχρείαν there is a short *vacat* similar to those in lines 1 and 2; possibly the amount of money advanced is lost.

Fr. II: The end of a tabella; not more than 4–6 letters are lost in lines 1–2, if the tabella was at all regular. ΚΑ in line 1 are quite uncertain, and the appearance of Cassianus here is not without difficulties, since he is listed in a later tabella (Fr. IV, lines 1–2) as one who has just arrived from Zeugma. In line 2, a slanting stroke after Μ, if it is not a flaw in making that letter, can only be read Α. The line then contains a Semitic name beginning with Εσμα-;[94] I have not found any other word or name containing these letters. This may then be the end of a list of proper names, perhaps arrivals; to such a text the πιστεύειν formula is a suitable addition.

Fr. III: No doubt an entry concerning arrivals. The restoration [Δ]ίου gives a normal width (0.166 m.) and eliminates the necessity of restoring a word preceding [ε]ἰσαγούσης. The end of line 1 (ιΟι) can only be combined with line 2 if we restore Γορ|[πια]ίου, but αι is an un-

---

[91] *R.E. s.v.;* Friedländer, I, pp. 344 ff.

[92] *Rep. VI*, pp. 176 f., no. 695, p. 275, and especially pp. 299–304 with full bibliography. See also *SEG*, IV, 560.

[93] *R.E. op. cit.*, p. 2182; Hesychius: σταθμοῦχος · ὁ τῆς οἰκίας κύριος καὶ ξενοδόχος.

[94] Wuthnow gives Εσμαηλος and Εσμαθου (genitive).

likely spelling, and a very short word would have to be inserted at the beginning of line 3. Dius 26 is a plausible date here (see p. 253). Σαββα [ε]ἰσαγούσης at the end of a paragraph (S) is strange, but can be understood as "Sabba was the leader," either as a genitive absolute or as the end of a longer construction.[95] The whole sentence may have been: [ἐξῆλθε ὁ δεῖνα κτλ. Δ]ίου Sκ', Σαββα [ε]ἰσαγούσης.

εἰσάγειν, sc. εἰς οἶκον (cf. Fr. I, col. 6, line 18) is used without an object apparently as a kind of technical term, as in Fr. IV, line 10.

Fr. IV, lines 1–3: Despite the singular[96] in this fifth notice of arrivals from Zeugma, both Cassianus and Rufus are presumably members of the group. The very doubtful letters ΕΛΛΕΟ have been taken to contain the date of arrival after the parallel entry in Fr. I, col. 5, A. But they might also be read ΚΑΛΕΟ, implying that these entertainers had come to Dura on an invitation. The name of the host would then be mentioned in the following lines. With neither reading is it possible to combine ΟC in line 9 with the letters in line 3. A longer gap must therefore intervene between these two lines, which might have been filled with further arrivals if ['Απ]ελλέο[υ] is correct.

Fr. IV, lines 10–16: A warning is appended to the list of arrivals as in the other texts; it is addressed to the same kind of people as the texts in Fr. I, cols. 5–6, B, because of the phrase εἰς οἶκόν σου which recurs in Fr. I, cols. 5–6, line 18, and in a similar form in Fr. I, col. 6, lines 11–12. The meaning appears to be a general maxim: "If for two months you bring (people) into your house, be careful not to trust anyone much, not even yourself, be careful." [Εἰσά]γων is restored after Fr. III, line 3. δύο μῆνας means "over a period of two months."[97] πιστεύειν ἑαυτῷ is frequent in literature,[98] always in the sense of being self confident, and occurs also in Syll.³ 985, the famous mystic inscription from Philadelphia, line 56. Here, however, the sense seems to be "do not trust even yourself" rather than "do not be self confident."

The graffiti to the right of Fr. IV, B, show part of a figure of some sort and a leaf; on **c** the strokes seem to be writing.

---

[95] The word order would then be of a not uncommon type represented e.g. by OGIS, 214; cf. the parallels cited by Welles, op. cit., p. 40.

[96] This use is very common in papyri, Mayser, II, 3, pp. 31 f.

[97] Kühner-Gerth, Grammatik der Griechischen Sprache, II, 1, p. 314; Mayser, II, 2, p. 32.

[98] See Stephanus, Thesaurus, and add Plato, Crat., 425 B, Phaed., 83 A, Rep. V, 450 D, Laches, 186 D, Prot., 348 E.

Fr. V, *Graffito:* This metrical, and almost certainly hexametrical, text is hardly restorable, since it does not seem to be a quotation. In line 4 - -]νιν should be the end of a word such as μῆνιν or κόνιν; the particle νιν is not properly epic. - -].[.]ωδια may be ἐ[π]ῴδια as Professor Welles suggests, or [τρ]ᾳ[γ]ῴδια, although these diminutives are not attested. The last letter of χρήματα is very badly preserved; possibly we should read χρῆμά τι or χρήματι. In line 5, ξίφος ὠκύ cannot be combined with the preceding line, since that would place χρήματα in the third foot of the hexameter. Therefore a new verse must have started with line 5 which was never completed, for nothing, it seems, was inscribed after ὠκύ. Presumably each line contained a verse; this arrangement centers the graffito in relation to the painted tabellae below. These were clearly written later, as is shown by their position below the red wall surface (above, p. 208) and by the fact that the bottom of the lower stroke of φ in line 5 is covered with black paint.

An original metrical inscription directly above, and seemingly related to, a text mentioning entertainers should be related to their activities. τρ]ᾳ[γ]ῴδια[99] may refer to songs and ξίφος ὠκύ to sword dancing or sword swallowing.[100] Since the text is in hexameters one might also consider the Ὁμηρισταί,[101] but in that case a quotation from Homer would be more likely, because the Ὁμηρισταί acted and recited scenes from Homer.[102] As a description of entertainers the poem may refer to almost any kind of acting.

*Dipinto,* col. 1, lines 1–6: The heading explains the contents of the following list as one of all the δουλοπαράσειτοι who had been with the group "since the time when the slaves came to Zeugma, or later."

Fr. V, col. 1, lines 1–2: δουλοπαράσειτοι, a new compound after the fashion of so many late compounds with δουλο-,[103] designates all the fol-

---

[99] Cf. Fr. V, col. 1, lines 7–9 and notes.

[100] H. Blümner, *Fahrendes Volk im Altertum,* Münchener Akademie der Wissenschaften, *Sitzungsberichte,* Phil.-hist. Klasse, 1918, no. 6, pp. 10 f.; L. Robert, *Rev. Ét. Gr.,* XLII, 1929, p. 436, note 1 and p. 437, note 1.

[101] Blümner, *op. cit.,* p. 5; *RE,* Suppl. III, *s.v.;* Friedländer, I, p. 253; L. Robert, *Rev. Ét. Gr.,* XLIX, 1936, p. 237, note 4; W. Heraeus, *Rhein. Museum,* LXXIX, 1930, pp. 395 ff.; Herondas, *Mimiambi,* ed. Crusius, 5th ed., 1914, p. 123; *P. Osl.* 189, line 12, lists an ἀπόδιξις Ὁμηρι[στῶν] in a calendar of festivals of the 3rd century A.D.: see the comments of S. Eitrem and L. Amundsen, *Papyri Osloenses,* fasc. III, 1936, note on p. 269. This interpretation was also suggested by Professor Nock.

[102] Petronius, ch. 59, 3.

[103] Stephanus, *Thesaurus* and F. Passow, *Handwörterbuch der griechischen Sprache.*

lowing men as slaves. παράσιτος is in Hellenistic and later literature used only in the sense of parasite.[104] The early Athenian institution of cult officials was in subsequent centuries known only to scholars.[105] In comedy and the mime, where we know them best, parasites share their masters' meals and act as entertainers and γελωτοποιοί. In the mime, this name came to be characteristic of the actor of the second rôle, and the Roman organization of *parasiti Apollinis* may derive its name therefrom.[106] It is clear, then, that the men listed here are not intended to be designated as "slave-associates"; in the absence of other evidence it must be decided from the context whether they are actors of mimes or dinner entertainers. It is true that in cols. 2–3, line 8, reference seems to be made to mimic plays. But the mention of a τρα(γῳδός) in col. 1, line 7, of a "glutton" in col. 2, line 1, and of a dice player in col. 3, line 1, makes the second hypothesis more plausible.[107] Our men then enter into a category of which the first example is the γελωτοποιός Philip at Xenophon's Symposium who, it will be remembered, acts also as a sort of mime.[108] In the later Roman Empire mimes and entertainers more and more restricted their activities to private celebrations such as weddings and funerals, and often formed part of the familia in wealthy houses.[109] Such a parasite is found as a member of the familia of slaves in the Oxyrhynchus mime Μοιχεύτρια (ll. 165, 167; in Herondas, *Mimiambi*, ed. Crusius, 5th ed., p. 114). No doubt writers like John Chrysostom depict actual conditions when they speak of παράσιτοι at the rich man's banquet.[110] Yet they were not professional mimes, but rather performers of

---

[104] O. Navarre in Daremberg-Saglio, *s.v.*

[105] Athen. VI, 234 D (Polemon); 235 b–c (Crates). Pollux VI, 34 f. *OGIS*, no. 195, a dedication by a certain Aphrodisius "the parasite" in honor of Marc Antony is probably to be taken as a form of flattery (cf. Dittenberger's comments *ad loc.*) rather than as evidence for a cult association of which the parasite was a member (F. Poland, *Geschichte des griechischen Vereinswesens*, pp. 55–56); the term parasite is therefore not to be connected with the early sense of this word. Compare similar sentiments voiced by Tiridates before Nero, Cassius Dio LXIII, 5, 2.

[106] A. Müller, *Philologus*, LXIII, 1904, pp. 342 ff. G. Cultrera, *Not. Scavi*, 1915, pp. 158 ff. with bibliography.

[107] See also p. 257.

[108] Xenophon, *Symp.*, II, 21. Cf. Reich, pp. 160–164, 417, 821.

[109] A. Müller, "Das Bühnenwesen in der Zeit von Constantin d. Gr. bis Justinian," *Neue Jahrbücher für das klassische Altertum*, XII, 1909, p. 49; E. S. Bouchier, *Syria as a Roman Province*, 1916, pp. 16 f. and 76.

[110] *Homilia in Matthaeum*, 6, 7 (Migne, vol. 57, p. 71); 48, 6–7 (Migne, vol. 58, pp. 494 ff.); *De Lazaro*, 6, 5 and 8 (Migne, vol. 48, pp. 1033 and 1039); *Ad Theo-*

jests and tricks. John Chrysostom was of course not interested in making this distinction. Generally speaking, our parasites should be regarded as close relatives of the people mentioned by him.[111]

Fr. V, col. 1, lines 3–4: ἀνέβη must be read because the space of two letters preceding Β in line 4, which is now largely broken away, appears to have been a *vacat*. There seems to have been a hole in the plaster which continued as a depression down to line 5 causing the irregular shape of the Δ which was partly written on the right side of the flaw; and it seems that the I was written on top of it. ἀναβαίνειν is used in papyri in the sense of going from the village to the city, καταβαίνειν being used for going to the village;[112] here the arrival of the group at their main center of activity is spoken of.

Fr. V, col. 1, line 5: Ζεῦγμ[α] : the υ, now somewhat blurred, is perfectly clear on the Dura photograph. Part of μ and the α, must have been on the black margin which is now badly preserved at this point.

Fr. V, col. 1, line 7: Ἀϲβόλιϲ : for the name, see Fr. I, col. 4, line 8. He is here specified as ὁ τρα(γῳδός) ; ο is certain on the Dura photograph. It is not surprising to find a tragedian as a member of a group of popular entertainers, if it is considered that tragedy long before this time had degenerated into a singing of separate songs or recitation of iambics.[113] Accordingly τραγῳδός came to mean singer of tragic choruses, and then simply singer.[114] Our man, then, is a singer, perhaps of tragic songs. Such a τραγῳδός with his ὑποκριτής, has already appeared at Dura as a member of the familia of the Dux Ripae.[115] But he was no doubt of a higher category than Asbolius and a real tragedian of late type.

Fr. V, col. 1, lines 8–9: Ῥωμανὸς ᾧ Θεοδώρα ὑποτρ(αγῳδεῖ) is apparently

dorum Lapsum, 1, 9 (Migne, vol. 47, p. 288) ; cf. also Alciphron III, 19, 9; Agathias, *Hist.* II, 29 C = *Hist. Gr. Min.*, II, p. 230.

[111] On γελωτοποιοί see the excellent article by P. Maas, *R.E.*, *s.v.*

[112] U. Wilken, *Grundzüge und Chrestomathie der Papyruskunde*, I, 2, 1914, no. 495, etc.

[113] Schmid-Stählin, *Geschichte der Griechischen Literatur*, II,[6] pp. 333, 635 and 958 f.; Schanz-Hosius, *Geschichte der römischen Literatur*, II,[4] pp. 293 f.; M. P. Nilsson, "Zur Geschichte des Bühnenspiels in der römischen Kaiserzeit," *Acta Universitatis Lundensis*, XL, 1, 3, 1906.

[114] K. Krumbacher, *Geschichte der Byzantinischen Literatur*, p. 647. As early as 336 B.C. Νεοπτόλεμος ὁ τραγῳδός sang at Philip of Macedon's banquet one of the ἐπιτετευγμένων ποιημάτων from an unknown tragedy (Diodorus Siculus, XVI, 92, 3). τραγῳδός = "singer" occurs in Dionysius Thrax (Bekker, *Anecd.*, p. 631, 21) and often in our scholia (Theocritus, Odyssey), cf. Goetz, III, p. 371, 77 and p. 504, 70.

[115] *Rep. VII/VIII*, p. 121. The inscription which will be published in *Rep. IX*, Part

another τραγῳδός helped by a woman. But it is curious that the profession is not mentioned again and it is tempting to read lines 7–9 as a continuous text. In that case, Romanus might be a second name of Asbolius which he used for his connections with the Roman soldiers.[116] But the position of the name after the profession is too awkward even in a text like the present. Much more likely would it be to see in ὁ τραγῳδός ῾Ρωμανός a Latinism for *tragoedus Romanus* and to think of Asbolius as a singer of Latin verse. In a much earlier time, 170 B.C., we find among the Latin jugglers who visited Delos a ῥωμαϊστής ᾿Αγαθόδωρος, i.e., an actor who spoke Latin.[117] Under the Empire Latin mimes are found in the East acting in Latin.[118] In the palace of the Dux at Dura Latin seems to have been recited, for a graffito records the first verses of the Aeneid.[119] Recitation of Latin verses would have been appreciated among the Roman soldiers. Nevertheless, this interpretation forces the meaning of ῾Ρωμανός unduly, and it has not been admitted into the text.

ὑποτραγῳδεῖν is quoted by Liddell and Scott as *v.l.* in Lucian, *Jupiter Trag.*, ch. 1,[120] where it is used figuratively, and from Philostratus, *Vit. Soph.*, I, 18, 2 (cf. Demosthenes, *On the Crown*, §262). It is very improbable that Theodora acted a second part in regular tragedy of the classical type. She probably was Romanus' ὑποκριτής, supporting her partner's solo arias by gestures or commenting on the action by recitation, a type of acting illustrated by the Dux inscription and most familiar from the Emperor Nero.[121] In Rome the separation of song and gesture in tragedy had been instituted by Livius Andronicus, who used a young boy to sing the cantica while he himself played the part by

2, has been mentioned several times and is quoted in full by F. Gilliam, "The Dux Ripae at Dura," *T.A.P.A.*, LXXII, 1942, p. 158.

[116] See pp. 260 f. ὁ καί is often omitted in double names. Lambertz, *Glotta*, V, 1913–1914, p. 133 and note 4.

[117] *IG*, XI, 2, 133, 81; cf. 132, 13. The same profession is found again in the 1st century B.C. at Delos, *Inscr. Délos*, no. 2618, d, line 8.

[118] Dessau 5208. The inscription from Iconium, *IGRR*, III, 1479, however, does not refer to a mime; cf. L. Robert, *Rev. Ét. Gr.*, XLIX, 1936, p. 243, who also shows that the evidence adduced by P. Perdrizet, *BCH*, XXIII, 1899, pp. 592 f. and F. Cumont, *Festschrift O. Hirschfeld*, 1903, p. 277 concerning Latin mimes in the Orient is erroneous.

[119] To be published in *Rep. IX*, Part 2. The quotation must be viewed in the light of the above mentioned actors' inscription.

[120] Adopted by Harmon, *L.C.L.*

[121] Suetonius, *Nero*, ch. 24. Lucian, *Nero or the Piercing of the Isthmus*, ch. 9; cf. G. Boissier, *Rev. Arch., N.S.*, IV, 1861, p. 340.

mere gesticulation.[122] An actor (Stephanio) of the time of Augustus used a Roman *matrona,* dressed as a boy, for a similar purpose and was punished by the Emperor.[123] A boy as ὑποκριτής probably appears on a consular diptych which shows a singing tragedian with his right arm raised; his left he rests on a small boy who makes a gesture appropriate to explanatory recitation.[124] The fact that a woman is associated with a tragedian in the inscription shows that it was a low type of entertainment and not real tragedy. Women had, however, long before entered the stage of the mime,[125] and occasionally they are found in the pantomime.[126] In comedy they are known from Donatus.[127] It is a common phenomenon that jugglers kept women as their assistants,[128] and one is particularly reminded of Tertia "the mime" and daughter of the mime Isidorus who lived with a Rhodian flute player in Sicily before Verres abducted her.[129] The evidence entitles us to see in Romanus and Theodora a typical pair of entertainers; the man sang tragic songs while the woman assisted him on the stage.

Fr. V, col. 1, line 10: Ἄχαβος: αχ were well preserved in Dura. "This masculine name is frequent in Dura.[130] It is probably a Hellenized form of an original Aḥ-Abû, 'brother of the father,' similar to the name of the famous Israelite king of Ahab."

[122] Livy, VII, 2.

[123] Suetonius, *Augustus,* ch. 45. It is commonly thought, however, that the matrona was the actor's servant at private parties, for Suetonius uses the word *ministrare;* cf. Friedländer, II, p. 137; *R.E., s.v.* "Stephanio," no. 1; Forcellini, *s.v.* "ministro." But cf. ὑπηρετεῖν used of the Empress Theodora, Procopius, *Hist. Arc.,* 9, 13.

[124] R. Delbrück, *Die Consulardiptychen,* Berlin, 1929, p. 126, N 18; M. Bieber, *History of the Greek and Roman Theater,* 1939, p. 425, fig. 564.

[125] Reich, pp. 28, 528–529, 601.

[126] A. Müller, *Neue Jahrbücher f. d. klass. Altert.,* XII, 1909, p. 45. M. Bieber, *History of the Greek and Roman Theater,* p. 414. John Chrysostom repeatedly makes reference to women as singers of couplets; see J. U. Vance, *Beiträge zur Byzantinischen Kulturgeschichte,* Diss. Jena, 1907, p. 52. Cf. Malalas, 288, 10. Dessau 5256 *a* (a *symphoniaca*), 5231 and 5232 (*monodiaria*).

[127] On Terence, *Andria,* 4, 3, 1.

[128] Cf. the boy and the girl in Xenophon's *Symposium. I.G.,* XI, 2, 115, 25; Strabo XIV, 648 (cf. *P. Enteux.,* 26); Athen. IV, 130 c; XIV, 621 b. In the mime: Ammian. Marcell., XXIII, 5, 3; J. Horovitz, *Spuren Griechischer Mimen im Orient,* pp. 38 ff.; R. Delbrück, *Die Consulardiptychen,* p. 132, N 21. The best example remains always that of the Empress Theodora.

[129] Cicero, *In Verrem,* II, III, 34, §78 and V, 12, §31, etc.; cf. III, 36, §83.

[130] *Rep. II,* H 43, p. 109; *Rep. V,* no. 517; *Rep. VI,* p. 429, *D.Pg.* 23; Cumont, *Fouilles,* no. 7 and note, no. 20 and note.

Fr. V, col. 1, line 11: Although the traces of the missing letters do not particularly favor [Φι]λόπα[ππ]ος, there is nothing against it. I have found no restoration which would give Achabos' profession in this line; the letters ΛΟΠΑ cannot be read ΛΟΓΟ.

Fr. V, col. 1, line 12: [Κ]ᾳρσιανός is restored after Fr. IV, line 1, and seems also to occur in Fr. II, line 1. The name, although Roman, seems to have been common in Semitic countries because of a phonetic similarity to Semitic names.[181]

Fr. V, col. 1, line 13: Here again one is tempted to restore something different from a proper name. [ἡ] γυνὴ αὐτο[ῦ] could perhaps be seen in the very badly blurred traces of the last three extant letters, and there seems to be a red spot on the black margin where the final υ should be. However, γ is quite doubtful, and a woman's name is needed after the line thus restored, but ο in Ὕμνος is certain.

Fr. V, col. 1, line 14: ὑμνολ[όγ(ος)] is very unlikely in this setting[182] but Ὕμνος is not uncommon as a man's name.[183] The lower part of col. 1, then, contains only proper names and we can only speculate as to the type of performers listed here. They may all have been τραγῳδοί but a number of at least eight tragedians seems disproportionate. It is much more probable that they were γελωτοποιοί with no special proficiency.

Fr. V, col. 2, lines 1–4: The entertainer Charisius is specified as a glutton and a good musician (?). καταφαγᾶς in Greek was hitherto known only from Attic poetry.[184] The word was rejected by the Atticists, perhaps, as Lobeck suggests, because formations in -ᾶς are not formed from compound verbs, and this type of word was thus unfamiliar.[185] But in popular literature the word is found in Latin. Trimalchio in the *Satyricon*, ch. 39, 9, goes through the signs of the zodiac: "In leone cataphagae nascuntur et imperiosi." In Goetz, the word is glossed: *ganeo* (II, 32, 15), *gulatores* (36, 44) and *nebulo* (132, 58), etc. As far as can be determined, καταφαγᾶς always means "glutton" as a jest, and is never a designation of a profession or of a type in the mime.[186] It is inter-

---

[181] Wuthnow, *s.v.*

[182] See Daremberg-Saglio, *s.v. hymnodus.*

[183] F. Bechtel, *Die historischen Personennamen des Griechischen*, Halle, 1917, p. 609; *IG*, XI, 4, 684, line 3; *IGRR*, I, 815 (cognomen).

[184] Aeschylus, fr. 428 Nauck; Myrtilus, fr. 4, Kock (I, p. 254); Menander, fr. 424, Kock (III, p. 123). Compare the κατωφαγᾶς in Aristophanes, *Birds*, 288 with scholia *ad. loc.* and Suidas, *s.v.*

[185] Phrynichus, *Epit.*, pp. 433 ff., Lobeck. Cf. Pollux, VI, 40.

[186] This is certainly true for the passage in Petronius and also for Myrtilus, fr. 4

esting to find the word in the Koine; the reason no doubt is the great productivity of the suffix -ᾱς in late Greek.[187] Although there is no evidence for the use of καταφαγᾱς as a rôle in the mime, it might be suggested that here the "glutton" represents a special type of entertainer. The voracious *Bucco* was of old a type in the Atellana and it is not surprising to find him among a group of entertainers of various kinds.

[μουσι?]κός has been conjectured in accordance with the mention of musicians as low-class entertainers in Egyptian papyri. While it is not altogether clear what kind of music they performed, they probably formed the bulk of the orchestra, since they are distinguished from flute-players on the one hand, and from secondary members on the other.[188]

Fr. V, col. 3, lines 1–2: κοττιστής, followed presumably by a proper name. κόττος, κοττίζειν, κοττιστής, etc., are regular late Greek words for κύβος, κυβεύειν, κυβιστής. As a profession, dice playing is mentioned by Theophrastus (*Charact.* VI, 5),[189] and is assured by the frequent mention of κυβευτήρια.[140] That dice-playing was one of the amusements at banquets, and as such is often mentioned together with other forms of entertainment is well known and may be illustrated by Libanius, *Or.*, LII, §38. Songs, flutes, etc., and dice are all constituents of the banquet. It is natural, then, that it often fell to the parasite to amuse his hosts with this game.[141]

Fr. V, cols. 2–3, lines 5–6: Two black lines written over two columns and so awkwardly spaced that ε in line 5 must originally have been written over κ in line 4. The writing suggests a warning of the kind found in Fr. I, cols. 5–6, B, Fr. II and Fr. IV, B.

Kock (I, p. 234). Cf. Herodiani Technici, *Reliquiae*, ed. Lentz, II, I, p. 51, l. 9; p. 657, l. 13; *Partitiones*, ed. Boissonade, London, 1819, p. 284.

[187] E. Schwyzer, *Griechische Grammatik,* p. 461. B. Olsson in *Aegyptus*, VI, 1925, pp. 247 ff.; XIII, 1933, p. 327, note 2.

[188] *P. Oxy.* 1275: ὁ προεστὼς συμφωνίας αὐλητῶν καὶ μουσικῶν; *P. Fior.* 74: μεθ' ἧς ἔχετε συμφωνίας πάσης μουσικῶν τε καὶ ἄλλων.

[189] Cf. Cicero, *Philipp.,* VIII, 9, §26.

[140] Cassius Dio, LXV, 2, 1; Plutarch, *Quaest. Conviv.,* I, 621b. See in general Daremberg-Saglio, *s.v. alea*, and H. Blümner, *Die Römischen Privataltertümer*, pp. 412 ff. For professional dice-players in the Talmud, see S. Krauss, *Talmudische Archäologie*, 1910–1912, III, p. 110.

[141] A parasite and a hetaera are playing dice in Diphilus, fr. 73, Kock (II, p. 565). Cf. also Alciphron, III, 6, 18.

Fr. V, cols. 2–3, lines 7–10, also can hardly be understood otherwise, if the independent placing of **b** is accepted (above, p. 209). The crucial letters in line 7, col. 3, are very faint, but starting with γ, which seems certain, I have found the letters ΠΟΥϹΓΕ the only possible reading. They cannot form the beginning of a word, and **b** likewise cannot be read continuously. Φίλω[ν..]ο|ϲ κὲ μῖμο[ϲ] seems therefore out of the question. The present restoration, which cannot claim certainty, can only be defended by a general reference to the frequent association of γέλωϲ and γελωτοποιία with μῖμοι in our literary texts.[142] The occurrence of a form of the word μῖμοϲ in this fragment is, however, of the greatest importance. Whether it refers to actors or to plays (as is more likely in the present restoration) it connects the δουλοπαράϲειτοι in some way with the mime. γελ[οίου|]ϲ entails some crowding at the end of line 7, and μῖμο[υ|ϲ] some irregular and wide spacing. But this is a very badly written series of tabellae.

The warning, then, may say: "If you like jests and mimes, be careful that (the group) do not - - - -: (because) the *optio* - - - (is) with Satyrillus." It is not clear to whom this is addressed. From φιλῶν it would seem that customers rather than parasites are meant. But on the analogy of the other warnings this assumption is not entirely plausible. Somebody is told to see to it that others do not misbehave, because an *optio* watches them. While the exact nature of that office here cannot be determined,[143] it seems reasonable to assume a supervision of the establishment by the army. In col. 3, line 9, a mistake was made by the scribe, the letters being almost certainly ϹΘΟΟΠΤΙΩΝ; ποιῆϲθ⟨ε⟩ · ὁ ὀπτίων may be read instead of the suggestion adopted in the text. Ϲατυρίλλῳ also makes difficulties, since I have not found this name. Possibly it is a corruption or Hellenization of Saturninus.[144] In that case, Saturninus may be the superior officer of the *optio,* although ὑπό rather than παρά is used in this connection in the papyri.[145] The ΛΛ are smeared and at present look more like ΑΛ or ΑΔ.

[142] The *locus classicus* is Demosthenes, *Olynth.*, 2, 19: μῖμοι γελοίων at Philip's court. The reference is probably to γελωτοποιοί, not to mimes, but the expression, often repeated, was later sometimes misunderstood to mean mimes.

[143] In general see *RE, s.v. optio.*

[144] This name is found in the following Greek spellings: Ϲατορνῖνος; Ϲατορνῖλος, a common spelling in Greek (cf. B. Keil, *Hermes,* XLIII, 1908, p. 561); Ϲατυρνῖλος (see Index to *CIG*). Cf. Pape, *Eigennamen, s.v.* Ϲατουρνῖνος.

[145] Preisigke, *Wörterbuch,* III, p. 216, *s.v.* ὀπτίων.

No. **941** is apparently a μνησθῇ text, perhaps put up when some repairs were made in the wall plastering. Three persons seem to be named, Aurelia (cf. Fr. I, col. 5, line 6), a person with a Semitic name, and - -]υτης, perhaps identical with - -]ʹ της in Fr. II, line 2. α]ὐτῆς is also possible, but the noun on which it depends can hardly be found. The text, it would seem, is not a dedication.

## GENERAL COMMENTS

### Date of the Inscriptions

On general grounds the inscriptions must be assigned to the period between 250 and 256 A.D., for the house in which they were found was last rebuilt about 250 and the attack of the Persians on Dura in 256 made communications between Dura and the outer world impossible. The excellent state of preservation of the best preserved fragments, moreover, seems to favor a date not long before the fall of the city. There is little in the texts themselves to indicate any definite date. The only reference to affairs outside the life of the group of entertainers is the frequent mention of Zeugma as the place from which members came to stay in Dura. In spite of the frequent occurrence of this name for places which had a river crossing, it cannot be doubted that Zeugma here is to be identified with the city on the upper Euphrates approximately three hundred miles northeast of Dura. This identification is strengthened by the discovery of a hoard containing coins from Zeugma in one of the adjacent houses, which may have been in the possession of one of the members of the group (see below, pp. 259 f.). The frequent mention of travel between Zeugma and Dura, then, shows that the inscriptions belong to a period of relative security. Professor Rostovtzeff has come to the conclusion that Dura was probably in the hands of the Persians for a short period in the summer of 253, but that there was a period of tranquillity from 253 until the final invasion in which the town fell.[146] Our inscriptions are in favor of the latter part of this hypothesis and in turn must be dated in accordance with the general political situation.

In Fr. I, col. 1, a list of months is appended to the date of arrivals of members from Zeugma on the 13th of Peritius. It may be conjectured that this list, which completes the year but begins anomalously with Peritius, was written down for reference for people unfamiliar with the

---

[146] "Res Gestae Divi Saporis and Dura," *Berytus*, VIII, 1943, pp. 17–60.

Dura calendar and may have been used in compiling the lists of arrivals (see below, p. 253). In A.D. 253 Dura, in all probability, still used the form of Seleucid calendar which has Dius as the first month;[147] Peritius then falls either in January or February of the Julian calendar. It is therefore legitimate to ask whether the first arrival of members did not for some reason coincide with the beginning of the Roman year; in that case, our list would represent a crude equation between the Roman and the Seleucid calendars. This coincidence could have occurred in A.D. 253 and in A.D. 256, when the new moons of Peritius fell on December 18, A.D. 252, and December 16, A.D. 255, respectively. In these two years only would Peritius 13 correspond closely to January 1, and it is possible to think that the caterva came to Dura to take part in the New Year's celebrations (cf. *R.E., s.v. Neujahr,* p. 152). The date A.D. 253, however, conflicts with Professor Rostovtzeff's hypothesis concerning the events of that year since our records will be seen to cover almost an entire year (below, p. 253). It is, in any case, well known that in many places in Syria and Asia Minor the Romans succeeded in equating the local Macedonian calendars with the Julian year; and if this was only partially true at Dura, and if, as suggested below, the members of our group may have been connected with the Roman garrison of Dura, it is possible that they needed guidance in the local usage. There are a number of peg calendars at Dura, and several unsuccessful double dates (*Rep. IV,* p. 110, no. 233; p. 123, no. 246; *Rep. V,* p. 155, no. 471a; *Rep. VI,* p. 490, no. 824).

[147] *Rep. IV,* pp. 105 ff., no. 232, and especially pp. 95 f., no. 220. It is true that two Dura papyri now show the Antiochene equation of the Roman calendar, with Hyperberetaeus 1 = October 1 (F. K. Ginzel, *Handbuch der mathematischen und technischen Chronologie,* III, 1914, pp. 20, 31). *D.P.* 74, however, is from Qatna, not from Dura (*Rep. VI,* pp. 433 ff.; C. B. Welles, *Harvard Theological Review,* XXXIV, 1941, p. 100, note 65), and only *D.P.* 73 gives evidence for the Dura civil archives: Ἐπὶ ὑπάτων τὸ γʹ καὶ τὸ αʹ πρὸ Ϛʹ Νωνῶν Ὀκτωβρ[ί]ων [- - - κατὰ δὲ] τ[ὸ]ν πρότερον ἀριθμ(ὸν) δευτέρου ξφʹ μηνὸς Ὑπερβερεταίου δευτέρᾳ, etc., i.e., October 2, 251 A.D. = Hyperberetaeus 2 (cf. *Rep. VI,* pp. 436 f.). The change from the Seleucid to the Julian calendar, however, was probably not generally practiced in Dura, for the very probable equation of *Rep. IV,* pp. 95 f., no. 220, postdates *D.P.* 74 and yet shows the Seleucid calendar still in force, and our μετέβημεν notices suggest that the company moved on Dius 1 because it was the first of the year: in Palestine, Nisan 1 was the usual moving date (S. Krauss, *Talmudische Archäologie,* I, p. 58, and p. 376, note 751), and the same tendency prevailed in Egypt where six out of twelve contracts examined begin with Thoth (*P. Teb.* 372; Wessely, *Studien,* XX, 53; *P. Oxy.* 911; 1036; cf. 502; *P. Rendel Harris,* 82; cf. A. C. Johnson, *Economic Survey,* II, 1936, p. 262).

### *Purpose and Classification of the Texts*

The text consists of a series of lists of members of a group which was certainly homogeneous, and considerable care seems to have been taken to make them conspicuous. Not only were they placed apparently at a convenient height and on a part of the wall of the main room in the house where much space was available, but some attention was paid to having them appear as a unit. This end was served by the enclosure of the texts in black dividers forming a series of double-paneled columns and still more by the use of black and red either for separate entries or within a single text. This can only have had an ornamental purpose. Six columns were put up as a unit shortly after the house had been rented, and the notice of arrival at the house was painted in large red letters in the upper right corner (Fr. I, col. 6, lines 1–3). The other panels were then filled with lists (Fr. I, cols. 1–4, and col. 5, A) and with warnings (mainly Fr. I, cols. 5–6, B); this may have been done from left to right and certain differences in the writing indicate that it was not all done at the same time. To the right of this main framework a series of shorter notices can be placed which deal in part with financial matters (Fr. I, col. 8 [?]), but mainly also with lists (Frs. II and III). We do not know whether these entries occupied only the lower panels (B) below the central horizontal divider which was certainly continued, or whether a whole series of texts has been lost from the upper panels (A). At the end, in any case, a column of texts in two panels was again painted; it again combines a list and a warning (Fr. IV). Fr. V, placed slightly lower on the wall because of a metrical graffito previously incised, and with dividers of different width, must be kept apart from the other texts not only because of its different form, but also because of its content. It was presumably painted last (below, pp. 253 f.).

The texts are not official, for their headings give no information intelligible to an outsider. But they were clearly issued by a kind of central management interested in keeping a permanent record of their group for themselves as well as for the members. Probably none of the texts was addressed to customers, and it is evident that the arrangement of texts was not made with a view to giving information to people who came to hire artists. Only Fr. V gives a systematic list of entertainers with their special proficiencies; the nicknames of the women in Fr. I, cols. 2–3, probably do not indicate their professions. Furthermore, no mention is made of prices or fees for services. Another possible interpretation, namely that the lists were made for the tax collector or other officials supervising the group (cf. the mention of an *optio* in Fr. V, col. 3, line 9), is also very unlikely. A wall would be an inappropriate place for records of that sort, and on a wall already provided with other decoration it would be impossible to keep a record complete, so that the inscriptions can only represent a selection of significant items which the management wanted to keep in evidence for the benefit of the members of the group and for themselves.

A division of the text into two large sections has already been implied in the previous remarks: the first consists of one text only, giving a systematic list of entertainers according to the acts they could put on (Fr. V); the other section consists of a series of notices of arrivals from, and departures for, Zeugma together with two notices connected with the occupation of the house (Frs. I–IV). The second section is clearly the more important, giving as it does a permanent record of the actual strength of the group at any given time. To most items of both sections, warnings are added. Grouped by content, the material is as follows: Announcement of occupation of the house and partial pre-payment of the rent (Fr. I, col. 6, lines 1–3, and col. 8 [?]); entries of arrival and departure (Fr. I, cols. 1–4, col. 5, A, Frs. II, III, IV); the δουλοπαράσειτοι text (Fr. V); and warnings (Fr. I, cols. 5–6; Frs. II, IV, and V).

The entries of the second group are all headed by ἐξῆλθε whenever the heading is preserved (Fr. I, col. 1, lines 1–2, col. 5, line 1, Fr. IV, line 1). In the first instance this word is connected with Zeugma. All these entries are therefore interpreted as referring to arrivals from Zeugma, an assumption greatly strengthened by the insertion in Fr. I, col. 5, A, of Fr. I, **h** which gives the letters ἔπεμσα [- - - -]α εἰς Ζεῦγμα, thus providing a second heading for Fr. I, col. 5, A. Yet the lists are probably not of exactly the same type. The first is by far the longest, giving names of 33 women and 14 men, and it has a systematic look, with its separation of these two groups. No doubt it contains the main body of members, and it seems therefore that the main part of the group came to Dura on one day, Peritius 13. Thus this list is in fact, though not in form, an *album,* but of an unofficial kind because of the absence of headings explaining the identity of the members and of the organization. The systematic character of the list is further strengthened by the heading τῶν ἡμετέρων (Fr. I, col. 2, line 15) which divides the women into two groups of 14 and 19 persons respectively. With the help of the restored passage, Fr. I, col. 3, lines 5–7, where two women of the same name are distinguished as belonging to Zeugma and belonging to "us" (see the notes *ad loc.*) we can determine the meaning of τῶν ἡμετέρων as implying that the women preceding this heading are Ζευγματίτιδες, like Badsemeia in Fr. I, col. 3, line 5. Taken by itself, this might mean that only the first 15 women arrived from Zeugma on Peritius 13, while the others had been in Dura for some time and were included in the list then drawn up. But it is better to assume that τῶν ἡμετέρων and Ζευγματίτιδες indicate a difference in ownership: some women belonged to an establishment of some sort located in Zeugma, others were owned by the people now located in the house at Dura. All of them, men and women, seem to have come down from Zeugma on Peritius 13.

The second ἐξῆλθε text (Fr. I, col. 5, A) continues the *album* and deals, it would seem, with arrivals and departures of three persons. All the following ἐξῆλθε texts likewise are to be understood as a continuation of the *album* (see Frs. II, III and IV). But in this, as restored, the chronological arrangement is curious. Because of the double mention of Sabba it has been suggested in the notes that the list constitutes a record of the stay in Dura of three persons and that this stay in each case was limited to a period of several months. One would then expect a list arranged according to persons, not according to dates. This arrangement shows more clearly than any of the other ἐξῆλθε texts that they are all connected with a chronological list of arrivals and departures which must have been kept at the house. Of this register the extant texts would then be merely copies, for it is impossible to assume that our records are identical with the register, which would presumably not contain material such as the nicknames and warnings.

The third group of texts, the list of slave parasites with a metrical graffito, is the only one with an explanatory heading. From it we learn that the entertainers in general were slaves (παιδία), that they had been in some other place before coming to Zeugma, and finally that some but not all of the parasites were registered with the company since the arrival of the group or groups in that place. If the following list was intended for customers, it was badly done; it is, in fact, the most carelessly written text. In col. 1 only three persons have their professions of tragedians indicated (one by implication), the others are left unidentified. In cols. 2–3, however, two parasites have longer descriptions, the glutton and the dice-player. It is surprising that out of nine names reasonably preserved only two are duplicated in the other lists. Whether this is an unlucky accident, or whether a number of tabellae have been lost after Fr. I in the upper panels, cannot be decided.

The fourth group of texts consists of a series of warnings appended to the lists of arrivals and to the list of parasites. They form the most difficult part of our material, and require some discussion. The first text of this kind occupies the lower portions of Fr. I, cols. 5–6, A, and all of Fr. I, cols. 5–6, B, and special care was taken in the execution of the letters. It seems to be composed of a number of short sentences, all addressed to someone in the singular; it has already been suggested in the notes that this is a member of the group because ἐξήχθης ὑπὸ Οὐικτωρίνου (Fr. I, cols. 5–6, lines 19–20) can hardly be addressed to a customer. Yet it cannot be a single entertainer, since in none of the texts of this kind is a name given, and the character of the notices is too general. I therefore assume that σύ refers to entertainers, not customers, and that each single entertainer is addressed. It is unfortunate that it has not been possible to recover the full meaning of the sentences. Members are forbidden to bring something into the house; nobody trusts (?) them; they shall be careful not to trust . . . what (?) they have given; "do not take (?) into your house, be careful; for nobody makes gifts to the other. You have been brought from Zeugma (?) by Victorinus"—these are the remnants of a bewildering series of warnings which may or may not have formed a continuous text. It is clear, however, that they were written by someone in authority, and this can only have been the management of the group.

It is of interest that the lower part of the two columns to the left of these warnings was left uninscribed, suggesting that a special relation exists between them and the shorter ἐξῆλθε text in Fr. I, col. 5, A, an assumption supported by the similarity of writing (above, p. 209). This makes more understandable the phrase ἐξήχθης ὑπὸ Οὐικτωρίνου, which seems to restrict the warnings to a particular group of people, which may be that listed in Fr. I, col. 5, A. The same relation also exists between the warning πιστευσε[-- and the remains of a list in Fr. II; from this fragment nothing else can be learned. Fr. IV, B, the only complete warning, is likewise connected with a list of arrivals; its meaning is the most general of all: "do not trust anybody, not even yourself." Yet the first part of the sentence is more specific: it is laid down that the entertainers addressed shall stay in their house for two months. This supports the belief that a relation exists between the warning and the preceding notice of Cassianus' and Rufus' arrival at Dura. So also the last warning, that appended to the δουλοπαράσειτοι text (Fr. V, cols. 2–3, lines 7–10) which contains a reference to mimes, is apparently a general caution against misbehavior. It also shows that a military official (*optio*) had something to do with the supervision of the group. Above this warning are the scanty remains of another of two lines; a considerable portion of the parasite text was therefore filled with these remarks.

It is very difficult to define more closely the character of the warnings and, as far as I am aware, impossible to point to parallel texts. We are faced with the question whether these are serious regulations, or at least are connected with the life of the group, or whether they are gnomic maxims, perhaps written down in a playful spirit quite appropriate in a theatrical milieu. Comparative material is almost wholly lacking. Generally speaking the warnings are colloquial in tone and such as a master might address to his inferiors or slaves. Similar phrases recur very frequently in papyrus letters,[148] and in the so-called mime Μοιχεύτρια from Oxyrhynchos the *archimima* in the rôle of the leader of the household addresses her slaves in βλέπε μή or ἰδοῦ sentences throughout the play.[149] Statutes of religious or secular organizations, or guilds, sometimes have a section of their regulations consisting of warnings against misbehavior.[150] Since our group is certainly not a formal association, its warnings are hardly comparable to statutes. Yet even private associations may have to issue regulations concerning the behavior of their members.[151] Similar phrases may have occurred in contracts by which hetaerae or the like became the property of a man for a certain time, if we can trust the mock contract drawn up by a parasite in Plautus, *Asinaria*, 751 ff. I am inclined to see in the warnings of our inscriptions

[148] E.g., *Papiri Greci e Latini*, V, no. 483, line 6; 494, lines 14 f.; (258/7 B.C.); B. Olsson, *Papyrusbriefe aus der frühesten Römerzeit*, 1925, p. 185, no. 67, lines 17–19.

[149] Herondas, *Mimiambi*, ed. Crusius, 5th ed., 1914, pp. 110 ff. Cf. e.g. lines 125 ff., 139 ff., etc.

[150] In general, see E. Ziebarth, *Das griechische Vereinswesen*, 1896, p. 145; F. Poland, *Geschichte des griechischen Vereinswesens*, 1909, pp. 446 ff.; W. Liebenam, *Zur Geschichte und Organisation des römischen Vereinswesens*, Leipzig, 1890, pp. 220 ff.; J.-P. Waltzing, *Étude historique sur les Corporations Professionnelles chez les Romains*, I, 1895, pp. 371 ff.

[151] Cf. e.g., the law of an ἔρανος from Athens, presumably of the 2nd century A.D. (*IG*,[2] II/III, 1369), and sections of the νόμος of a guild of Zeus Hypsistos from Egypt of the 1st century B.C. (C. Roberts, T. C. Skeat, A. D. Nock, "The Guild of Zeus Hypsistos," *Harvard Theological Review*, XXIX, 1936, pp. 40 f., lines 15 ff.).

regulations issued by the management of the group and addressed in the first place to the entertainers mentioned in the lists to which they are appended, but also applicable to each of the other entertainers.

Of course, gnomic maxims are common in comedy and the literature of the mime, and one may recall the fondness of the third century A.D. for moralizing sentences as exemplified by the *dicta Catonis* written for use in schools at about this time.[152] But I have found no parallels to our texts in the literary sources.

### *Relative Chronology of the Texts*

Fr. I, col. 6, lines 1–3, and col. 8 (?), B, give a date, Dius 1, for the occupation of the house which must serve as a *terminus post quem* for all the other inscribed texts. It would then seem probable at first glance that all other dates postdate the date of arrival, but the fact that the list dated Peritius 13 presents itself as the main album suggests that the main body of entertainers did not arrive until three months after the house had been rented. However, it has been suggested that Fr. I, cols. 1–6, were conceived as a unit and it may therefore be concluded that the first arrival of the company preceded Dius 1 and was not to the present house but to some other place in Dura. If it be assumed that everything to the left of the large μετέβημεν notice precedes Dius 1 while the short and irregular notices on the right were inscribed later and deal with arrivals after Dius 1, the following scheme results:

Fr. I, col. 1, line 3: Peritius 13: arrival.
    col. 5, line 3: Daesius 2: arrival.
        line 4: [Daesius 3 (?)]: arrival.
        line 5: [ - - - - ]: arrival.
        lines 7–8: [ - - - - ]: departure.
        lines 9–10: Hyperberetaeus 1: departure.
        lines 10–11: Hyperberetaeus 2: departure.
    col. 6, lines 1–3, and col. 8 (?), B: Dius 1: renting of the house.
Fr. III, line 2: Dius 26: arrival.
Fr. IV, line 3: Apellaeus (?): arrival.

The undated entry of Fr. II then must be thought to fit into this scheme and it seems certain that Cassianus in Fr. IV, lines 1–2, is one

---

[152] E. Baehrens, *Poetae Latini Minores*, III, pp. 205–242. Of a similar kind are the distichs written on the walls of the house of Vettius Valens at Pompeii telling his guests how to behave (*Not. Scavi*, 1927, pp. 93 f., nos. 21–23).

of the latest arrivals. This would date the list of δουλοπαράσειτοι in Fr. V after all the other preserved texts, for Cassianus appears there in col. 1, line 12.

### Classification of the Entertainers

In spite of the fact that some portions of the text remain unexplained, some conclusions can be drawn regarding the type of establishment in which the entertainers lived and their professions can perhaps be indicated more clearly. The unity of the group is shown by the form μετέβημεν, used in Fr. I, col. 6, line 1, and in Fr. I, col. 8 (?), line 1, and repeated reference has already been made to the existence of a central management, one of the members of which was the person who speaks in the first person in Fr. I, col. 5, line 6 (ἔπεμσα). It is interesting that she is a woman, Aurelia, and the only person known to have been a Roman citizen. She may therefore be the owner of the establishment, but we cannot be sure whether she ran it alone. The other two persons who put up the text (No. **941**) with her may belong to the same category.

A number can be distinguished as having been in a responsible position. In the first place, the warnings twice seem to speak of εἰσάγειν εἰς οἶκόν σου (Fr. I, cols. 5–6, line 18, and Fr. IV, lines 10–11) which probably means that the person addressed acts as the leader of a group taking residence in another house. It is clear that as large a body of people as the present—altogether about 63 names are listed—could not have been accommodated in one small private house. It must therefore be assumed that the company broke up into smaller groups living in other houses.[153] These units would have needed someone to take charge of them, and to such leaders the εἰσάγειν phrases are addressed. The clearest indication of the existence of smaller groups is the sentence ἰδέ - - - μὴ ποιῆσθε in Fr. V, cols. 2–3, lines 8–9, in which someone is held responsible for a number of people. Such an εἰσάγουσα is Sabba (see Fr. III) concerning whom we know that she arrived in Dura first perhaps in Daesius and left again for Zeugma in Hyperberetaeus (Fr. I, col. 5, A), but that she was back on Dius 26 with a group of people (Fr. III). Fr. I, col. 5, A, then, contains at least one instance of an entertainer of a higher order than the *plebs* of the group. It is not improbable that other persons in the lists to which warnings are appended were also εἰσάγοντες. Τά[τιος ?], the lost name in Fr. I, col. 5, A, Cassianus, who is also listed

---

[153] Cf. the discussion of the hoard, below, pp. 259 f.

as a slave parasite, and Rufus may all be conjectured to be leaders of groups.

More difficult to define is the position of Victorinus who brought down some people, presumably from Zeugma. In Fr. V, col. 3, an *optio* is mentioned who was certainly not an entertainer. It is then possible that we should recognize in Victorinus also an outsider under whose supervision the entertainers travelled. But it is more probable that he was a business manager of some kind in charge of groups going from Zeugma to Dura.[154] The people whom he brought down should be those listed in Fr. I, col. 5, A.

In addition to these scanty notices, the texts preserve the names of many among the *caterva* or *grex* who worked under the *principales*. Of these, the greater number, if not all, were slaves, as shown by the term παιδία used in Fr. V, col. 1, lines 4–5, in reference to the entertainers as a whole, and by the term δουλοπαράσιτοι in the same list. They fall into two groups of 34 women and 24 men, not counting εἰσάγοντες. But the men are clearly more important: they are listed as parasitoi in Fr. V where Theodora, the only woman, is merely an assistant; and they are more carefully described as regards their proficiencies than the women; in Fr. I, cols. 1–4, two men are classified as σκηνικοί while the women are only distinguished by epithets.

We know of one woman that she assisted an entertainer; this is Theodora who worked for the singer Romanus (Fr. V, col. 1, lines 8–9). The 33 women who formed the *caterva* in the main *album* are not as clearly distinguished. It has been said that 15 of them belonged to an establishment in Zeugma while the remaining 18 belonged to the Dura establishment. But they are clearly a homogeneous group, and no differences can be detected as to their names or epithets. To judge by the names, the women are probably of local Syrian stock and of low origin.

Epithets are added to at least 26 names; only 7 women have none and, of these Ἄννα Βαδοισαία in Fr. I, col. 2, line 21, and Βα[δοη(μεία)] ἡμετέ(ρα) in Fr. I, col. 3, line 7, are special cases. Most of the epithets are uncomplimentary adjectives or nouns, though a few are complimentary. The greater number are common adjectives and therefore not to be regarded as precisely nicknames.[155] They are rather to be regarded as jests

---

[154] Professor A. D. Nock (by letter) calls Victorinus "an entrepreneur . . . who made it his business to provide amusements for the garrison."

[155] Possible exceptions are κάππα and κόππα which have no immediately apparent meaning.

written down when the list was made and may best be compared with similar epithets in erotic inscriptions all through classical antiquity. These are really acclamations, and the custom is best known from Attic graffiti and painted vases, though it is prevalent in a laudatory or depreciatory sense in all kinds of inscriptions.[156] However, they are at least in part of a kind which in late antiquity easily developed into nicknames, and it is well known how large a part was played by nicknames in the breakdown of the Greek and Roman name systems. In this development, a large part was played by the popular theater, as best shown by the example of Alexandria, famous for both mimes and nicknames. Similar conditions prevailed in Syria, and our list thus becomes a significant example of these tendencies.[157]

Or it may be suggested, alternatively, that the epithets were connected with the performances of the women, and their rôles may be conjectured to have been as follows: the μωραί may have played parts in which they were ridiculed, and the καλαί may have been dancers. The ἱλαραί may have sung ἱλαρὰ ᾄσματα;[158] the μωροκυστα may have performed tricks with the bladder which were so common in the mime;[159] σπάθη may conceivably be a reference to sword dancing or similar feats; ἡ παλαιοπόρνη may be the type of an old hetaera, and γραίοψις that of an old woman.[160] εὔπ[ους] would again be a dancer, and for κηλητρία various possible connections with the Atellana have already been suggested. It may be, then, that the essential qualities of the women are summed up in the epithets. A parallel for this use of adjectives may be seen in the

[156] Cf. in particular the graffiti from the brothels of Pompeii, e.g., CALOS PARIS (*C.I.L.*, IV, 2179), CALOS CASTRENSIS (*ibid.*, 2180), φουτοῦτρις (*ibid.*, 2204), and *Scordopordonicus* (*ibid.*, 2188), the last an improvised nickname similar to Σκορδοσφράντης (Alciphron, III, 25).

[157] For Syria cf. especially Dio Cassius, LXXIX, 4, 1, and also LXXVIII, 31, 1 (on Comazon Eutychianus). A complete and classified list of nicknames does not exist. But cf. L. Grasberger, *Die Griechischen Stichnamen,*[2] 1883, and *Studien zu den Griechischen Ortsnamen,* 1888, pp. 309 ff. *R.E. s.v. Spitznamen.* Lambertz, *op. cit.* (p. 231, note 75). L. Robert, *Études Épigraphiques et Philologiques,* 1938, pp. 151 ff. J. N. Truesdale, *A Comic Prosopographia Graeca,* Diss. Duke, 1940.

[158] Athenaeus, XV, 697d; Eustathius *ad Od.* ψ 134; cf. Paulus e Festo, p. 101 (p. 78 ed. Thewrewk), where *hilarodos* is defined as *lascivi et delicati carminis cantator.*

[159] Athenaeus, I, 20A; cf. Alciphron, III, 12, 3.

[160] A type common in the mime; cf. Claudian's epigram quoted by Reich, p. 613, note 1; Pliny, *N.H.,* VII, 48, §158; Athen. IV, 130c; Reich, *op. cit.,* pp. 602, note 2; 735, 766.

ephebic inscriptions where χρηστός, γοργός, φιλόξενος, γαῦρος describe the essential qualities of the ephebes.[161] But I do not feel confident that it is possible to adopt the hypothesis that our list is descriptive of the women's professions: it seems indicative that the epithets are much vaguer than those describing the men. It is, then, difficult to decide whether they were performers or mere prostitutes. In actual fact, the combination was common in antiquity, and this type of low-class female performer is largely responsible for the confusion between the terms for dancers and prostitutes in our sources.[162]

We may then assume that the women could dance and do turns of various sorts as well as act as prostitutes. With the former competence the professions of the men would agree well, for none of the professions ascribed to them are such as we should expect to find in a cast of mimes; they belong to the same class of miscellaneous entertainers. But it is not without significance that the proportion of Greek and Latin names among them is much higher than it is for the women. This shows that the men are clearly superior. The main information concerning them comes from the systematic list of slave parasites in which we find a tragedian or singer, and a man and woman of the same profession, and a "glutton," probably a type from the Atellana who was a musician (?); in addition there is a dice-player. These terms are a peculiar mixture drawn from the stage, from tragedy, and from the light kinds of entertainment common at banquets. It is impossible that these men should form a theatrical cast or that the texts were intended to list a group of people acting together. They are entertainers acting singly or in small groups whenever occasion arose, but presumably mainly in private houses. They are not regular mimes, and the term μίμο[υς] in Fr. V, cols. 2–3, line 8, must be understood loosely as small παίγνια or skits acted by one or a few. It is hardly necessary to present evidence for this use of the term μῖμος, since in later antiquity it became synonymous with almost any type of light performance.

---

[161] L. Robert, *Hellenika*, pp. 127 ff. It cannot be conceded that our epithets are technical terms, and the use of adjectives to designate a profession is very rare; cf. however, ἱλαρός above, p. 222, note 19, and L. Robert, *Rev. Ét. Gr.*, XLIX, 1936, pp. 253 ff. (a σπουδαιογέλοιος, i.e., a παρῳδός).

[162] W. W. Tarn, *The Greeks in Bactria and India*, Cambridge, 1938, p. 374, note 4. Machon, *Convivium Atticum*, line 121 (Athen. IV, 137c).

## *History and Organization of the Establishment*

The inscriptions contain some enigmatic remarks on the life of the group previous to its stay in the Dura house and some inferences can also be drawn from them regarding the life of the entertainers at Dura. It may be taken for granted that all the members listed had come down from Zeugma on the upper Euphrates. But they did not originate in that place, as is shown by the phrase in Fr. V, col. 1, lines 3–5 : ἀφ’ ὅτε ἀνέβη τὰ πεδία εἰς Ζεῦγμα. From the names of the women, as well as from general probabilities, it may be conjectured that the group had come from Syria, the homeland of mimes and entertainers, whence they went, as is well known, all over the Roman Empire. It may be recalled that, as early as 187 B.C., low-class entertainers had come to Rome from Asia,[163] and that the emperor Claudius had ’Ασιανοὶ παῖδες μετάπεμπτοι dance the *pyrriche* after his campaign in Britain.[164] Horace has given a famous picture of the collegia of Syrian *ambubaiae* in Rome,[165] and equally noted were the girls from Gades.[166] Lucius Verus brought many mimes to Rome from his Eastern campaigns.[167] A list of Syrian cities with their specialties in the field of entertainment is given in the *Totius Orbis Descriptio*, §32.[168] Our entertainers, then, were connected with a lively trade in the theatrical world emanating from Syria.[169]

They went to Zeugma, the crossing point of the Euphrates into Mesopotamia, and a natural place for entertainers to stop and organize groups to be sent down the river. It may be assumed that Dura was only one of many towns furnished with entertainment from Zeugma.[170] We appear to have to do with a large organization which sent out smaller groups to the surrounding cities, as suggested by the prominence of Zeugma in the headings of our lists, by the fact that 15 women of the first list of arrivals were kept distinct from the Dura group as persons belonging to Zeugma, and by the fact that members of the Dura estab-

---

[163] Livy, XXXIX, 6, 8.          [164] Cassius Dio, LX, 23, 5.

[165] *Sat.*, I, 2, 1–2.

[166] Cf. H. Blümner, *Die Römischen Privataltertümer*, p. 412.

[167] *S.H.A.*, Verus, 7, 4; 8, 7 and 11.

[168] Müller, Geogr. Graec. Min., II, p. 519.

[169] Cf. also M. Bieber, "Mima Saltatricula," *A.J.A.*, XLIII, 1939, pp. 642 f.

[170] A passage in Philostratus, *Apollonius of Tyana*, I, 20 (quoted by J. Johnson, *Rep. II*, p. 157) shows how customary was the passage of slave girls and the like through Zeugma.

lishment not only came from Zeugma but were also sent back there by the management.

The 33 women and 14 men who arrived in Dura on Peritius 13 were under a kind of central management, among the members of which was Aurelia. They stayed for nine months in one or more houses unknown to us, and during that period several other small groups arrived and stayed in Dura for several months before they were sent back to Zeugma by Aurelia. During their travel some entertainers were in charge of a business manager, Victorinus, who was no doubt responsible both to the management in Zeugma and to that in Dura for their proper consignment. Possibly he was one of the heads of the organization in the former place. On Dius 1, the central management moved into House C in Section G5 of the agora and at once had the previous records painted on the walls. But since arrivals from Zeugma continued, the number of inscriptions gradually grew, all painted by the same man. Among the late arrivals we find one person who had already stayed several months in Dura previous to the renting of the house: namely Sabba of Fr. III.

While the entertainers stayed in Dura, the management had to provide living quarters for many of them outside of the small house used as headquarters. Under the leadership of one or another of the members, small groups rented houses or rooms in the vicinity. In these houses the leaders were in charge, but certain warnings were given them by which the management apparently freed itself from any responsibility for carelessness or misdemeanor. That the houses referred to in these warnings were those rented by the entertainers and not houses of customers in which they went to work seems indicated by the repeated phrase εἰς οἶκόν σου. It would then appear that the entertainers were hired out only for short periods as need arose, so that they had to have their own living quarters. This finds some confirmation in the discovery of a hoard of coins already referred to.[171] It was found in G5, D3, i.e., the house on the other side of the block from ours, with the entrance from the south side. (See above, p. 121, fig. 48.) The hoard consisted of: 1 tetradrachm of Elagabalus from Antioch, 2 bronzes of Gordian and Abgar from Edessa, 7 of Philip Sr. and Jr., from Cyrrhus, 14 of the same from Hierapolis, 5 of Elagabalus and 20 of Philip Sr. and Jr. from Zeugma. The types appear elsewhere in Dura, but only in small numbers and the

---

[171] Hoard XI, *Rep. VII/VIII*, pp. 422 f.; see above, p. 121.

hoard is far from typical. The large number of coins from Zeugma is explicable only on the assumption that the hoard was the property of some person recently arrived from that region, for the proportions are quite impossible for any body of money accumulated in Dura in ordinary trade. The fact that the coins stop in 249 A.D. does not speak against connecting the hoard with our inscription, for Cyrrhus, Hierapolis and Zeugma issued no coins after that date. It is very probable that the owner of the hoard was connected with our establishment and that he was one of the entertainers living in the vicinity. Such persons, for some reason unknown to us, generally stayed in Dura only for short periods: compare [εἰσά]γων δύο μῆνας εἰς οἶκόν σου in Fr. IV, lines 10–11 with the list of arrivals and departures in Fr. I, col. 5, A. Some, however, seem to have stayed longer, for Asbolius who arrived in Dura on Peritius 13 is the same, in all probability, as the one listed among the slave parasites, and this list was apparently drawn up at least ten months later.

After the renting of the house, the stay of the entertainers in Dura appears to have been fairly short. The latest entry of arrivals from Zeugma seems to be dated in Apellaeus, i.e. between one and two months after Dius 1. It is tempting to connect this abrupt stopping of further arrivals and the excellent state of preservation of some of the texts with some external event, and this would be the beginning of the siege of Dura and its final fall, if the date of 256 could be given for the inscriptions with some confidence. The numerous well preserved fragments give the impression that the inscriptions had been buried soon after they were written and hence deliberately destroyed. The arrival of the Persians could not then antedate Apellaeus, i.e. December 256.

It is unfortunate that the texts tell us so little about the doings of the entertainers in Dura. Why had they come there and with whom was their business? It seems very improbable that such a large group with its continuous reinforcements would have stayed in a place as small as Dura to do business with the local inhabitants. The inscriptions, it will be remembered, are from a house in the northern section of the agora at the shortest possible distance from the Roman camp, which is, in fact, less than two blocks away, as will be seen from the general plan of Dura. In the same block, Terentius *tribunus* had his residence in one of the adjacent houses,[172] and a number of rooms in several houses were con-

[172] Above, pp. 103–105.

verted into shops in the last period, a fact connected with the proximity of the Roman garrison by Professor Brown.[173] It is therefore probable that the entertainers served the needs of the garrison stationed at Dura, and it may even be suggested that they were supervised by the military authorities. This may have been the function of the *optio* mentioned in Fr. V, col. 3, line 9, and the term σταθμοῦχος in Fr. I, col. 8 ( ? ), line 3, may imply that quarters were provided by the military command. Furthermore, our group seems to be from Syria; Syria was also the homeland of the majority of the soldiers stationed at Dura.[174]

It may be well at the end of this section to give an estimate of the numerical strength of the group, which presents itself as follows: about 68 names we know to have stood in the texts, about 63 are preserved. Of these, 9 may be conjectured to have been in a more prominent position. Of the 36 women, there is a group of 15 from Zeugma, another of 18 from the Dura establishment. Of the 27 men, there is one group of 14 consisting of arrivals; another of 10 or more slave parasites. An estimate of the real size of the whole group depends on how much inscribed space has been lost between Frs. I and IV. Assuming that we have lost none, the gaps in Frs. II, III, and V, col. 1, would easily bring the number to 80–90.

### Comparison of the Dura Group with Other Types of Low-Class Entertainers

It remains to find a place for the establishment among the various types of groups which made entertainment their business in Hellenistic and Roman times. It seems clear that, in spite of the strong possibility that prostitution was practised in our group, it is not an organized brothel of the kind known from Greece and Italy. Nor is it a professional association of the kind treated by Poland and Liebenam, but it seems to belong to a class of organization like that of gladiators, jugglers and mimes. The outstanding characteristic of this class is that it consists of slaves and freedmen, owned by or connected with one man who is a professional himself and at the same time acts as the business manager of his *caterva*. In other cases such groups form part of the *familia* of a wealthy man. This type of organization is most familiar from gladiators who, it will be remembered, often formed privately

[173] Above, p. 116.
[174] Rostovtzeff, *Dura-Europos and its Art,* 1938, pp. 50 and 88.

owned bands travelling around and lending their services for certain periods.[175] Low-class entertainment and especially the mime was also organized on this basis, so fundamentally different from that of the Dionysiac *technitae*. The *archimimus* was at once the director, the business manager and the main actor of his troupe.[176] Such bands could also form part of the *familia* of a wealthy man; a good example is Trimalchio's troupe of Atellani. These *greges* were sometimes very large; the famous inscription from Bovillae gives a list of 60 members of a cast of mimes.[177] But since we also have evidence for travelling mimes,[178] it must be supposed that such companies could break up into smaller units, for the evidence from extant plays does not favor very large casts of mimes performing together. The appearance of women in leading positions where men are present can be paralleled from the Oxyrhynchus mime Μοιχεύτρια in which the cast consists of the *archimima* and a group of male actors as members of her household. It must also be remembered that mimes in the East lead a more ephemeral and obscure life than the Roman mimes in Italy, since as a rule their plays were not admitted in Greek contests as was done in Rome at an early time.[179] It is, then, not so much the internal organization as the type of professions mentioned as well as the preponderance of women in the *caterva* which makes the identification of our group as a company of mimes impossible.

The evidence from Egypt affords a much closer parallel. Small companies of entertainers lived in the cities and were called to the villages for certain brief periods of time. The directors were regularly professional entertainers themselves who seem to have received the greater part of the profits.[180] Most often the group went as a whole but sometimes a few artists were rented from the entrepreneur.[181] The variety of performers is not dissimilar to our document; most of them are musi-

---

[175] In general, see Friedländer, II, pp. 56 f.; cf. pp. 64 f. L. Robert, *Les Gladiateurs dans l'Orient grec,* Paris, 1940, pp. 283 ff.

[176] Reich, pp. 530, 603 ff.; 701 ff.; *RE, s.v. Mimus,* p. 1748. Cf. esp. Dessau 5208.

[177] *CIL,* XIV, 2408 (= Dessau 5196).

[178] Dessau 5223: *Libela scenicus viarum, etc.*

[179] *R.E., s.v. Mimus,* p. 1744.

[180] W. L. Westermann, "The Castanet Dancers of Arsinoe," *Journal of Egyptian Archaeology,* X, 1924, pp. 137, 142, and "Entertainment in Villages of Graeco-Roman Egypt," *ibid.,* XVIII, 1932, pp. 16 ff.; Teresa Grassi, "Musica, Mimica e Danza," *Studi della Scuola Papirologica di Milano,* III, 1920, pp. 117 ff.; A. C. Johnson, *Economic Survey,* II, 1936, pp. 297 ff.

[181] Wilcken, *Chrestomathie,* no. 497.

cians, dancers and pantomimes. The smaller groups, of 3–4 dancers, are comparable to our small groups stationed in their own lodgings. But there seems to be no indication of a larger organization in the cities.

An interesting illustration comes from the Palestinian Talmud, recently commented on by S. Liebermann.[182] In Caesarea in Palestine, Rabbi Abbahu wanted a man called Παντόκακος to pray for rain and asked him about his occupation. "Pantokakos said (referring to himself): 'This man commits five sins every day: he adorns the theater, engages the hetaerae, brings their clothes to the bath-house, claps hands and dances before them, and clashes the cymbals before them.' "[183] The man is certainly not a regular mime or pantomime as Liebermann thinks, but in all probability the owner and director of a small group of dancing girls, himself a musician and dancer. In his capacity as director he takes care of the girls and fixes up the theater. Professor Obermann, who has kindly helped me in this matter, tells me that the term used for "adorning" is very generic. He also thinks that "dances before them," etc. refers to the public rather than the girls. This story of which only part has been quoted gives an intimate picture of a Palestinian entertainer of much lower social standing even than those found in the Egyptian documents, and shows that in that milieu not much distinction was made between different types of acting, and that the personal union of director, owner, artist and entrepreneur was quite common.

But our inscription represents a company far bigger than those discussed. The large organization in Zeugma which sent smaller groups into the neighboring districts seems to offer the only point of comparison with the Dionysiac *technitae* who supplied artists for public festivals. Such groups may have had temporary centers of their activities, but they were never stationary, and thus they belong to the well-known travelling companies on which information is abundant, and which wandered far beyond Hellenized countries.[184] A pantomime from Antioch, forced to leave the city, took his troupe as far as Gaul and when

[182] Taanith, I, 4, 64a. Liebermann, *Greek in Jewish Palestine*, New York, 1942, pp. 31 ff., from which the quotation is taken.

[183] The point of the story, of course, is that Jews were forbidden to have any dealings with the pagan theater, in accordance with Leviticus 20, 23.

[184] Cf. also the stories connected with travelling dealers in prostitutes, Dio Chrysostom, or. 60 (77), 4; Clemens Alex., *Paedagogus*, III, III, 22, 1; Kaibel, *Epigr. Graeca*, no. 613; and esp. Strabo, XII, 578 (§17). On travelling troupes of mimes see

he needed a κοτυλιστής (whatever that is) sent for one from Antioch.[185] An Ionian appears at Babylon,[186] and Greek mimes went as far as India; conversely, Indian jugglers are found at Alexander's court and later in the Near East.[187] After Crassus' death, the Parthians had Greek singers at court.[188] In general, foreign entertainers were always valued more highly than native performers, a fact often mentioned in inscriptions.[189] Thus a very lively trade must have existed between Asia Minor and Mesopotamia and India. In fact, Posidonius speaks of shiploads of μουσικὰ παιδισκάρια καὶ ἰατροὺς καὶ ἄλλους τεχνίτας going to India,[190] and there is evidence from Indian sources to support this.[191]

Our entertainers as members of this "Fahrendes Volk" of ancient times presumably followed the routes of the Roman soldiers and thus are part of a larger phenomenon: the decrease of military morale and discipline in the 3rd century which was particularly acute in Syria.[192] Although the subject of popular entertainment is not treated in the works on military antiquities, it can be stated that the roots of this degeneration lie in Hellenistic times.[193] For the period under consideration, the preoccupation with the licentiousness of the soldiers is attested by a law forbidding soldiers to enter the stage;[194] but this is almost contemporary with two famous inscriptions of the sailors from Misenum who acted as mimes (Dessau 2178 and 2179). Likewise we know that soldiers kept their own entertainers with or without the consent of higher authorities. Thus, two inscriptions show that legions some-

Reich, pp. 558 ff. and 698 ff. H. Blümner, *Die Römischen Privataltertümer*, p. 370, note 1. H. Blümner, *Fahrendes Volk im Altertum*, p. 41, note 96.

[185] Julian, *Misopogon*, 359D. I owe this reference to Dr. F. Lenz.

[186] Max. Tyr., *Diss.*, 35, 4. Reich, pp. 698 ff.

[187] Athenaeus, XII, 538e; cf. Aelian, *Varia Historia*, VIII, 7.

[188] Plutarch, *Crassus* 33 = Polyaenus, VII, 41.

[189] L. Robert, "Pantomimen im Griechischen Orient," *Hermes*, LXV, 1930, pp. 114–116.

[190] Strabo, II, 99.

[191] W. W. Tarn, *The Greeks in Bactria and India*, pp. 373 ff.; cf. also the remarks on export of prostitutes from Syria, p. 374; W. L. Westermann, *RE, s.v. Sklaverei*, Suppl. VI, p. 936.

[192] E. S. Bouchier, *Syria as a Roman Province*, p. 68. A. S. Hoey, *Harvard Theological Review*, XXX, 1937, pp. 32–33.

[193] Some material will be found in Reich, p. 776, note 1, and pp. 559–560. Cf. esp. Plutarch, *Cleomenes*, ch. 12.

[194] Dig., XLVIII, 19, 14.

times kept their own troupes of gladiators.[195] The presence in military camps of popular magicians together with the stock characters of the Atellana may perhaps be inferred from a difficult passage in the Babylonian Talmud.[196] But from Syria itself, though in a later time, comes almost complete confirmation of the conditions conjectured to have prompted our enigmatic texts. Libanius, in describing the injuries suffered by the local innkeepers of Antioch, says that they were inflicted not only by the soldiers, but also by their entertainers who frequented the inns with their animals and played the flute or syrinx impersonating Pan, Silenus, or Bacchus.[197] These entertainers, not themselves soldiers, are apparently hired by soldiers to assist in the entertainment at drinking parties with their miscellaneous acts, and they seem to be under the soldiers' control; all these facts are closely paralleled by the Dura dipinti.

[195] L. Friedländer, II, p. 58.

[196] *Abodah Zarah,* 186 (transl. by Mishcon and Cohen, Soncino Press edition, London, 1935, pp. 93 ff.). But cf. *Monumenta Talmudica,* ed. S. Krauss, V, II, 2, pp. 164 f., no. 397.

[197] Libanius, Or. XLVI, §13–14. Cf. R. A. Pack, *Studies in Libanius and Antiochene Society under Theodosius,* Diss. Michigan, 1935, p. 17.

# INDICES TO THE GREEK INSCRIPTIONS

## A. *Deities*

ψυχαὶ θεαί   no. 939, p. 177

## B. *Geographical Terms*

Ζεῦγμα   no. 940 I 5 A, p. 214; V 1 A,
   p. 217

Ζευγματῖτις   no. 940 I 3 A, p. 213
Θάσιος   no. 938, p. 169

## C. *Persons*

### 1. Dura

’Απολλώνιος ’Αρχελάου   no. 935, p. 168
Αὐρηλία ’Αρρία   w. of Julius Terentius
   no. 939, p. 177
Πολύμηλος Διοκλέους τοῦ Δανύμου   no.
   937, p. 168

’Ιούλιος Τερέντιος   *trib. Coh. XX Pal.*
   no. 939, p. 177
Τίτος Φρόντων   no. 934, p. 168

### 2. Thasos

Πρηξίπολις   no. 938, p. 169

### 3. Entertainers (no. 940, pp. 212–220)

[’Αβάσκ?]αντ(ος)   I 4 B
’Αντιοχίδης   I 4 A
’Ασβόλιος   I 4 A; V 1 A
”Αχαβος   V 1 A
Γαῖος(?)   I 4 A
Εσμα - -   II
ΙΑΓΑΠΕΛΘΟΣ   I 4 A
Καῖος   I 4 B
Κασσιανός   II; IV A; V 1 A
Μαρ - -   I 4 A
Ομανας   I 4 A
Οὐάλης   I 4 A
Οὐικτωρῖνος   I 5 B
‘Ροῦφος   IV A
‘Ρωμανός   V 1 A
Σαμακους   I 4 A
Σατυρίλλος   V 2 B
Τάτιος   I 5 A

”Υμνος   V 1 A
Φιλόπαππος   V 1 A
Χαρίσιος   V 2 A

Αβεδσιμεια   I 3 A
Αβσαλμας   I 3 A
’Αλβῖνα   I 2 B
”Αννα   I 2 B
Αὐρηλία   I 5 A; no. 941, p. 221
’Αφροδισία   I 2 A
Βαδσημεια (*bis*)   I 3 A
Βαδσισαια   I 2 B
Βλ. . . .ς   I 2 A
Δόμνα   I 2 B
Θεννις   I 2 B
Θεοδώρα   V 1 A
Θικιμη   I 2 A; B
Καμαθη   I 2 A

Κάστα  I 3 A

Κλεοπάτρα  I 2 A

Κυρίλλα  I 3 A

'Ολυμπιάς  I 2 A

Ρε..υθη  I 2 A

Σαββα (*bis*)  I 5 A; III

Σαλιφθας  I 2 B

Σαλμαθη (*bis*)  I 2 A

...αβαιθα  I 2 B

.ανθελους  I 3 A

.αρβαιθη  I 3 A

..ισιιθας  I 2 B

.μις  I 2 A

..νκυβις  I 2 A

.ΝΟΜΑΣ  I 3 A

.....ους  I 2 B

## D. *Months* (no. 940, pp. 212–220)

'Απελλαῖος  I 1 B; IV A

'Αρτεμίσιος  I 1 A

Αὐδυναῖος  I 1 B; 7 A

Γορπιαῖος  I 1 A

Δαίσιος  I 1 A; 5 A

Δῖος  I 1 B; 6 A; 8 B; III

Δύστρος  I 1 A

Λῶος  I 1 A

Ξανδικός  I 1 A

Πάνημος  I 1 A

Περίτιος  I 1 A

'Υπερβερεταῖος  I 1 B; 5 A

## E. *Military Units*

Σπεῖρα κ' Παλμυρηνῶν  no. 939, p. 177

## F. *Officials*

ἀγορανομικὸς τόμος, ὀπτίων, ταμιευτικὸς τόμος, χειλίαρχος, χρεοφυλακικὸς τόμος

## G. *Stage and Entertainment*

γραίοψις, δουλοπαράσιτος, καταφαγᾶς, κοττιστής, μῖμος, μωροκυστα, παλαιοπόρνη, σκηνικός, σπάθη, τραγῳδός, ὑποτραγῳδέω

## H. *Miscellaneous*

Abecedarium  no. 936, p. 168

Dates, 125 B.C.–A.D. 198  no. 410, pp. 169–173

## I. *Greek Words*

ἀγαθός  no. 940 V 2 A, p. 217

ἀ(γορανομικὸς τόμος)  cf. p. 175

ἀναβαίνω  no. 940 V 1 A, p. 217

ἀνήρ  no. 939, p. 177; 940 V, p. 217

ἄξιος  no. 939, p. 177

ἀπό  no. 940 I 1 A, p. 212; V 1 A, p. 217

βλαρός  no. 940 I 2 A, p. 212; 3 A, p. 213

βλέπω  no. 940 I 5 B, p. 214; (*bis*) IV B, p. 216

γαῖα  no. 939, p. 177

γάρ  no. 940 V, p. 217

γέλοιος  no. 940 V 2 A, p. 217

γραίοψις  (*bis*) no. 940 I 2 B, p. 213

δεύτερος  (*bis*) no. 940 I 5 A, p. 214

δέχομαι  no. 939, p. 177

δίδωμι  (*bis*) no. 940 I 5 B, p. 214

φιλέω   no. 940 V 2 A, p. 217
φίλιος   no. 939, p. 177
χειλίαρχος   no. 939, p. 177
χρ(εοφυλακικὸς τόμος)   cf. p. 175

χρῆμα   no. 940 V, p. 217
ψυχή   no. 939, p. 177
ὧδε   no. 940 I 8 B, p. 215
ὠκύς   no. 940 V, p. 217

## J. *Phonology and Morphology*

### αι>ε

δέξασθε   no. 939, p. 177
Δέσιος   no. 940 I 1 A, p. 212; 5 A, p. 214
Γορπιέος   no. 940 I 1 A, p. 212
Ὑπερβερετέος   no. 940 I 1 A, p. 212; 5 A, p. 214
Ἀπελλέος   no. 940 I 1 A, p. 212; IV A, p. 216
Ἐδυνέος   no. 940 I 1 A, p. 212; Αἰδυνέος   no. 940 I 7 B, p. 215
παλεοπόρνη   no. 940 I 2 B, p. 213
γρέοψις   no. 940 I 2 B, p. 213
πεδία   no. 940 V 1 A, p. 217

### ι>ει

χειλίαρχος   no. 939, p. 177
Δείου   no. 940 I 6 A, p. 214; 8 A, p. 215
δουλοπαράσειτοι   no. 940 V 1, p. 217

### αυ>ε

Ἐδυνέος   no. 940 I 1 A, p. 212

### αυ>αι

Αἰδυνέος   no. 940 I 7 B, p. 215

### θ>τ

στεναρός   no. 939, p. 177

### μψ>μσ

κόμση   no. 940 I 2 B, p. 213; ἔπεμσα 5 A, p. 214

### ιος>ις

Ἀσβόλις   no. 940 I 4 A, p. 214; V 1 A, p. 217

* * * * *

μικκός = μικρός   no. 940 I 2 B, p. 213
εἰσενίκῃς = εἰσενέγκῃς   no. 940 I 6 A, p. 214
δίδει = δίδωσι   no. 940 I 6 B, p. 214

I

2

I) G3, A2. REMAINS OF THE SELEUCID SHOPS.   2) G3, A2. PERIOD II. CHREOPHYLAKEION

1

2

1) G3, A3. REMAINS OF THE SELEUCID SHOP, SOUTH END.   2) G3, A3. REMAINS OF THE
SELEUCID SHOP, NORTH END

1

2

1) G3, A3. PERIOD II. CHREOPHYLAKEION.    2) G3, A AND F. FINAL STATE

I

2

I) G3, F3 AND A4.   2) G3, G2. VAULTED CELLARS

I

2

1) G3, B2.   2) G3, H3

1

2

1) G3, S5. EXTERIOR CORNER.   2) G3, K2

I

2

1) G3, S3. SHOP FITTINGS.   2) G3, L. SOUTH FAÇADE

1

2

1) G3, M2.   2) G3, MI

1

2

1) GI, SII6 AND SIII. NORTH FAÇADE.   2) GI, AREA 70–71¹, 83–102, 126

1

2

1) GI, SII6.   2) GI, SII8

1

2

1) GI, GI03.   2) GI, FI09

1

2

1) G5, AIR VIEW.   2) G5, B3. EXTERIOR CORNER

1

2

1) G2, SHOPS S5 AND S8, HOUSES C AND B.    2) G6, ROMAN MARKET

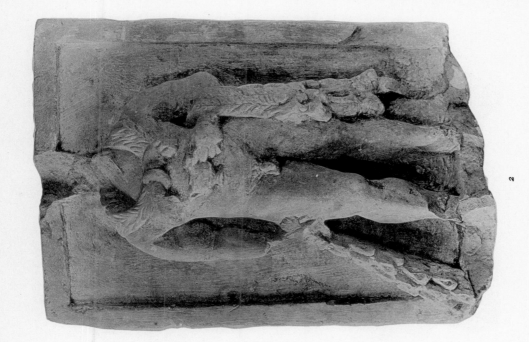

2

1

1) G3, M2. RELIEF OF HERCULES.   2) G3, M4. RELIEF OF HERCULES

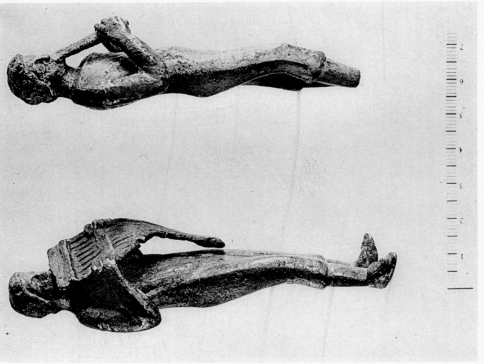

1) G3, L3. BRONZE STATUETTES. FRONT VIEW.   2) G3, L3. BRONZE STATUETTES SIDE VIEW

1) G3, H10. RELIEF OF GODDESS.   2) G3, J1. STATUETTE.   3) G3, H5. PLASTER
RELIEF PLAQUE

1) G7, H1. ANTEFIX.   2) G7, H7. PLASTER RELIEF OF HERCULES.   3) G5, F4. RELIEF
OF GODDESS.   4) G5, B3. STATUETTE

XIX

G5, C2. PLASTER RELIEF PLAQUE. VENUS ANADYOMENE

1) G3, A3. INSCRIPTION 938. STAMPED AMPHORA HANDLE.   2) G3, A3. INSCRIPTION
410(A) AND (C).   3) G3, A3. INSCRIPTION 410(D).   4) G3, A3. INSCRIPTION 410(E)

G5, HI. INSCRIPTION 939

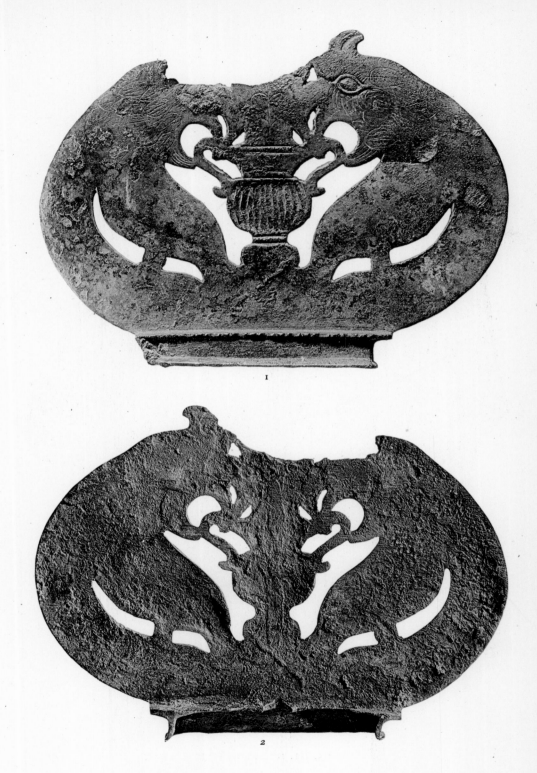

1) G3, H4. BRONZE PLAQUE. OBVERSE.    2) G3, H4. BRONZE PLAQUE. REVERSE

1) FRAGMENT OF RELIEF.   2) FRAGMENT OF RELIEF. VIENNA.   3) SARCOPHAGUS. YORK.

4) BRONZE FRIEZE. AUGST

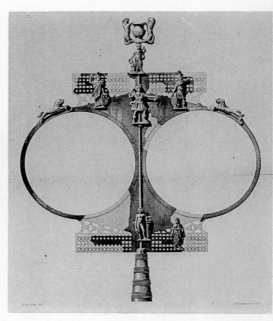

1) BRONZE HINGE. LAURIACUM.　2) BRONZE HANDLE. BONN.　3) BRONZE HANDLE.
ATHENS.　4) STANDARD FINIAL. PARIS

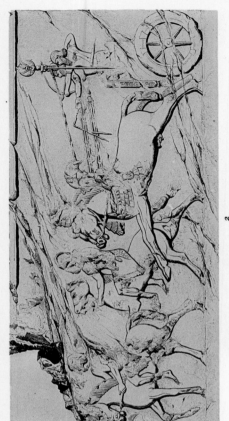

1) SIGNA. COLUMN OF TRAJAN. 2) RELIEF. NINEVEH. 3) CORNICINES. COLUMN
OF TRAJAN

DIPINTI FROM G5, C2; NO. 940, FRAGMENT I, a, b

DIPINTI FROM G5, C2; NO. 940, FRAGMENT I, a–e

DIPINTI FROM G5, C2; NO. 940, FRAGMENT I, f–p

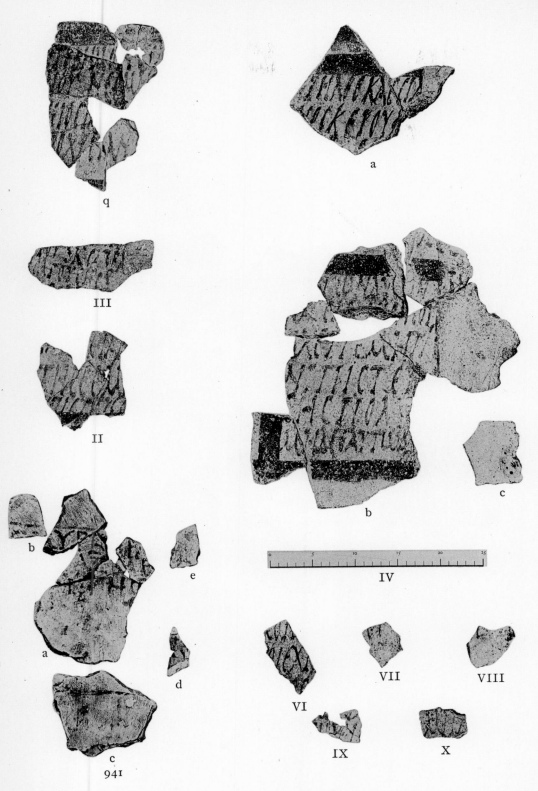

DIPINTI FROM G5, C2; NO. 940, FRAGMENT I, q, FRAGMENTS II–IV, VI–X; NO. 941, a–e

DIPINTI FROM G5, C2; NO. 940, FRAGMENT V, a, b